组编 | 湖北升本信息服务中心

专升本核心语法：
上岸必备

ZHUAN SHENG BEN HEXIN YUFA
SHANGAN BIBEI

主编：徐霄龙　刘　娟

编委：杜芳菲　张扬扬　陈　戈　姜　倩
　　　姜玲玲　谭云云　李楚焰　李　俊

华中师范大学出版社

新出图证(鄂)字 10 号

图书在版编目(CIP)数据

专升本核心语法:上岸必备/湖北升本信息服务中心组编.—武汉:华中师范大学出版社,2023.4
(2024.7 重印)
 ISBN 978－7－5769－0095－8

Ⅰ.①专… Ⅱ.①湖… Ⅲ.①英语—语法—成人高等教育—升学参考资料 Ⅳ.①H319.35

中国国家版本馆 CIP 数据核字(2023)第 054418 号

专升本核心语法:上岸必备
ⓒ 湖北升本信息服务中心组编

编 辑 室:综合(数字)分社	电 话:027－67867370
丛书策划:杨 宁　　责任编辑:董云梅	封面设计:张 捷 胡 灿
出版发行:华中师范大学出版社	责任校对:王 胜
社　　址:湖北省武汉市洪山区珞喻路 152 号	邮　　编:430079
销售电话:027－67861549(发行部)	
网　　址:http://press.ccnu.edu.cn	电子邮箱:press@mail.ccnu.edu.cn
印　　刷:湖北新华印务有限公司	督　印:刘 敏
开　　本:787mm×1092mm　1/16	印　张:13
版　　次:2023 年 4 月第 1 版	印　次:2024 年 7 月第 3 次印刷
字　　数:200 千字	定　价:59.00 元

欢迎上网查询、购书

敬告读者:欢迎举报盗版,请打举报电话 027－67867353

前　言

本书适用于参加湖北省普通专升本大学英语考试的考生。大学英语科目主要考查考生是否具备一定的英语知识技能与语言水平,而英语语法的学习则会贯穿考生学习、备考专升本英语的始终。学好语法是考生在单项选择、阅读理解、翻译、写作四大考试题型中获得理想分数的基石。本书根据湖北省普通专升本大学英语考试大纲的要求,结合湖北省专升本英语历年真题,帮助考生建立英语语法的知识体系,掌握专升本考试中必备的语法知识点。

一、本书主要内容

本书的第一部分是基础语法,即英语语法体系中的词法,对英语中的九大词性及其功能和用法进行了系统的阐释。第二部分是核心语法,即英语语法体系中的句法,对英语中的简单句、复合句、特殊句型等进行了全面的梳理。每一章和每一节的所有知识点都配有与专升本考试难度一致的例词或例句,针对与知识点相关的重点考查内容还设置了表格总结,对考生掌握较薄弱的易错点、难点以"补充提示"给出。此外,每一章都配有"实战演练",及时检测考生对每个章节内容的掌握情况。

二、本书几大特点

1. 内容全面,针对性强

本书涵盖了湖北省专升本英语几乎所有可能涉及的语法知识点。市面上各类英语语法书层出不穷,但鲜有针对专升本考生的专门的语法书。本书目标明确、针对性强,从湖北省专升本英语的大纲要求和历年真题实际考查出发,在不遗漏与考试相关的知识点的同时,力求框架逻辑清晰、语言简洁易懂、难度适宜。

2. 紧扣考纲,循序渐进

本书重视英语语法学习中语法体系的构建,在学习的难度上循序渐进,从词法过渡到句法,帮助考生全面掌握语法体系和知识点的同时,打好语法基础。无论是基础语法还是核心语法,每一章节都紧扣专升本的考纲要求。基础语法中的代词、冠词、数词、形容词、连词、介词等内容,是近年来湖北省专升本英语考试中单项选择部分的热门考点,而核心语法中的时态、语态、主谓一致、从句、非谓语动词、特殊句型等内容,均为湖北省专升本英语考试历年真题中单项选择部分的重点考查内容。本书让考生在学完语法之后,真正感觉学有所用,也助力考生提升在大学英语科目上的成绩。

3. 层次分明,重点突出

本书通过大量的表格对重难点细节进行总结,让考生一目了然的同时印象深刻。本书在语言上力求简洁易懂,抽丝剥茧般把复杂的语法知识拆解开来,便于考生理解、消化和吸收。此外,针对考生掌握薄弱的易错点、难点进行"补充提示",真正做到解决考生在语法学习中的各种疑难困惑。

三、本书使用方法

考生可根据章节对学习进度进行规划,比如每周学习一章,三个月即可学完本书的全部内容,也可适当加快进度,每周学习两章,一个半月即可学完全书。当然,作为一本语法书,本书也可以作为一本工具书,考生可在遇到语法困惑需要查阅的时候跳读和查读部分章节内容。

目　录

第一部分　基础语法

第一章　名词、代词 ... 1
　一、名词 ... 1
　二、代词 ... 8
　实战演练 ... 22

第二章　冠词、数词 ... 23
　一、冠词 ... 23
　二、数词 ... 28
　实战演练 ... 34

第三章　动词 ... 36
　一、实义动词 ... 36
　二、系动词(link-v.) ... 39
　三、助动词 ... 42
　四、情态动词 ... 44
　实战演练 ... 53

第四章　形容词、副词 ... 55
　一、形容词 ... 55
　二、副词 ... 56
　三、比较级与最高级 ... 61
　实战演练 ... 65

第五章　连词、介词 ... 67
　一、连词 ... 67
　二、介词 ... 71
　实战演练 ... 83

第二部分　核心语法

第一章　简单句 ······ 84
　一、句子成分 ······ 84
　二、简单句的五种基本句型 ······ 87
　三、句子类型 ······ 90
　实战演练 ······ 101

第二章　时态 ······ 103
　一、一般时态 ······ 103
　二、进行时态 ······ 108
　三、完成时态 ······ 112
　四、完成进行时态 ······ 115
　实战演练 ······ 116

第三章　语态 ······ 117
　一、被动语态的构成 ······ 117
　二、被动语态的转换 ······ 118
　三、被动语态的用法 ······ 120
　四、被动语态的注意事项 ······ 121
　实战演练 ······ 122

第四章　主谓一致 ······ 124
　一、语法一致原则 ······ 124
　二、意义一致原则 ······ 128
　三、就近一致原则 ······ 131
　实战演练 ······ 132

第五章　从句 ······ 133
　一、名词性从句 ······ 133
　二、定语从句 ······ 138
　三、状语从句 ······ 148
　实战演练 ······ 155

第六章　非谓语动词 ······ 156
　一、非谓语动词的形式 ······ 156

二、非谓语动词的句法功能 ·· 159
　　实战演练 ·· 173

- **第七章　特殊句型** ·· 175
　　一、强调句 ·· 175
　　二、虚拟语气 ·· 178
　　三、倒装句 ·· 182
　　实战演练 ·· 186

- **第八章　其他结构** ·· 188
　　一、割裂 ··· 188
　　二、插入语 ·· 188
　　三、否定 ··· 190
　　实战演练 ·· 192

实战演练参考答案 ·· 193
附录　不规则动词变化表 ·· 195

第一部分　基础语法

第一章　名词、代词

一、名词

名词是表示人、事物、地点或抽象概念等名称的词。名词可以分为专有名词和普通名词,也可分为可数名词和不可数名词。

(一) 专有名词与普通名词

1. 专有名词

专有名词主要指人、地点、事物、机构、组织、星期、月份、节日等特有的名称,其首字母必须大写。
- John 约翰　　China 中国　　WTO 世界贸易组织　　Friday 星期五

【补充提示】
① 部分由两个及以上的普通名词构成的专有名词,前面需加定冠词 the。
- the United Nations 联合国　　　　the Great Wall 长城
- the Olympic Games 奥运会　　　　the United States 美国

② 姓氏复数前加 the 表示该姓氏一家人。
- the Greens 格林一家人　　　　the Whites 怀特一家人

2. 普通名词

普通名词表示一类人或事物或抽象概念的名称。普通名词又可以分为四类:个体名词、集体名词、物质名词和抽象名词。

分类	定义	例词		
个体名词	表示单个人或事物的名词	book 书 child 孩子 student 学生	school 学校 doctor 医生 tree 树木	city 城市 girl 女孩 uncle 叔叔
集体名词	表示一群人或一些事物总称的名词	police 警察 cattle 牛	people 人们 team 队伍	family 家 army 军队
物质名词	表示无法分成个体的材料、食品、液体、气体、金属等的名词	water 水 silk 丝绸 wood 木头	milk 牛奶 cotton 棉花 money 钱	gold 金子 gas 天然气 tea 茶
抽象名词	表示人或事物的品质、情感、状态、动作等抽象概念及学科、疾病等的名词	love 关爱 coldness 寒冷 worry 担心	thought 思想 success 成功 politics 政治	happiness 快乐 kindness 善良 diabetes 糖尿病

(二) 可数名词与不可数名词

1. 可数名词

可数名词(countable nouns 或[C.])指能以数目来计算的人或事物,有单复数之分。可数名词单数一般不能单独使用,要用冠词、指示代词等限定词修饰。表示两个及以上的数量时,可数名词要用复数形式,复数形式变化分为规则变化和不规则变化。

(1) 可数名词单数。

① 可数名词单数常用不定冠词 a/an 限定,表泛指或表示数量"一"。

- There is **a** beautiful **girl** over there.
  那边有一个漂亮的女孩。
- It is **a tool** for getting fruit.
  这是一个用来摘水果的工具。
- Lao She is **an** extraordinary **writer**.
  老舍是一位杰出的作家。
- Lucy comes from **an** English-speaking **country**.
  Lucy 来自一个说英语的国家。

【补充提示】

可数名词单数前 a/an 的使用,详见基础语法第二章冠词。

② 可数名词单数也可用定冠词 the 限定,和指示代词 this、that 含义相近,表示特指"这个、那个"。

- **The/That/This girl** in red is my daughter.
  这(那)个穿红色衣服的女孩是我的女儿。
- John is **the monitor** in our class.
  John 是我们班的班长。
- I heard about **the accident** on the radio.
  我从广播里听说了这场事故。

(2) 可数名词复数。

① 可数名词复数的规则变化。

一般情况在词尾直接加-s。

- book—books 书　　girl—girls 女孩　　desk—desks 书桌　　chair—chairs 椅子
  tree—trees 树木　　door—doors 门　　house—houses 房子　　pen—pens 钢笔

以 s、x、sh、ch 结尾的名词在词尾加-es。

- dress—dresses 裙子　　fox—foxes 狐狸　　dish—dishes 盘子　　watch—watches 手表
  class—classes 班级　　box—boxes 盒子　　brush—brushes 刷子　　bench—benches 长凳

以"辅音字母加+y"结尾的名词,变 y 为 i,再加-es。

- family—families 家庭　　lady—ladies 女士　　factory—factories 工厂
  baby—babies 婴儿　　city—cities 城市　　candy—candies 糖果
  pony—ponies 矮马　　country—countries 国家

以 f 或 fe 结尾的名词,变 f 或 fe 为 v,再加-es。
- leaf—leaves 树叶　self—selves 自己　wife—wives 妻子　wolf—wolves 狼

以"辅音字母加+o"结尾的名词一般加-es。
- hero—heroes 英雄　potato—potatoes 土豆　tomato—tomatoes 番茄

【助记】"英雄爱吃土豆和番茄"

【补充提示】
① 以"元音字母+y"结尾的名词,直接加-s。
- boy—boys 男孩　　toy—toys 玩具　　key—keys 钥匙

② 一些以 f 或 fe 结尾的名词,变复数时直接加-s。
- proof—proofs 证据　roof—roofs 屋顶　belief—beliefs 信仰　chief—chiefs 首领

③ 一些以"元音字母+o"结尾的名词和以 o 结尾的外来词,变复数时直接加-s。
- zoo—zoos 动物园　photo—photos 照片　piano—pianos 钢琴　bamboo—bamboos 竹子

② 可数名词复数的不规则变化。

变化情况	常见例词		
元音发生变化的名词	man—men 男人 foot—feet 脚	woman—women 女人 tooth—teeth 牙齿	mouse—mice 老鼠 goose—geese 鹅
词尾发生变化的名词	child—children 孩子 basis—bases 基础 ox—oxen 公牛	datum—data 数据 crisis—crises 危机 phenomenon—phenomena 现象	analysis—analyses 分析 medium—media 媒介

③ 可数名词复数的特殊情况。

单复数同形的名词。

有些名词单数形式和复数形式相同。
- sheep 绵羊　　deer 鹿　　aircraft 飞机　　means 方法
  Chinese 中国人　Japanese 日本人　crossroads 十字路口　series 系列
- What I need is a **sheep**.
  我需要的是一只羊。
- They have ten minutes to shear five **sheep**.
  他们有10分钟的时间来给5只羊剪毛。
- There are many **means** of contacting him.
  有很多方法和他取得联系。

【补充提示】
① fish 表鱼的数量时,单复数同形;表鱼的种类时,其复数为 fishes;表"鱼肉"时,为不可数名词。
② 除 Chinese、Japanese 等表某国人的名词单复数同形外,还有部分表某国人的名词复数形式有变化。

- Englishman—Englishmen 英国人   Frenchman—Frenchmen 法国人
- German—Germans 德国人   American—Americans 美国人

【助记】口诀：中日不变，英法变，其余复数加 s

以复数形式出现的名词。

有些名词常以复数形式出现，通常不用具体的数字及不定冠词 a/an 限定，但可以用 a pair of、two pairs of、many 等单位量词和数量词修饰。

- chopsticks 筷子   glasses 眼镜   clothes 衣服   scissors 剪刀
- trousers 裤子   pants 裤子   jeans 牛仔裤   shorts 短裤
- socks 短袜   headphones 耳机   pyjamas 睡衣裤   twins 双胞胎

- We need a pair of chopsticks.
  我们需要一双筷子。
- He gave me two pairs of shoes.
  他给了我两双鞋。
- She bought many socks in the department store.
  她在百货商店买了很多袜子。

【补充提示】
另外还有一类名词，它们总是以复数形式出现，但不用具体的数字、不定冠词 a/an 及单位量词 a pair of 等修饰，只能用 many、a great many、a lot of 等修饰。

- arms 武器   goods 商品   belongings 所有物   earnings 收入
- thanks 感谢   savings 积蓄

- We never used to import so many goods.
  我们过去从来没有进口过这么多货物。
- A lot of his belongings were burnt in the fire.
  他的很多财物在大火中付之一炬。

集体名词。

有些集体名词只有复数意义，不能用具体的数字或不定冠词 a/an 修饰；作主语时，谓语动词用复数。

- people 人们   police 警察   cattle 牛   personnel 人员

- The police are also looking for the second car.
  警察也在寻找第二辆车。
- The people here are very friendly.
  这里的人们非常友好。

【补充提示】
① 表示"一个人"时需用"person"。people 意为"人们"时，是集体名词，只有复数意义，没有形式变化；但 people 意为"民族"时，是可数名词，有单复数形式变化，其复数为"peoples"。

- This is a proud and independent people.
  这是一个有尊严且独立的民族。

> There are a lot of exchanges between our two **peoples**.

我们两个民族之间有很多交流。

② 有些集体名词既有单数意义又有复数意义。一般说来,当这些集体名词被视为一个整体时,表单数意义,其作主语时,谓语动词用单数;当强调这个群体中的成员时,表复数意义,其作主语时,谓语动词用复数。

    family 家庭   class 班级   group 组,群   crew 全体船员
    crowd 人群   staff 全体员工   army 军队   team 队,组

> Our **family** is small.

我们的家庭很小。(指家庭这个整体)

> My **family** are watching TV.

我的家人们正在看电视。(指家庭里的每个成员)

2. 不可数名词

不可数名词(uncountable nouns 或[U.])是指不能以数目计算的概念、状态、品质、感情或表示物质、材料等的名词。其一般没有复数形式,前面不能用不定冠词 a/an 限定,但可以用数量词或单位量词等加以限定。

> We need to buy **some furniture**.

我们需要买一些家具。

> If you are thirsty, you can drink **some water**.

如果你渴了,你可以喝一些水。

> He drank **a bottle of milk** in the morning.

他早上喝了一瓶牛奶。

> He gave me **three pieces of advice**.

他给了我三条建议。

常见的不可数名词:

weather 天气	luggage 行李	information 信息	news 消息
furniture 家具	advice 建议	wealth 财富	health 健康
work 工作	knowledge 知识	happiness 幸福	courage 勇气
music 音乐	wood 木头	paper 纸张	progress 进步
rice 大米	water 水	meat 肉	salt 盐
beer 啤酒	air 空气	money 钱	time 时间

【补充提示】

① 有些以 -s 结尾的名词形式上是复数,但实为不可数名词。

> maths 数学   politics 政治   physics 物理   economics 经济学   news 消息

② 有些名词既可以作可数名词,也可以作不可数名词,但含义不同。

> room [C.]房间 [U.]空间   paper [C.]论文;试卷 [U.]纸张
    time [C.]次数;倍数 [U.]时间   experience [C.]经历 [U.]经验
    glass [C.]玻璃杯;一杯 [U.]玻璃

③ 有些不可数名词以复数形式出现时有特殊的含义。
➢ wood 木头—woods 树林   water 水—waters 水域
  sand 沙子—sands 沙滩   work 工作—works 作品；工厂

（三）名词的修饰词

可数名词的数量常通过复数形式或"数量词/单位量词+复数形式"来体现，不可数名词则需要借助数量词、单位量词等使之数量化。

1. 数量词

数量词分类	常见数量词		
只修饰可数名词复数	many 许多 a few 几个	a number of 许多 few 很少，几乎没有	a great many 许多 several 几个
只修饰不可数名词	much 许多 a bit of 一点儿	a little 有一点儿 a good/great deal of 很多	little 很少，几乎没有 a large amount of 大量的
既可修饰可数名词复数又可修饰不可数名词	some 一些 most 大多数 plenty of 充足的 quantities of 大量的	all 全部 a lot of 很多 tons of 大量的 masses of 大量的	enough 足够的 lots of 很多 a quantity of 大量的 loads of 大量的

2. 单位量词

不可数名词/可数名词复数除了可以用数量词来修饰、限定外，也可用单位量词来修饰、限定。单位量词有单复数形式变化，结构为"a/an+量词单数+of+不可数名词/可数名词复数"或"数词(大于1)+量词复数+of+不可数名词/可数名词复数"。

常见单位量词	a cup of 一杯 a bottle of 一瓶 a loaf of 一条 a pile of 一堆 a sum of 一笔（钱）	a piece of 一件；一条 a bar of 一块，一条 a box of 一箱，一盒 a drop of 一滴 a meter of 一米	a pair of 一副；一双 a glass of 一杯 a crowd of 一群 a ton of 一吨 a kilo of 一千克
例词	a glass of milk 一杯牛奶 a piece of advice 一条建议 two cups of tea 两杯茶	a bottle of water 一瓶水 a crowd of people 一群人 five pairs of shoes 五双鞋	a piece of news 一则新闻 a sum of money 一笔钱 two boxes of apples 两箱苹果

【补充提示】

"a/an+量词单数+of+不可数名词"结构中的 a/an 也可用 one 代替。
➢ a/one bottle of water 一瓶水
  a/one cup of tea 一杯茶

（四）名词的所有格

名词所有格是表示名词所属关系的形式，包括-'s 所有格、of 所有格和双重所有格。

1. -'s 所有格

-'s 所有格一般表示有生命的名词的所属关系，是英语中构成名词所属关系最常见的形式。

-'s 所有格的用法	例词
普通单数名词词尾加 's	my father's pen 我父亲的笔 the girl's name 那个女孩的名字
在以-s 或-es 结尾的复数名词后加 '	students' books 学生们的书 heroes' names 英雄们的名字
不以-s 结尾的可数名词复数，直接在其后加 's	men's clothes 男士服装 children's toys 儿童玩具
表示某人的店铺、住宅及诊所等场所时，常省略-'s 所有格后的名词	at the doctor's 在诊所 at my sister's 在我姐姐家
表示两者或多者共同拥有时，只将最后一个名词变为所有格形式	Mary and Jane's room Mary 和 Jane 共有的房间（共同拥有）
如果是各自拥有，则每一个名词都要变为所有格形式	Mary's and Jane's rooms Mary 和 Jane 各自的房间（各自拥有）
表示国家、城市、时间、距离、价格、节日等名词所有格常用-'s	China's future 中国的未来 today's newspaper 今天的报纸 ten minutes' walk 步行十分钟的路程 Women's Day 妇女节

2. of 所有格

of 所有格一般表示无生命名词的所属关系，其结构为"名词+of+名词"。

(1) 一般来说，无生命的名词表示所属关系常用 of 所有格。

➢ the center of this city 这个城市的中心　　the roof of the house 房子的屋顶
　the name of the movie 电影的名字　　　 the door of the room 房间的门

(2) of 所有格有时也用于表示有生命的名词的所属关系。

➢ the advice of my parents 我父母的建议　　the opinion of her friends 她朋友们的观点
　the guidance of their teacher 他们老师的指导　the help of his classmate 他同学的帮助

【补充提示】

-'s 所有格与 of 所有格有时可以通用。

➢ the boy's name/the name of the boy 那个男孩的名字
　the old lady's story/the story of the old lady 那个老妇人的故事

3. 双重所有格

双重所有格由"of+-'s 所有格/名词性物主代词"构成,表示部分概念或特殊的情感。

(1) 表示部分概念。

表示部分概念时,双重所有格中-'s 所有格的名词必须是明确限定的、指人的,且 of 前的名词通常被 a/an、数词、some 等词限定。

> a friend of my mother's 我妈妈的一位朋友(妈妈所有朋友中的其中一个)
> two photos of mine 两张我的照片(我所有照片中的其中两张)

【补充提示】

当 of 前面的名词为 picture、photo、portrait 等词时,后接 of 所有格与双重所有格句子的意义有区别。

> a picture of my mother's 一张我妈妈的照片(照片为妈妈所有,但不一定是她本人)
> a picture of my mother 一张我妈妈的照片(照片上的人是妈妈本人)

(2) 表示特殊的情感。

表特殊情感时,双重所有格 of 前面的名词常与指示代词 this、that、these、those 连用,表达出赞赏、厌恶、不满等感情色彩。

> I like **this car of my sister's**.
> 我喜欢我姐姐的这辆车。
> **That daughter of your cousin's** is always complaining.
> 你表哥的那个女儿总是在抱怨。

二、代词

代词是替代名词或名词短语以及相当于名词、名词短语或句子的词。根据指代对象的不同,代词主要分为人称代词、物主代词、反身代词、指示代词、相互代词、不定代词、疑问代词、连接代词和关系代词九种。

(一) 人称代词、物主代词、反身代词

1. 人称代词

人称代词是用于替代人或物的词,有人称、数、格的变化。

数 格 人称	单数		复数	
	主格	宾格	主格	宾格
第一人称	I	me	we	us
第二人称	you	you	you	you

续表

数 格 人称	单数		复数	
	主格	宾格	主格	宾格
第三人称	he	him	they	them
	she	her		
	it	it		

(1) 人称代词主格用作主语,宾格用作宾语。

➢ I have many friends. **They** are all kind to me.

　我有许多朋友。他们都对我很友好。(主格作主语)

➢ **We** never know what will happen tomorrow.

　我们永远不知道明天会发生什么事情。(主格作主语)

➢ I lost my bike. Now I'm looking for **it**.

　我的自行车丢了。我现在正在找它。(宾格作宾语)

➢ You can ask **him**.

　你可以问他。(宾格作宾语)

【补充提示】

主格 I 在句中的任何位置都要大写。

➢ **I** want to be a teacher when **I** grow up.

　我长大后想当一名教师。

➢ **I** think **I**'d better go now.

　我想我最好现在就走。

(2) 人称代词 it 的用法。

① 指代上文提到的事物。

➢ Where is my pen? I left **it** right on the desk.

　我的笔去哪儿了？我就把它放在书桌上了。(指上文中提到的 my pen)

➢ I like playing basketball. **It** is my favorite sport.

　我喜欢打篮球。它是我最喜欢的运动。(指上文中提到的 playing basketball)

② 指代前文提到的某件事情。

➢ You helped me a lot. I shall never forget **it**.

　你帮了我很多。我永远也不会忘。(指前文的整个句子)

③ 指代性别、身份不明的人。

➢ The baby is crying. **It** must be hungry.

　宝宝在哭。它一定是饿了。(指婴儿,尤指性别不详或无所谓时)

➢ Is **it** Tom over there?

那是 Tom 吗?(指身份不明的人)

④ 指代时间、距离、天气等。

➢ What time is **it** now?

现在几点了?(表时间)

➢ **It** is 202 miles from here.

距这里 202 英里。(表距离)

➢ **It** is sunny today.

今天天气晴朗。(表天气)

⑤ 作形式主语或形式宾语,代替句中的不定式短语、动名词短语或从句等。

➢ **It** is no use **crying over spilt milk**.

覆水难收。(真正的主语是动名词短语 crying over spilt milk)

➢ **It** took me a week **to rewrite the paper**.

重写这篇论文花了我一周的时间。(真正的主语是不定式短语 to rewrite the paper)

➢ I think **it** a pity **that you didn't pass the exam**.

你没有通过考试,我觉得很遗憾。(真正的宾语是 that 引导的从句)

➢ I consider **it** important **to practice more**.

我认为多练习很重要。(真正的宾语是不定式短语 to practice more)

⑥ 用于强调句句型。

➢ **It** was Smith that broke the window.

打破窗户的正是 Smith。(it 本身没有词义,只起引出被强调部分 Smith 的作用)

➢ **It** was in the park that I met her.

正是在公园,我遇见了她。(it 本身没有词义,只起引出被强调部分 in the park 的作用)

2. 物主代词

物主代词是表示所属关系的代词,是人称代词的属格形式。物主代词分为形容词性物主代词和名词性物主代词。形容词性物主代词只用作定语修饰名词,不能代替名词;名词性物主代词具有名词的性质,相当于"形容词性物主代词+名词",可作主语、宾语、表语等成分。

含义 分类	我的	你的	他的	她的	它的	我们的	你们的	他/她/它们的
形容词性物主代词	my	your	his	her	its	our	your	their
名词性物主代词	mine	yours	his	hers	its	ours	yours	theirs

(1) 形容词性物主代词。

➢ Thank you for **your** letter.

谢谢你的来信。

➢ **My** mom has changed **her** idea.

我妈妈改变了主意。

- **Our** plans are quite useful.
  我们的计划相当有用。
- **My** whole family came to **my** graduation.
  我的家人都来参加了我的毕业典礼。

【补充提示】
形容词性物主代词后可加 own 表示强调,意为"(某人)自己的"。
- Jane has **her own** room.
  Jane 有她自己的房间。
- I want to have **my own** business.
  我想拥有自己的事业。

(2) 名词性物主代词。
- Your coat is green, but **mine** is yellow.
  你的外套是绿色的,但我的(外套)是黄色的。(mine = my coat,作主语)
- He was not in my room. He might be in **his**.
  他不在我的房间。他可能在自己的(房间)。(his = his room,作宾语)
- Those books are **yours**.
  那些书是你的(书)。(yours = your books,作表语)
- Their house is almost opposite **ours**.
  他们的房子几乎正对着我们的(房子)。(ours = our house,作宾语)

【补充提示】
名词性物主代词用作主语时,谓语动词的数应随物主代词所指代的人或事物的数而定。
- —Is this bag yours or hers?
  —It's mine. Hers **is** over there.
  —这个包是你的还是她的?
  —是我的。她的(包)在那边。(Hers = Her bag)
- My books are new but his **are** old.
  我的书很新,但他的(书)很旧。(his = his books)

3. 反身代词

表示反身或强调的代词叫作反身代词,含义为"……自己"。当主语和宾语所指的人或物为同一个人或物时,通常用反身代词,需在人称和数上保持一致。

数 \ 人称	第一人称	第二人称	第三人称
单数	myself 我自己	yourself 你自己	himself 他自己 herself 她自己 itself 它自己

续表

数 \ 人称	第一人称	第二人称	第三人称
复数	ourselves 我们自己	yourselves 你们自己	themselves 他/她/它们自己

(1) 反身代词在句中可作宾语、表语、同位语,但一般不作主语。

➢ Help **yourself**!
请自便!(作宾语)

➢ The old woman often talks to **herself**.
这位老太太经常自言自语。(作宾语)

➢ That poor boy was **myself**.
那可怜的孩子就是我自己。(作表语)

➢ She is not **herself** today.
她今天跟平常判若两人。(作表语)

➢ I **myself** did that.
那是我自己做的。(作 I 的同位语,表强调)

➢ Tom's mother taught him **herself**.
Tom 的母亲亲自教他。(作 Tom's mother 的同位语,表强调)

【补充提示】

反身代词没有所有格形式,但可以用"形容词性物主代词+own"来表示其所有格的含义。

➢ Please retell the story in **your own** words.
请用你自己的话来复述这个故事。

(2) 含有反身代词的常用短语。

➢ by oneself 独自　　　　　　　devote oneself to 致力于
　help oneself to 随便吃/用　　come to oneself 苏醒过来
　for oneself 独自　　　　　　 seat oneself 坐下
　teach oneself 自学　　　　　 enjoy oneself 玩得开心
　talk/speak to oneself 自言自语　make oneself at home 不受拘束

(二)指示代词

指示代词是用来指代或标记人或事物的代词,在句中可以作主语、宾语、表语、定语等成分。

指示代词	含义
this	这个
that	那个

续表

指示代词	含义
these	这些
those	那些

1. 指代人或物

➢ I'll mention **this** next class.

下一节课我将讲到这一点。(指代物,作宾语)

➢ **That** is my mom.

那是我的妈妈。(指代人,作主语)

➢ What I want to say are **these**.

我想说的是这些。(指代物,作表语)

➢ **Those** pencils are my brother's.

那些铅笔是我弟弟的。(指代物,作定语)

2. 表近指和远指

this、these 指在时间或空间上较近的人或物;that、those 指在时间或空间上较远的人或物。

➢ **This** is my seat and **that** is yours.

这是我的座位,那是你的。

➢ I don't like **these** flowers. Could you please show me **those** ones?

我不喜欢这些花。你把那些拿给我看一看好吗?

3. 指代上下文中的事情

that 或 those 常指上文提到过的事情,this 或 these 常指下文将要提到的事情。

➢ He broke his leg yesterday. **That** is why he didn't show up.

他昨天摔断了腿。那就是他没有出现的原因。(指上文提到过的事情)

➢ I want you to remember **this**: practice makes perfect.

我希望你们记住这一点:熟能生巧。(指下文将要提到的事情)

4. 指代不知名的人或事物

打电话时,常用 this 指自己,that 指不明身份的对方。

➢ Hello. **This** is Mike. Who is **that** speaking?

你好。我是 Mike。你是哪位?

5. that 和 those 的其他用法

that、those 常用在比较结构中以避免重复,代指前面提到的同类名词,that 特指不可数名词或者可数名词单数,those 特指可数名词复数。

➢ The weather in Beijing is much colder than **that** in Wuhan.

北京的天气比武汉的(天气)冷得多。(that = the weather,代指前面提到的同类名词"天气")

➢ The library in my school is not so large as **that** in yours.

我学校的图书馆没有你们学校的(图书馆)大。(that = the library,代指前面提到的同类名词

"图书馆")

> The days in summer are much longer than **those** in winter.
> 夏天的白天比冬天的(白天)长得多。(those = the days,代指前面提到的同类名词"白天")

(三) 相互代词

英语中的相互代词只有 each other 和 one another 两个,意为"互相、相互"。相互代词在句中只能作宾语,其所有格形式为 each other's 或 one another's,可在句中作定语。

1. 相互代词作宾语

> We should help **each other**.
> 我们应当互相帮助。(作动词的宾语)
> Jeffrey and I often write emails to **each other**.
> 我和 Jeffrey 经常互相给对方写电子邮件。(作介词的宾语)
> We understand **one another** perfectly.
> 我们彼此非常了解对方。(作动词的宾语)
> We communicate with **one another** in this special language.
> 我们用这种特殊的语言互相交流。(作介词的宾语)

2. 相互代词的所有格形式

> They looked into **each other's** eyes, without a word.
> 他们看着彼此的眼睛,一言不发。
> The children are chasing **each other's** shadows.
> 孩子们追逐着彼此的影子。
> We received **one another's** postcards before New Year.
> 新年前夕,我们收到了彼此的明信片。
> They were always together and were **one another**'s best friends.
> 他们经常在一起,互相是对方最好的朋友。

(四) 不定代词

用于指代不确定或不定数量的人或物的代词称为不定代词。不定代词可以代替名词和形容词,有指代或修饰可数名词和不可数名词之分,但没有主格和宾格之分,在句中可作主语、宾语、表语、定语等。

1. all 和 both 的用法

all 指"(三者或三者以上)所有,全部",both 指"两者都"。

> I know **all** of the four British students in their school.
> 他们学校的四个英国学生我全认识。
> **All** my plants grow well.
> 我的花草都长得很好。
> —Would you like this one or that one?
> —**Both**.
> ——你要这个还是那个?

——两个都要。
- **Both** of my parents are doctors.
  我的父母都是医生。

2. neither、none、either 的用法

neither 指"两者都不"，none 指"没有任何，都不"，either 指"（两者中的）任何一个"。

- —Will you go there by bus or by car?
  —**Neither**. I will go there by train.
  ——你坐公交车去还是坐轿车去？
  ——都不坐，我坐火车去。
- **Neither** you nor I will go on a business trip.
  你和我都不去出差。
- We have three sons but **none** of them lives/live nearby.
  我们有三个儿子，但他们都不住在附近。
- **None** of these pens works/work.
  这些钢笔都不能用。
- I don't care much for what to drink. **Either** of the two will be OK.
  我不介意喝些什么，两个之中随便一个都行。
- Sightseeing is best done **either** by tour bus or by bicycles.
  观光最好要么乘游览巴士，要么骑自行车。

【补充提示】

不定代词 all、both、every 等与 not 连用时，构成部分否定，表示"不是所有、并非全部"；若要表示完全否定，则需使用 none、neither、no one 等。部分否定相关内容详见核心语法第八章。

- **Not all** of the students like the novel.
  不是所有学生都喜欢这本小说。
- **Not every** expert was interested in it.
  不是每个专家都对此感兴趣。
- **None** of the students like the novel.
  学生中没有一个喜欢这本小说。
- **No one** doubted his capability.
  没有人质疑他的能力。

3. some 和 any 的用法

(1) some 一般用于肯定句中，意思是"几个，一些"，后可接可数名词复数或不可数名词。

- He went to fetch **some** books.
  他去取来一些书。
- I have **some** work to do today.
  今天我有一些工作要做。
- **Some** people like pop music, but **some** don't.
  有些人喜欢流行音乐，但有些人不喜欢。

（2）some 表示"某个，某种"，后可接可数名词单数。
> She won the first prize in **some** competition.
  她在某个比赛中获得了一等奖。
> She is playing chess with **some** boy.
  她正在和某个男孩下棋。

【补充提示】

some 用于疑问句时，表示建议、请求。
> Would you like **some** coffee with sugar?
  你要加糖的咖啡吗？

（3）any 一般用于否定句或疑问句中，意思是"任何一个，任何一些"，后可接可数名词复数或不可数名词。
> There isn't **any** money in my wallet.
  我的钱包里一点儿钱也没有了。
> Did you have **any** questions to ask?
  你有问题要问吗？

【补充提示】

any 也可用于肯定句，含义为"任一，任何"。
> If you have **any** question, you can ask me.
  如果你有任何问题，可以来问我。
> **Any** color is OK.
  任何颜色都可以。

4. every 和 each 的用法

every 含义为"每个"，只能作定语修饰单数名词。each 含义为"每个，各个"，可以放在单数名词前作定语，也可以作代词，后直接跟 of 短语，而 every 后面不能直接跟 of 短语。
> She knows **every** student in the school.
  她认识学校里的每一个学生。
> **Each** book is beautifully illustrated.
  每本书都配有精美的插图。
> They are very busy. **Each** of them has something to do.
  他们很忙，人人都有事干。
> **Every** one of the students in his class studies very hard.
  他班上每个学生学习都很用功。

5. many 和 much 的用法

many 和 much 都表示"许多"，many 代替或修饰可数名词复数，much 代替或修饰不可数名词。
> His name is familiar to **many** people.
  他的名字很多人都熟悉。

➢ How **many** books do you have?
你有多少本书？
➢ The children have too **much** homework to do.
孩子们有太多的家庭作业要做。
➢ I don't have **much** money with me.
我没带很多钱。

【补充提示】
many 的其他常见用法：
① a great many 表示"许多的"，后接可数名词复数，作主语时谓语动词用复数。
➢ **A great many** parents were present at the meeting.
许多家长出席了会议。
② many a 后接可数名词单数，作主语时谓语动词用单数，且相当于 many 后接可数名词复数，如 many a girl = many girls。
➢ **Many a** boy and **many a** girl wishes to attend the party.
许多男孩和女孩都希望参加派对。

6. other、the other、others、the others、another 的用法

(1) other 意思是"别的，其他的"，泛指"其他的（人或物）"。
➢ There are **other** ways of doing it.
做这事还有其他的办法。
➢ The teacher criticized **other** students.
老师批评了其他的学生。

(2) the other 特指"两者中的另一个"，常与 one 连用，构成"one...the other..."，表示"一个……另一个……"。
➢ He has two daughters. One is a nurse; **the other** is a worker.
他有两个女儿。一个是护士，另一个是工人。
➢ He raised one arm and then **the other**.
他先举起一只手，然后举起另一只。

【补充提示】
the other 后可接单数名词，也可接复数名词，此时的 other 作形容词。
➢ On **the other** side of the street, there is a tall tree.
在街道的另一边，有一棵大树。
➢ Mary is much taller than **the other** girls.
Mary 比其他的女孩高得多。
➢ She shared her candies with **the other** kids.
她把她的糖分享给其他的孩子。

(3) others 意思是"另外一些，其他的"，常构成"some...others..."，意思是"一些……另一些……"。

- Some of us like singing and dancing; **others** go in for sports.
  我们中的一些人喜欢唱歌和跳舞,另一些人爱好体育。
- Some came by car; **others** came on foot.
  一些人坐车来,另一些人步行来。

(4) the others 意思是"其他东西,其余的人",特指某一范围内的"其他的(人或物)"。

- Two boys will go to the zoo, and **the others** will stay at home.
  两个男孩将去动物园,其余的人留在家里。
- For some reason, she thinks that **the others** don't like her.
  由于某种原因,她认为其他人不喜欢她。

(5) another 意思是"另一个,又一个",表泛指,接可数名词单数,也可以不接名词,直接使用。

- I have eaten an apple, but I still want **another** (apple).
  我已经吃了一个苹果了,但我还想再吃一个。
- We need **another** computer.
  我们还需要一台电脑。

【补充提示】

若 another 后有数词或 few 修饰时,也可接复数名词。
- I've got **another** three minutes.
  我还有三分钟。
- They met **another** two students later.
  他们后来又遇到了另外两个学生。
- I'm staying for **another** few weeks.
  我还要再待几个星期。

7. one 和 it 的用法

(1) one 常泛指前面提到的可数名词的同一类人或物,相当于"a/an+名词",其复数为 ones。

- I prefer a university in Shanghai to **one** in Beijing.
  比起北京的大学,我更喜欢上海的大学。(one = a university,泛指北京的任意一所大学)
- Our TV set was broken. Let's buy a new **one**.
  我们的电视机坏了。我们去买一台新的吧。(one = a TV set,泛指任意一台电视机)
- New fashions drive out old **ones**.
  新款式淘汰旧款式。(ones = fashions,泛指款式)

(2) it 常特指前面提到的具体的一个名词(和前面提到的名词是同一个),相当于"the+名词"。

- I have lost my pen and I am looking for **it**.
  我的钢笔丢了,我正在找它。(it = my pen,特指前面提到的我的笔)
- I bought a new car. **It** is black.
  我买了一辆新车。它是黑色的。(it = a new car,特指前面提到的新车)

8. few、little、a few、a little 的用法

few	几乎没有(否定)	代替或修饰可数名词复数
a few	一点儿,一些(肯定)	代替或修饰可数名词复数
little	几乎没有(否定)	代替或修饰不可数名词
a little	一点儿,一些(肯定)	代替或修饰不可数名词

➤ **Few** people live in that polar region.
　几乎没有人住在那个极地地区。

➤ You can get **a few** sweets from him.
　你可以从他那儿弄到一些糖果。

➤ He is very poor and he has **little** money.
　他很穷,几乎没有什么钱。

➤ Don't worry. There is still **a little** time left.
　别着急,还有一点儿时间呢。

9. 复合不定代词

由 some、any、no、every 加上 body、one、thing 构成的代词叫作复合不定代词。当复合不定代词作主语时,谓语动词用单数。somebody、someone、something 一般用于肯定句中;anybody、anyone、anything 一般用于疑问句、否定句中。复合不定代词主要有 12 个:somebody(某人)、someone(某人)、something(某事)、anybody(任何人)、anyone(任何人)、anything(任何事)、nobody(没有人)、no one(没有人)、nothing(没有事)、everybody(每个人)、everyone(每个人)、everything(一切)。

➤ There is **someone** at the door.
　门口有个人。

➤ Did you meet **anyone** just now?
　你刚才遇到什么人了吗?

➤ He did **nothing** at the weekend.
　他周末什么也没干。

➤ **Nobody** seems to be bored.
　似乎没有人感到无聊。

【补充提示】

形容词修饰复合不定代词时,常放在复合不定代词之后。

➤ Do you have **anything interesting** to tell us?
　你有什么有趣的事要告诉我们吗?

➤ I have **nothing important** to deal with now.
　我现在没有什么重要的事情要处理。

(五)疑问代词、连接代词、关系代词

1. 疑问代词

用来表达疑问或构成特殊疑问句的代词叫疑问代词。英语中常用的疑问代词有 who、whom、whose、which、what 等。

(1) who、whom、whose 的用法和功能。

who 意为"谁",可在句中作主语、宾语和表语;whom 意为"谁",在句中只能作宾语,一般可与 who 互换,但直接跟在介词后时,只能用 whom;whose 意为"谁的",既可在句中作定语修饰名词,也可在句中作表语,单独使用。

➢ **Who** would like to go with me?
　谁愿意和我一起去呢?(作主语)

➢ **Whom/Who** are you writing to?
　你在给谁写信?(作宾语,whom 可用 who 代替)

➢ With **whom** did you discuss the question?
　你和谁一起讨论这个问题?(位于介词 with 后作宾语,whom 不可用 who 代替)

➢ **Who** is the girl standing outside?
　站在外面的女孩是谁?(作表语)

➢ **Whose** bag is this?
　这是谁的书包?(作定语)

➢ **Whose** are those apples?
　这些苹果是谁的?(作表语)

(2) which 的用法和功能。

which 意为"哪一个,哪一些",既可指代人或物,也可修饰人或物;在句中作主语、宾语、定语等,可与 of 连用。

➢ **Which** is cheaper, the blue or that green coat?
　蓝色和绿色外套,哪一个更便宜?(作主语,指代物)

➢ **Which** is your sister?
　哪个是你的姐姐?(作主语,指代人)

➢ **Which** do you prefer, coffee or tea?
　咖啡和茶,你更喜欢哪一种?(作宾语,指代物)

➢ **Which** book has she read?
　她读过哪本书?(作定语,修饰物)

➢ **Which** of the three cities do you like most?
　三个城市中你最喜欢哪个?(与 of 连用)

(3) what 的用法和功能。

what 意为"什么",可以指代或修饰物;在句中可作主语、宾语、表语和定语。

➢ **What** has happened?
　发生了什么事?(作主语)

➢ **What** do English people eat?
　英国人吃什么?(作宾语)

➢ **What** is your father?
　你父亲是做什么工作的?(作表语)

➢ **What** kind of music do you like?
　你喜欢什么样的音乐?(作定语)

【补充提示】

① what 和 which 的用法区别:what 范围较广,which 常用于在指定的范围内进行选择。

➤ **What** fruit do you like?
你喜欢什么水果?(没有指定选择的范围)

➤ **Which** fruit do you like better, apples or oranges?
苹果和橙子,你更喜欢哪一个?(在指定的范围内进行选择)

② what 和 who 指人时的区别:用 what 提问时,一般是对职业进行提问;用 who 提问时,一般是对身份进行提问。

➤ **What** is your father?
你父亲是做什么工作的?

➤ —**Who** is the man?
—He is my father.
——那个人是谁?
——他是我的父亲。

2. 连接代词

连接代词是指引导主语从句、宾语从句、表语从句、同位语从句的代词。常见的连接代词有 who、whom、which、whose、what、whoever、whichever、whatever 等。

➤ **What** I want to talk about is this.
我想谈的事情就是这个。(引导主语从句)

➤ I can't tell **which** picture is more beautiful.
我分辨不出哪张画更漂亮。(引导宾语从句)

➤ That is **what** we are going to finish this evening.
那就是今晚我们要完成的。(引导表语从句)

【补充提示】

连接代词相关内容详见核心语法第五章第一节名词性从句。

3. 关系代词

关系代词常用来引导定语从句。关系代词一方面在定语从句中充当成分,如主语、宾语、表语或定语,另一方面又指代定语从句所修饰的名词或代词(通常称为先行词)。常见关系代词有 who、whom、whose、which、that、as 等。

➤ The foreigner **who** visited our school yesterday is from Italy.
昨天来参观我们学校的那位外国人是意大利人。(在定语从句中作主语)

➤ He is no longer the man **that** he was.
他已经不是过去的那个他了。(在定语从句中作表语)

【补充提示】

关系代词相关内容详见核心语法第五章第二节定语从句。

实 战 演 练

1. The boy was lost and his parents were worried about his _____.
   A. attention　　　　B. advice　　　　C. safety　　　　D. chance
2. The encouragement from her friends gave her great _____ to face the challenge.
   A. confidence　　　　B. regret　　　　C. result　　　　D. admission
3. There are three elegant _____ in that coffee shop.
   A. woman　　　　B. womans　　　　C. womens　　　　D. women
4. The room on the second floor is _____.
   A. Jack's and Mike's　　　　B. Jack's and Mike
   C. Jack and Mike's　　　　D. Jack and Mikes'
5. There are _____ on the table in the living room.
   A. three bowls of soup　　　　B. three bowl of soup
   C. three bowl of soups　　　　D. three bowls of soups
6. My little brother is seven years old and he can go to school by _____.
   A. oneself　　　　B. he　　　　C. himself　　　　D. his
7. —Is this _____ pen? I found it under the table.
   —Yes, it's _____. Thank you very much.
   A. yours; me　　　　B. your; mine　　　　C. you; my　　　　D. your; my
8. He told us two jokes, but _____ of them is funny.
   A. either　　　　B. both　　　　C. all　　　　D. neither
9. There is _____ with his eyes. He is all right.
   A. something wrong　　B. wrong something　　C. nothing wrong　　D. wrong nothing
10. He gave me _____ suggestions and _____ help.
    A. many; much　　B. many; many　　C. much; many　　D. much; much
11. _____ of my parents are fans of Na Ying, because they think she sings very well.
    A. Both　　　　B. Either　　　　C. None　　　　D. All
12. —Is there _____ food in the box?
    —No, there isn't. There are only _____ books.
    A. some; any　　B. any; any　　C. some; some　　D. any; some
13. There are a lot of plants on _____ side of the street.
    A. both　　　　B. all　　　　C. either　　　　D. none
14. This article is very difficult for us. There are _____ new words in it.
    A. few　　　　B. a little　　　　C. much　　　　D. many
15. He bought two bikes. One was for his wife, and _____ was for his daughter.
    A. other　　　　B. the other　　　　C. others　　　　D. the others

第二章 冠词、数词

一、冠词

冠词是一种虚词,本身不能单独使用,常放在名词前起限定作用。冠词分为不定冠词 a/an、定冠词 the 和零冠词(无冠词的情况)。

(一) 不定冠词

不定冠词 a/an 常用于可数名词单数前,表示泛指或表示数量"一"。

1. 不定冠词 a/an 的区分

a 用于以辅音音素开头的单词前面,an 用于以元音音素开头的单词前面。

- **a** book 一本书　　　　**a** day 一天　　　　　　**a** table 一张桌子
  a car 一辆车　　　　 **a** house 一所房子　　　**a** jacket 一件夹克
- **an** apple 一个苹果　　**an** umbrella 一把雨伞　**an** English book 一本英语书
  an egg 一个鸡蛋　　　**an** orange 一个橙子　　**an** interesting story 一个有趣的故事

【补充提示】

英语中共有 26 个字母,其中元音字母有 5 个,分别是 a、e、i、o 和 u,其余 21 个为辅音字母。一般来说,元音字母发元音,辅音字母发辅音,但要注意一些特殊情况:

① 拼写以辅音字母开头,读音却以元音音素开头的单词,如 hour /ˈaʊə(r)/、honest /ˈɒnɪst/ 等单词虽然以辅音字母 h 开头,但读音却以元音音素开头,故这类单词前面需要用 an。

② 拼写以元音字母开头,读音却以辅音音素开头的单词,如 university /ˌjuːnɪˈvɜːsəti/、European /ˌjʊərəˈpiːən/ 等单词虽然以元音字母开头,但读音却以辅音音素开头,故这类单词前面需要用 a。

2. 不定冠词 a/an 的用法

(1) 泛指一类人或物中的一个。

- I met **a** beautiful girl yesterday.
  昨天我遇见了一个漂亮的女孩。
- He started eating **an** apple.
  他开始吃苹果。
- He brings **a** sleeping bag.
  他带了一个睡袋。

(2) 表示数量"一",但其数的概念没有 one 强烈。

- The bridge can support **a** heavy truck.
  这座桥能承受一辆重型卡车。
- Rome was not built in **a** day.
  罗马非一日建成。

(3) 用在一些固定搭配中。

- a lot of 许多
- make an effort 努力
- have a good time 玩得开心
- a little 一点儿，一些
- a bit 一点儿
- have a cold 感冒
- in a hurry 急匆匆
- take a walk 散步
- have a rest 休息一会儿

(4) 用于表示价格、时间、速度等单位，意为"每"，相当于 every。

➢ He goes to the library four times a week.
   他每周去图书馆四次。

➢ I can type 35 words a minute.
   我每分钟能打 35 个单词。

➢ He was driving at 30 miles an hour.
   他以每小时 30 英里的速度驾车。

➢ It costs 50 pence a kilo.
   价格是每公斤 50 便士。

(5) 表示某种身份、职业、地位。

➢ Lucy is an English teacher.
   露西是一名英语老师。

➢ You are a student.
   你是一名学生。

➢ She's a Buddhist.
   她是一个佛教徒。

(6) 用在集体名词、物质名词、专有名词、抽象名词前。

① 用在集体名词前，对整体进行描述。

➢ Lucy and Mark are a couple.
   Lucy 和 Mark 是一对夫妇。

➢ His speech attracted a large audience.
   他的演讲吸引了一大批观众。

② 用在 rain、snow、tea、coffee 等物质名词前，使之转化为具体名词，表示"一场，一杯"等含义。

➢ They were caught in a heavy snow on their way home last night.
   昨晚他们在回家的路上遇到了一场大雪。

➢ I made a coffee.
   我冲了一杯咖啡。

③ 用在指人的专有名词前，表示某个不认识的人或具有某种特征的人等。

➢ I want to be a Lu Xun.
   我想成为鲁迅那样的人。

➢ A Mr. White wants to see you this afternoon.
   一位 White 先生今天下午想见你。

④ 用在抽象名词前，使抽象名词具体化，表示与该词相关的具体的人或事物。

> Yesterday's performance was **a** great success.
> 昨天的演出是一个巨大的成功。
> Working with Jane has been **a** great joy.
> 和 Jane 一起工作是一件令人愉快的事。

(二) 定冠词

定冠词 the 用于名词前,表示特指的人或物,常见用法如下:

1. 特指某人或某物

> **The** girl in red is my sister.
> 穿红色衣服的女孩是我的妹妹。
> He took **the** medicine.
> 他把药吃了。

2. 谈话双方都明确的人或物

> Could you please help me open **the** window?
> 你可以帮我打开窗户吗?
> Six of **the** 38 people were U.S. citizens.
> 38 人中有 6 个是美国公民。

3. 用于复述上文提到过的人或事物(首次提到的名词前用 a/an,再次提到的名词前用 the)

> There is a book on the table, and **the** book is used for learning English.
> 桌上有一本书,这本书是用来学习英语的。
> They bought a hotel. I have visited **the** hotel.
> 他们买了一家酒店。我曾经去过那个酒店。

4. 用在序数词或形容词最高级前

> I got **the** first prize in the competition.
> 我在比赛中获得了一等奖。
> I live on **the** second floor.
> 我住在二楼。
> Jack is **the** tallest student in our class.
> Jack 是我们班上最高的学生。
> I am **the** happiest man in the world.
> 我是世界上最幸福的人。

5. 用在西洋乐器前(民族乐器前不加)

> Mark can play **the** piano, but he can't play Erhu.
> Mark 会弹钢琴,但不会拉二胡。
> Do you play **the** guitar?
> 你弹吉他吗?

6. 用在某些形容词前,表示某一类人或物

➢ the young 年轻人　　　　the old 老年人　　　　the sick 病人
　the wounded 伤员　　　　the poor 穷人　　　　the disabled 残疾人

7. 用于比较级结构"the+比较级…,the+比较级"中,表示"越……就越……"

➢ The harder you study, the higher score you will get.
　你学习越努力,获得的分数就越高。

➢ The more she learns, the more she wants to learn.
　她学得越多,就越想学。

8. 用在表示地点、方位和时间等的一些固定用法中

➢ in the north 在北方　　　　in the morning 在早上　　　　in the future 未来
　around the corner 在附近　　at the top of 在……的顶端　　on the left 在左边

9. 用在姓氏复数前,表示该姓氏一家人或夫妇二人

➢ The Greens love each other deeply.
　格林夫妇深爱着彼此。(the Greens 表示格林夫妇)

➢ The Blacks are on holiday now.
　布莱克一家正在度假。(the Blacks 表示布莱克一家)

10. 用在独一无二的事物前

➢ the sun 太阳　　　　the earth 地球　　　　the moon 月球

11. 用在由普通名词构成的专有名词前

➢ the Great Wall 长城　　　the Silk Road 丝绸之路　　　the University of Cambridge 剑桥大学

12. 用在江河、湖泊、海洋、山脉、群岛等地理名词前

➢ the Yellow River 黄河　　　the Pacific Ocean 太平洋　　　the English Channel 英吉利海峡

13. 用在党派、团体、机构等名词前

➢ the Communist Party 共产党　　the Democratic Party 民主党　　the United Nations 联合国

【助记】定冠词记忆口诀:
特指双熟悉,上文已提及,世上独无二,序数最高级,某些专有名,习语及乐器,党派及地理。

(三) 零冠词

零冠词是指名词前不使用冠词的情况,具体用法如下:

1. 表示一日三餐、球类运动、棋类游戏、学科、语言的名词前

➢ have breakfast 吃早饭　　play chess 下象棋　　play basketball 打篮球
　learn English 学英语　　speak Chinese 讲汉语

2. 表示季节、月份、星期、节日的名词前

➢ in summer 在夏天　　　in July 在七月　　　on Monday 在星期一
　on Children's Day 在儿童节　　at Christmas 在圣诞节

3. "by+交通工具"结构中的名词前

➢ by bus 乘公交　　　　　by train 乘火车　　　　　by airplane 乘飞机

【补充提示】

表示交通工具的名词不接在介词 by 后时,则名词前要使用冠词、物主代词、指示代词等限定。

➢ I take **a** bus to work every day.
　我每天乘公交车上班。

➢ I've left my bag on **the** bus.
　我把包丢在公交车上了。

➢ She often goes to school on **her** bike.
　她经常骑自行车上学。

4. 名词前已有形容词性物主代词、指示代词及所有格等限定词时

➢ On **his** birthday she sent him presents.
　他生日那天,她送了他礼物。

➢ This is **Lily's** car.
　这是 Lily 的车。

➢ I'm checking **this** bag.
　我正在检查这个包。

5. 某些固定搭配中

➢ lose heart 灰心　　　　on foot 步行　　　　on fire 着火

【补充提示】

注意部分加定冠词与不加冠词时含义大不相同的常见词组:

take place 发生	take the place 代替
on earth 究竟	on the earth 在地球上
by sea 乘船	by the sea 在海边
in charge of 负责……	in the charge of 由……负责
in class 在上课	in the class 在班上

6. 物质名词前,表示泛指

➢ Water boils at 100℃.
　水在一百摄氏度沸腾。

➢ Plastic is hard to break down.
　塑料很难分解。

➢ The price of oil and petrol rose rapidly.
　石油和汽油的价格迅速上涨。

➢ Glass contracts as it cools.
　玻璃遇冷收缩。

7. 抽象名词前,表示泛指

➢ Work is a necessary thing in life.
  工作是人生中必不可少的一件事。
➢ Unity is strength.
  团结就是力量。
➢ Failure is the mother of success.
  失败是成功之母。

8. 表示人名、城市名、街道名、大多数国名等的专有名词前

➢ Beijing is the capital of China.
  北京是中国的首都。
➢ Joan lives in Bridge Street.
  Joan 住在大桥街。

9. 表示一类人或事物的复数名词前

➢ Students should study hard.
  学生应该努力学习。
➢ Horses need to be exercised regularly.
  马需要经常锻炼。

【补充提示】

复数名词前加定冠词时表示特指。
➢ The teachers in this school should attend the meeting.
  这个学校的教师应该参加会议。

10. 表示独一无二的职位、头衔的名词前

➢ William was elected president of the company.
  William 当选为公司总裁。
➢ Lincoln, president of the United States, was murdered in 1865.
  美国总统林肯于 1865 年被谋杀。

【助记】 零冠词用法口诀:

下列情况应免冠,代词限定名词前;
专有名词不可数,学科球类三餐饭;
复数名词表泛指,节日星期月份前;
颜色语种和国名,称呼习语及头衔。

二、数词

数词是表示数目多少和顺序多少的词。数词分为基数词和序数词,基数词表示数目,序数词表示顺序。

（一）基数词

1. 基数词的写法

1－10	11－19	20－90(整数)	100 及以上
1 one	11 eleven		100 one hundred
2 two	12 twelve	20 twenty	1,000 one thousand
3 three	13 thirteen	30 thirty	1,000,000 one million
4 four	14 fourteen	40 forty	1,000,000,000 one billion
5 five	15 fifteen	50 fifty	
6 six	16 sixteen	60 sixty	
7 seven	17 seventeen	70 seventy	
8 eight	18 eighteen	80 eighty	
9 nine	19 nineteen	90 ninety	
10 ten			

【补充提示】

① 13－19 基数词由 3－9 加后缀 teen 构成，注意 eighteen 只保留一个 t，thirteen、fifteen 分别由 three、five 转化而来。

② 20－90 整十基数词由 2－9 加后缀 ty 构成，注意 eight 只保留一个 t，twenty、thirty、forty、fifty 分别由 two、three、four、five 转化而来。

③ 21－99 非整十基数词由整十数加上 1－9 基本数词作个位数构成，十位数和个位数之间加连字符"-"，如 twenty-four。

2. 基数词的基本用法

基数词用于描述事物数量的多少，在句中常作主语、宾语、表语、定语等。

➢ **Two** of the girls are from Wuhan.
   女孩子中有两个来自武汉。

➢ There are **four** students in our group.
   我们组里有四名学生。

➢ Over **one thousand** people died during the war.
   有一千多人在这场战争中丧命。

➢ The city has a population of **two million**.
   这个城市有两百万人口。

➢ Two and two is **four**.
   二加二等于四。

（二）序数词

1. 序数词的写法

1-10	11-19	20-90（整数）
first	eleventh	
second	twelfth	twentieth
third	thirteenth	thirtieth
fourth	fourteenth	fortieth
fifth	fifteenth	fiftieth
sixth	sixteenth	sixtieth
seventh	seventeenth	seventieth
eighth	eighteenth	eightieth
ninth	nineteenth	ninetieth
tenth		

【补充提示】

① 除 first、second、third 外，序数词通常由基数词加后缀 th 构成，注意 fifth、eighth、ninth、twelfth 的拼写形式。

② 序数词的缩写形式是在阿拉伯数字后直接加上序数词的最后两个字母，如 1st、2nd、3rd、4th、21st 等。

③ 两位数及以上的词变序数词，只需把个位数变序数词，十位数、百位数等均不变，如 twenty-third、one hundred and fifty-sixth 等。

2. 序数词的基本用法

序数词用于描述事物的排列顺序，在句中常作主语、表语、定语等。

➤ I am always the **first** to come to the classroom.
  我总是第一个来教室的人。

➤ I live on the **third** floor.
  我住在三楼。

➤ The **eighth** of this month is my birthday.
  这个月的 8 号是我的生日。

➤ Mary was the **second** to arrive.
  Mary 是第二个到的。

【补充提示】

① 序数词前通常需要加定冠词 the，但当序数词前有形容词性物主代词、名词所有格等修饰时，

则省略定冠词 the。
- **The second** man on the left in the picture is my brother.
  照片上左数第二个人是我弟弟。
- Today is **my eighteenth** birthday.
  今天是我十八岁生日。
- He is **Lily's third** boyfriend.
  他是 Lily 的第三任男朋友。

② 当表示"又一、再一",不强调顺序时,序数词前用不定冠词。
- He has bought two cars, but he wants to buy **a third** one.
  他已经买了两辆车,但他还想再买一辆。
- You have had four apples. You can't have **a fifth** one.
  你已经吃了四个苹果了,不能再吃第五个了。

③ 在某些固定搭配中,序数词前不用冠词。
- first of all 首先 　　　at first 起初 　　　at first sight 乍一看

(三) 数词的其他用法

1. 表确切和不确切数目

(1) 表确切数目。

hundred(百)、thousand(千)、million(百万)、billion(十亿)、dozen(一打;十多个)、score(二十个)等词前有具体基数词且表确切数目时,这些词不用复数形式。
- **two hundred** students 两百名学生　　　**two dozen** eggs 两打鸡蛋
  six billion dollars 六十亿美元　　　**ten million** workers 一千万工人

(2) 表不确切数目。

hundred、thousand、million、billion、dozen、score 等词构成短语表示不确切数目时,这些词需变复数形式,其后与 of 连用,表示"数百"、"数千"、"数百万"、"数十亿"、"几十"或"许多"等含义。
- **hundreds of** teachers 数百名老师　　　**thousands of** people 数千人
  dozens of eggs 几十个鸡蛋　　　**scores of** young doctors 许多年轻的医生

【补充提示】
当这些词前有 some、several、a few、many 等词限定时,其用单数或复数形式均可。用单数形式时,其后 of 可省略;用复数形式时,其后 of 不可省略。
- many thousand (of) books/many thousands of books 几千本书

2. 表分数和百分数

(1) 表分数。

表示分数时,分子用基数词,分母用序数词。当分子是 1 时,分母用单数;当分子大于 1 时,分母用复数。
- one third 三分之一　　　two fifths 五分之二　　　seven tenths 十分之七

【补充提示】

① 二分之一常用 a half 表示；四分之一和四分之三也可用 one/a quarter 或 three quarters 表示。
② 分数表达中，基数词与序数词之间可加连字符"-"也可不加。
➢ two thirds/two-thirds 三分之二
③ 分数限定名词时需在名词前加 of。
➢ three fourths of students 四分之三的学生
④ 整数和分数之间常用 and 连接。
➢ four and one third 四又三分之一

(2) 表百分数。

表示百分数时，由基数词加 percent 构成，限定名词时需在名词前加 of。
➢ forty percent of the students 百分之四十的学生

3. 表倍数

表示倍数时，两倍用 twice/double，三倍及以上用"基数词+times"。
➢ seven times 七倍　　　fifteen times 十五倍　　　thirty times 三十倍

【补充提示】

倍数常见句型详见核心语法第五章状语从句。

4. 表年龄

(1) 表确切年龄。

用"基数词(+years old)"或"at the age of+基数词"表示某人的确切年龄。
➢ He is **ten(years old)** this year.
　他今年十岁。
➢ **At the age of twenty-eight**, I got married.
　在我二十八岁时，我结婚了。

【补充提示】

当基数词与 year old 用连字符"-"连接时可当作形容词使用，常作定语修饰可数名词，此时 year 只能用单数形式，即"基数词-year-old"。
➢ a **ten-year-old** boy 一个十岁的男孩

(2) 表大概年龄。

用"in+one's+整十的复数的基数词"表示某人的大概年龄。
➢ in my twenties 在我二十多岁时

5. 表时间

(1) 表日期。

日期的写法为月、日、年或日、月、年；其中年用基数词，日可用基数词也可用序数词，月需用英文拼写或使用缩写形式;年和月、日必须用逗号隔开。

➢ October 1(st), 2010 = 1(st) October, 2010
  2010 年 10 月 1 日

【补充提示】

各月份及其缩写形式:

January(Jan.) 一月	February(Feb.) 二月	March(Mar.) 三月	April(Apr.) 四月
May 五月(无缩写)	June(Jun.) 六月	July(Jul.) 七月	August(Aug.) 八月
September(Sep.) 九月	October(Oct.) 十月	November(Nov.) 十一月	December(Dec.) 十二月

(2) 表世纪和年代。

① 表示"……世纪……年代"时,常用"the+表示年份的阿拉伯数字+s/'s"。

➢ the 1980s/the 1980's 20 世纪 80 年代

② 单独表示"……世纪"时,常用"the+序数词+century",也可以用"the+百位进数+s/'s"表示。

➢ the eighteenth/18th century 18 世纪　　　the 1900s/the 1900's 20 世纪

(3) 表时刻。

① 表示整点常用"基数词+o'clock(可省略)"。

➢ ten(o'clock) 10:00

② 表示"几点几分"时,如果分钟数在 30 以内(包括 30),用"分钟数 + past + 钟点数";如果分钟数超过 30,用"(60-分钟数)+to+(钟点数+1)";半小时可用 half,一刻钟可用 a quarter。

➢ two past nine 9:02　　　　　　five to ten 9:55
➢ half past two 2:30　　　　　　a quarter to six 5:45

或者也可直接用"时钟数+分钟数"表示。

➢ nine two 9:02　　　　　　　nine fifty-five 9:55

(4) a.m.和 p.m.。

a.m.表示"上午",p.m.表示"下午",其前不加 o'clock,且不与 morning 和 afternoon 同时使用。

➢ 8:10 a.m.(= 8:10 in the morning) 上午 8 点 10 分
  6:00 p.m.(= 6:00 in the afternoon) 下午 6 点

6. 表编号

编号可用基数词或序数词表示,常用结构为"the+序数词+名词"或"名词(首字母大写)+基数词",基数词可用阿拉伯数字或英文单词,若用英文单词表示,首字母也需要大写。

➢ Room 403 403 房间
➢ Number 8/Eight 第 8 号
➢ Chapter 7/Seven = the seventh chapter 第 7 章
➢ Lesson 5/Five = the fifth lesson 第 5 课
➢ Act 3/Three = the third act 第 3 幕

7. 表加减乘除

(1) 加法。

常用 and/plus 表示,结构为"基数词+and/plus+基数词+is+基数词"。

➤ One and/plus two is three.　　1+2=3

(2) 减法。

常用 minus 表示,结构为"基数词+minus+基数词+is+基数词"。

➤ Eight minus three is five.　　8−3=5

(3) 乘法。

常用 times 表示,结构为"基数词+times+基数词+is+基数词"。

➤ Two times three is six.　　2×3=6

(4) 除法。

常用 divided by 表示,结构为"基数词+divided by+基数词+is+基数词"。

➤ Ten divided by two is five.　　10÷2=5

8. 表小数

小数用阿拉伯数字或者基数词表示,小数点读作 point,小数点后的数字按顺序依次读出。

➤ zero point four　　0.4　　　　two point six eight four　　2.684

实 战 演 练

1. There is _____ old bike in _____ corner of that room.
   A. a; the　　　　　B. an; the　　　　　C. an; an　　　　　D. a; a

2. _____ world we live in should be protected by all of us.
   A. /　　　　　　　B. An　　　　　　　C. The　　　　　　D. A

3. We often play _____ ping-pong after _____ class.
   A. the; the　　　　B. /; /　　　　　　C. the; /　　　　　　D. /; an

4. There is _____ new mobile phone and _____ mobile phone is Mike's.
   A. a; the　　　　　B. an; /　　　　　　C. the; an　　　　　D. a; an

5. I got _____ second prize in the English Translation Contest.
   A. a　　　　　　　B. an　　　　　　　C. /　　　　　　　D. the

6. He is _____ tallest boy in our class.
   A. the　　　　　　B. a　　　　　　　　C. an　　　　　　　D. /

7. He likes playing _____ guitar, but he doesn't like play _____ chess.
   A. /; the　　　　　B. the; /　　　　　　C. the; the　　　　　D. /; /

8. I usually visit my grandma by _____ air in _____ summer.
   A. an; the　　　　 B. /; /　　　　　　C. the; an　　　　　D. /; the

9. Miss Green was my _____ first teacher in high school.
   A. the　　　　　　B. a　　　　　　　　C. an　　　　　　　D. /

10. Today is Lucy's _____ birthday, so she is very happy.

   A. eighteen　　　　B. eighteenth　　　　C. the eighteen　　　　D. the eighteenth

11. There are two _____ desks, but _____ of them are broken.

   A. thousand; three fifths　　　　　　B. thousand; three fifth

   C. thousands; three fifths　　　　　　D. thousands; third fifths

12. —Lily, did you see all the acts?

   —No, when I got to the theater, they were playing _____ .

   A. Act Three　　　　B. third act　　　　C. the act third　　　　D. the act three

13. The newly built library is _____ than the old one.

   A. three time bigger　　　　　　　　B. three times bigger

   C. third time bigger　　　　　　　　D. three times biggest

14. —When was the Communist Party of China founded?

   —It was founded on _____ .

   A. 1921, July 23　　B. July, 1921, 23　　C. 1921, 23 July　　D. July 23, 1921

15. Though she is a _____ girl, she behaves like a child.

   A. twenty-year-old　　B. twenty years old　　C. twenty-years-old　　D. twenty-year-olds

第三章 动　　词

动词是用来表示动作或状态的词,是句子的重要组成部分;可在句子中担当谓语,说明主语是什么或做什么。英语中的动词有不同的形态,且通过不同的形态可以体现动作或状态发生的时间(时态),动作的发出者和承受者间的主被动关系(语态),以及体现说话人的情感态度(情态)等。根据动词的词义及其在句中的功能,通常可分为实义动词、系动词、助动词和情态动词。

一、实义动词

实义动词又称行为动词,表示具有实际意义的动作,可在句中独立充当谓语。根据动词后是否需接宾语,可分为及物动词与不及物动词。

（一）及物动词(vt.)

及物动词后面可以直接跟宾语,根据其后接的宾语可分为接单宾语的及物动词、接双宾语的及物动词和接复合宾语的及物动词。

➢ He **reads** newspapers every day.
　他每天都读报。
➢ I **watched** the movie.
　我看了那部电影。
➢ I could **hear** her laughter.
　我可以听见她的笑声。
➢ I **sent** John a postcard during the holiday.
　放假期间我给 John 寄了一张明信片。
➢ He **considers** himself an expert on the subject.
　他认为自己是这门学科的专家。

1. 接单宾语的及物动词

只接一个宾语的及物动词,即为单宾语及物动词,英语中的及物动词大多数是单宾语及物动词。

➢ She **loves** Chinese literature.
　她喜爱中国文学。
➢ I **accept** your apology.
　我接受你的道歉。
➢ Most people **hate** him.
　大部分人恨他。

2. 接双宾语的及物动词

可以接两个宾语的及物动词,即为双宾语及物动词。两个宾语中,直接宾语表示动作的承受者,间接宾语表示动作的方向或目标(给谁或为了谁)。一般来说,直接宾语是物,间接宾语是人,间接宾语一般位于直接宾语之前；但是当直接宾语置于间接宾语之前时，需在间接宾语前加介词 to/for。

- ➢ My parents bought **me a nice dress**.
- = My parents bought **a nice dress for me**.

  我的父母给我买了一条漂亮的裙子。(a nice dress 是直接宾语，me 是间接宾语)

- ➢ The mayor awarded **her the prize** for both films.
- = The mayor awarded **the prize to her** for both films.

  因为她的两部电影，市长为她颁奖。(the prize 是直接宾语，her 是间接宾语)

- ➢ I paid **him ＄5000** yesterday.
- = I paid **＄5000 to him** yesterday.

  我昨天付给他 5000 美元。(＄5000 是直接宾语，him 是间接宾语)

- ➢ She showed **me her ticket**.
- = She showed **her ticket to me**.

  她给我看了她的票。(her ticket 是直接宾语，me 是间接宾语)

直接宾语置于间接宾语之前时，需在间接宾语前加 to 的常见双宾语及物动词：

| give 给 | bring 带来 | hand 递 | pass 传递 | tell 告诉 |
| read 读 | return 归还 | lend 借 | teach 教授 | show 展示 |

直接宾语置于间接宾语之前时，需在间接宾语前加 for 的常见双宾语及物动词：

| buy 买 | make 制作 | save 保留 | cook 烹饪 | order 订购 |
| draw 画 | spare 抽出 | fetch 拿来 | play 演奏 | sing 唱歌 |

3. 接复合宾语的及物动词

有些及物动词接了宾语但句子意义仍不完整，还需要在宾语后加上其他的词或短语作宾语补足语，来补充说明宾语的特征、状态、身份或动作等，这种"宾语+宾语补足语"的结构称为复合宾语。

- ➢ We must keep **the classroom clean**.

  我们必须保持教室干净。(clean 是宾语补足语，补充说明宾语 the classroom 的状态)

- ➢ We should make **our city more beautiful**.

  我们应该让我们的城市更美丽。(more beautiful 是宾语补足语，补充说明宾语 our city 的特征)

- ➢ My mother names **me Peter**.

  我母亲给我取名叫 Peter。(Peter 是宾语补足语，补充说明宾语 me 的身份)

- ➢ I find **this job very relaxing**.

  我发现这份工作非常令人放松。(very relaxing 是宾语补足语，补充说明宾语 this job 的特征)

常见的接复合宾语的及物动词：

| make 使 | leave 使 | keep 使保持 | consider 认为 | find 认为 |
| think 认为 | call 称呼 | name 命名 | appoint 任命 | elect 选举 |

(二) 不及物动词(vi.)

不及物动词后面不能直接跟宾语,部分不及物动词后接介词之后可跟宾语。

➢ An honest boy never **lies**.
  诚实的男孩从不说谎。
➢ The little boy **smiled** at his mother.
  这个小男孩对着他妈妈笑。
➢ A year later my cat **died**.
  一年后,我的猫死了。
➢ The sun **rises** in the east.
  太阳从东方升起。

常见的不及物动词:

agree 同意	appear 出现	apologize 道歉	arrive 到达	come 来
die 死亡	dream 梦想	exist 存在	fall 落下	go 去
happen 发生	jump 跳	laugh 笑	lie 说谎	listen 听
live 居住	occur 发生	rain 下雨	rise 升起	run 跑
sit 坐	sleep 睡觉	smile 微笑	wait 等待	work 工作

【补充提示】
英语中有很多动词既可作及物动词也可作不及物动词,特别要注意一些动词在作及物动词和不及物动词时意义不同。

有些动词作及物动词和不及物动词时,意义相同:

begin   vi. & vt. 开始   change vi. & vt. 改变   drive vi. & vt. 驾驶
help   vi. & vt. 帮助   leave   vi. & vt. 离开   sing   vi. & vt. 唱

➢ Let's **begin** at 8 o'clock.
  我们八点开始吧。(begin 作不及物动词)
➢ He **begins** his lesson with a big smile.
  他带着灿烂的笑容开始上课。(begin 作及物动词)
➢ They **left** last week.
  他们上周离开了。(leave 作不及物动词)
➢ I **will leave** Beijing tomorrow.
  我明天将离开北京。(leave 作及物动词)
➢ The climates **change**.
  气候发生变化。(change 作不及物动词)
➢ I **'ve changed** my mind.
  我已经改变了主意。(change 作及物动词)

有些动词作及物动词和不及物动词时,意义不同:

play　　*vi.*玩耍　*vt.*打;演奏
grow　*vi.*生长　*vt.*种植
ring　　*vi.*(电话、铃)响　*vt.*打电话

hang　*vi.*悬挂　*vt.*绞死
beat　*vi.*跳动　*vt.*敲打
speak　*vi.*讲话　*vt.*说(语言)

- The phone **is ringing**.
  电话正在响。(ring 作不及物动词)
- I **will ring** you soon.
  我很快就会给你打电话。(ring 作及物动词)
- Tomatoes **grow** best in direct sunlight.
  西红柿在阳光直射下生长得最好。(grow 作不及物动词)
- Farmers **grow** rice in the rich soil.
  农民们在肥沃的土壤里种植水稻。(grow 作及物动词)
- Doctors **operated** on Max.
  医生给 Max 做了手术。(operate 作不及物动词)
- They **operated** a medical machine.
  他们操作一台医疗器械。(operate 作及物动词)

二、系动词(*link-v.*)

系动词本身有一定的词义,但不能单独作谓语,后必须接表语构成系表结构,说明主语的身份、性质、状态等。

(一) 状态系动词

状态系动词一般表示主语的状态,这类系动词只有 be 动词(am/is/are,was/were)。

- He **is** a student.
  他是个学生。
- She **was** a teacher.
  她曾是一名教师。

(二) 持续系动词

持续系动词表示主语继续或保持的一种状态,主要有 keep、remain、stay 等,含义为"保持,仍然,持续"。

- They **kept** silent at the meeting.
  他们在会上保持沉默。
- He still **remains** single.
  他仍然是单身。
- He should **stay** calm.
  他应该保持镇定。

（三）表像系动词

表像系动词表示"看起来,好像,似乎",主要有 seem、appear 等。

➢ He **seems** very anxious.
  他似乎很焦虑。
➢ They **seemed** an ideal couple.
  他们似乎是一对完美的夫妻。
➢ She **appeared** tired after a long journey.
  长途旅行后她看起来很累。

（四）感官系动词

感官系动词表示"……起来",主要有 look(看起来)、feel(摸起来;感觉)、smell(闻起来)、sound(听起来)、taste(尝起来)。

➢ The dress **feels** soft.
  这裙子摸起来很柔软。
➢ They **look** very excited.
  他们看起来很兴奋。
➢ Food **smells** delicious.
  食物闻起来真香。
➢ She **sounded** a little worried.
  她听起来有点焦虑不安。

（五）变化系动词

变化系动词表示主语状态的变化,主要有 become、grow、get、go、turn 等,含义为"变得,成为"。

➢ He **becomes** a doctor.
  他成了一名医生。
➢ Her face **turned** red.
  她的脸变红了。
➢ I **grew** a little afraid of the man in black.
  我变得有点害怕那个穿黑衣服的男人。
➢ The girls **get** tired.
  女孩子们变得疲惫起来。

（六）终止系动词

终止系动词表示"结果是,证明是",主要有 prove、turn out 等。

➢ The news **proves** (to be) false.
  这消息证明是假的。
➢ Improving yourself **proved** (to be) a difficult task.

提升自己证明是个困难的任务。
- His choice **turned out** (to be) right.

  他的选择证明是正确的。

【补充提示】

① 英语中有部分动词既可以作系动词,也可以作实义动词,但意义不同:

get *link-v.* 变得 *vt.* 得到;让　　　go *link-v.* 变得 *vi.* 去　　　grow *link-v.* 变得 *vi.* 生长 *vt.* 种植

look *link-v.* 看起来 *vi.* 看　　　　turn *link-v.* 变得 *vt.* & *vi* 转动

- The car **looks** new.

  这辆车看起来很新。(look 作系动词)
- He **looks** at me angrily.

  他生气地看着我。(look 作不及物动词)
- My father **got** angry.

  我父亲生气了。(get 作系动词)
- I **got** a letter from Mary this morning.

  今天早上我收到了 Mary 的一封信。(get 作及物动词)
- Sometimes food **goes** bad.

  有时食物会变质。(go 作系动词)
- The years **go** so quickly!

  一年年过得真快!(go 作不及物动词)
- It **turns** cold.

  天变冷了。(turn 作系动词)
- He **turned** and walked away.

  他转身走开了。(turn 作不及物动词)

② 英语中的动词根据其持续性,可分为延续性动词与非延续性动词。

● 延续性动词。

延续性动词又称持续性动词,表示可以持续的行为或状态,常与表示时间段的时间状语连用且句子常使用完成时态。

常见的延续性动词:

| study 学习 | learn 学习 | work 工作 | wait 等待 | watch 看 |
| read 阅读 | sleep 睡觉 | live 居住 | stay 停留 | walk 散步 |

- She **has lived** here for 10 years.

  她已经在这里住了 10 年了。(live 是延续性动词,与表示时间段的 for 10 years 连用)
- I've **been waiting** for twenty minutes.

  我等了二十分钟了。(wait 是延续性动词,与表示时间段的 for twenty minutes 连用)
- He's **worked** in Wuhan since 1959.

  他自 1959 年以来一直在武汉工作。(work 是延续性动词,与表示时间段的 since 1959 连用)
- I've **learned** English since I was seven.

  我从七岁起就开始学英语了。(learn 是延续性动词,与表示时间段的 since I was seven 连用)

- 非延续性动词。

非延续性动词又称短暂性动词、终止性动词，表示行为过程是短暂的、瞬间完成的，常与表示时间点的时间状语连用，一般不能与表示时间段的时间状语连用。

常见的非延续性动词：

| die 死亡 | open 打开 | close 关闭 | begin 开始 | start 开始 |
| finish 结束 | borrow 借出 | buy 买 | leave 离开 | arrive 到达 |

➤ Her husband **died** suddenly last week.

她的丈夫上周突然去世了。(die 是非延续性动词，与表示时间点的 last week 连用)

➤ They **had to leave** at midnight.

他们不得不半夜离开。(leave 是非延续性动词，与表示时间点的 at midnight 连用)

➤ Her brother **achieved** his goal in 2010.

她的哥哥在 2010 年实现了自己的目标。(achieve 是非延续性动词，与表示时间点的 in 2010 连用)

➤ Jack **bought** himself a mountain bike yesterday morning.

Jack 昨天早上给自己买了一辆山地自行车。(buy 是非延续性动词，与表示时间点的 yesterday morning 连用)

- 延续性动词与非延续性动词的转化。

非延续性动词在完成时中不能与表示时间段的时间状语连用，但可以将非延续性动词转化成延续性动词后，再与表示时间段的时间状语连用。

常见的延续性动词与非延续性动词的转化：

| die→be dead | borrow→keep | buy→have | open→be open |
| finish→be over | leave→be away | marry→be married | close→be closed |

➤ The old man has died for four years. (错误)

The old man **has been dead** for four years. (正确)

这位老人已经去世四年了。

➤ I have bought the book for five days. (错误)

I **have had** the book for five days. (正确)

这本书我已经买了五天了。

➤ He has left for 10 minutes. (错误)

He **has been away** for 10 minutes. (正确)

他已经离开了十分钟。

三、助动词

助动词用于帮助主要动词构成各种时态、语态、疑问句和否定句等。助动词本身无词义，不可单独使用。英语中常见的助动词有 be (am/is/are/was/were)、have (has/had)、do (does/did)、will/shall/would 等。

（一）构成时态

1. 进行时：be（助动词）+doing（现在分词）

➢ He **is singing** now.
　他正在唱歌。

➢ I **am studying** English.
　我正在学英语。

➢ They **were playing** football.
　他们正在踢足球。

➢ Lily **was cleaning** the room.
　Lily 正在打扫房间。

2. 完成时：have（助动词）+done（过去分词）

➢ I **have finished** my work.
　我已经完成了工作。

➢ We **have made** great progress in science and technology.
　我们在科技方面取得了巨大进展。

➢ She **has** already **got** married.
　她已结婚了。

➢ The train **had left** before we arrived.
　在我们到达之前，火车已经开走了。

3. 将来时：will/shall/would（助动词）+do（动词原形）

➢ He **will go** to Shanghai tomorrow.
　他明天将去上海。

➢ The ship **will be** ready in two months.
　这艘船两个月后将准备就绪。

➢ I **shall see** him soon.
　我很快就会见到他。

➢ He said he **would wait** for us at the bus stop.
　他说他将会在公共汽车站等我们。

（二）构成语态

被动语态：be（助动词）+done（过去分词）

➢ He **was sent** to school when he was 3 years old.
　他三岁的时候就被送去了学校。

➢ Firewood will **be collected** by two young girls.
　两位年轻女孩将采集柴火。

➢ The award **was established** in 2020.
　该奖设立于 2020 年。

（三）构成疑问句

- **Have** you **read** the book *The Little Prince*?
  你读过《小王子》这本书吗？（一般疑问句）
- What **will** you **do** tomorrow?
  你明天会做什么？（特殊疑问句）
- **Is** she a housewife or a nurse?
  她是一个家庭主妇还是护士？（选择疑问句）
- You were late today, **weren't** you?
  你今天迟到了，不是吗？（反义疑问句）

（四）构成否定句

- He **is not** listening to music.
  他没有在听歌。
- Cathy **has not** written to me recently.
  Cathy 最近没有给我写信。
- I **do not** like her voice.
  我不喜欢她的声音。
- We **will not** go on an outing.
  我们将不去郊游。

四、情态动词

情态动词用于表示说话人的情感和态度。情态动词本身有词义，但不能单独作谓语，必须与实义动词或系动词的原形一起构成谓语。常见的情态动词有 can/could、be able to、may/might、must、have to、should、ought to、need、shall、will/would、dare、used to、had better 等。

（一）情态动词的基本用法

1. can, could

（1）表示能力(会，能)。

- I **can** type 50 words a minute.
  我一分钟能打 50 个字。
- I **can** take care of myself.
  我能照顾好自己。
- I **could** drive a car when I was at university.
  读大学的时候我就会开车了。
- I **could** not speak English fluently last year.
  去年我还不能流利地说英语。

【补充提示】
could 是 can 的过去式,表示过去的能力。

(2) 表示请求或许可(可以)。

➢ **Can/Could** you please open the window?
   你能把窗户打开一下吗?(表请求)

➢ You **can** park your car here.
   你可以把车停在这儿。(表许可)

➢ You **can** use my phone.
   你可以使用我的手机。(表许可)

【补充提示】
① can/could 都可用于表请求,此时 could 不是 can 的过去式,而表示委婉语气。
② could 表请求时,回答常用 can。

➢ — **Could** you show me the way?
   —Yes, I **can**.
   ——你能告诉我怎么走吗?
   ——好的。

(3) 表示推测(可能)。

➢ The news **can't** be true.
   这消息不可能是真的。

➢ Where **can** he have gone?
   他可能去哪儿了呢?

➢ It **couldn't** be their decision.
   这不可能是他们的决定。

【补充提示】
can/could 表示推测,多用于疑问句和否定句,can't/couldn't 此时译为"不可能,一定不"。

(4) 表示惊讶,常用于疑问句与否定句。

➢ How **can** you believe such news?
   你怎么会相信这样的消息?

➢ You **can't** be serious!
   你不是认真的吧!

2. be able to

be able to 用于表示能力(会,能),be able to 中的 be 动词需要根据时态和主语的人称、数进行选择。

➢ I **am able to** play the piano.
   我会弹钢琴。

> He **was able to** drive a truck when he was young.
> 他年轻的时候会开卡车。

> They **will be able to** finish the work soon.
> 他们很快就能够完成工作。

【补充提示】

can/could 和 be able to 的用法区别:
① can/could 和 be able to 都可表能力,两者在意思上相同,可互换。

> He **can** answer the question. = He **is able to** answer the question.
> 他能回答这个问题。

② 表示过去成功做到了某件事,只能用 was/were able to,不用 could。

> The fire spread quickly in the hotel last night, but luckily everyone **was able to** get out.
> 昨天晚上大火在宾馆里快速蔓延,但幸运的是,大家都出来了。

> They **were able to** flee to Europe before the war broke out.
> 他们在战争爆发之前逃去了欧洲。

③ be able to 可用于多种时态,can/could 一般用于现在时和过去时。

> She **will be able to** come to the party tomorrow.
> 她明天会来参加聚会。

> I **was able to** understand what you said yesterday.
> 我能理解你昨天说的话。

> He **has been able to** speak three languages.
> 他已经会讲三门语言了。

3. may, might

(1) 表示推测(可能)。

> He **may** miss the train.
> 他可能错过火车。

> Some big firms **may** close.
> 一些大公司可能会关闭。

> He **might** be busy now.
> 他现在可能很忙。

> Smoking **might** be banned in most workplaces.
> 大部分的工作场所有可能禁止抽烟。

【补充提示】

① might 是 may 的过去式,但表示推测时,一般不区分时态,might 表示比 may 的可能性小。
② may/might 表示推测时一般用于肯定句中,may/might 的否定形式 may/might not 译为"可能不,也许不"。

(2) 表示请求或许可(可以)。

> **May/Might** I borrow your book?

我可以借你的书吗？（表请求）

> You **may** leave now.
> 你现在可以离开了。（表许可）

> **May** we come in?
> 我们可以进去吗？（表请求）

【补充提示】
① 表示请求时，may/might/can/could 可以互换，其中 might/could 表示委婉语气；肯定回答一般用 can/may，不用 could/might，否定回答用 can't 或 mustn't（不允许，禁止）。

> — **May/Might/Can/Could** I open the window?
> —Yes, you **can/may**.
> —No, you **can't/mustn't**.
> ——我可以打开窗户吗？
> ——是的，你可以。
> ——不，你不可以（打开窗户）。

② 表许可时，may 与 can 可以互换，但一般不用 might/could。

> You **may/can** go home now.
> 你现在可以回家了。

(3) 表示祝愿。

常用句式结构：May+sb.+动词原形+其他+!

> **May** you have a nice day!
> 祝你度过愉快的一天！

> **May** you succeed!
> 祝你成功！

> **May** you return soon!
> 愿你早日归来！

(4) may/might 的固定用法。

may/might as well do sth. 不妨，不如做某事

> We **may/might as well** finish the work now.
> 我们不妨现在就完成这项工作。

> You **may/might as well** try again.
> 你不妨再试一遍。

> We **may/might as well** get started.
> 我们不妨开始吧。

4. must, have to

(1) 表示主观看法（必须、一定）。

> All passengers **must** wear their seat-belts.

= All passengers **have to** wear their seat-belts.
所有乘客必须系上安全带。
➢ The candidate **must** satisfy the general conditions for the job.
= The candidate **has to** satisfy the general conditions for the job.
应试者必须满足这项工作的一般条件。

【补充提示】

① must 引导的一般疑问句的肯定回答用 must，否定回答用 needn't 或 don't have to。
➢ — **Must** I go with you?
　　—Yes, you **must**.
　　—No, you **needn't/don't have to**.
　　——我必须和你一起去吗？
　　——是的，你必须。
　　——不，你不必。

② must 的否定形式 must not，缩写为 mustn't，表示"禁止，不允许"。
➢ Children **mustn't** swim in the pool.
禁止小孩在该泳池游泳。
➢ You **mustn't** play with strangers.
禁止你和陌生人玩耍。

③ must 和 have to 的区别：
● must 和 have to 都可表"必须"，从含义上来看，must 强调主观性，have to 强调客观性。
➢ We **must** study English hard.
我们必须努力学英语。
➢ It's too late so she **has to** take a taxi.
太晚了，所以她不得不打车。
➢ Nurses **have to** wear a uniform.
护士必须穿制服。

● must 没有人称和时态的变化，而 have to 有人称和时态的变化，且 have to 变否定句或一般疑问句时需借助助动词。
➢ She **has to** stay at home and look after her sister.
她不得不待在家照顾她的妹妹。
➢ He **will have to** finish his work tomorrow.
他明天不得不完成他的工作。
➢ They **didn't have to** come here yesterday.
他们昨天不需要来这里。
➢ **Do** you **have to** treat him like that?
你必须要那样对待他吗？

(2) must 表示推测（肯定、一定）。
➢ He **must** be at home because the light is still on.

他肯定在家,因为灯仍然亮着。
- He **must** have done a good job.
  他一定做得很好。

【补充提示】
注意 have to 不能用于表示推测。

5. should, ought to

(1) 表示责任、义务、劝告、建议(应该,应当)。
- You **should/ought to** take care of your children.
  你应该照顾你的孩子。
- You **should/ought to** go to school right now.
  你应该马上去学校。
- He **should/ought to** exercise more.
  他应该多锻炼。

(2) 表示推测(应该,可能)。
- They **should/ought to** be home by now.
  他们现在应该到家了。
- The doctor said I **should/ought to** be fine tomorrow.
  医生说我明天应该会康复。

【补充提示】
ought to 的一般疑问句的表达以及回答:
- — **Ought** he **to** start now?
  —Yes, he **ought to**.
  —No, he **ought** not **to**.
  ——他现在应该开始吗?
  ——是的,他应该。
  ——不,他不应该。

(3) should 表示惊讶、愤怒和失望等强烈的情感(竟然)。
- He **should** be late for such an important meeting.
  这么重要的会议他竟然迟到了。
- You **should** be so rude to a lady!
  你竟然对一位女士如此无礼!

6. need

need 既可作情态动词也可作实义动词。need 作情态动词表示必要性(需要)时,没有人称和时态变化,常用于疑问句或否定句中,其句式结构如下:
一般疑问句结构:Need+sb.+动词原形+其他+?

否定句结构:sb.+needn't (= need not)+动词原形+其他

➢ — **Need** he do it at once?
　—Yes, he **need**.
　—No, he **needn't**.
　——他需要马上就做吗?
　——是的,他需要。
　——不,他不需要。

➢ You **needn't** make two copies.
　你不需要打印两份。

➢ We **needn't** finish that work today.
　我们不必今天做完这项工作。

【补充提示】

need 作实义动词时表示必要性(需要),有人称和时态变化,变否定句或一般疑问句时需借助助动词,后面常接名词、to do、doing 作宾语,主语分人和物两种情况:

① 主语是人时,后接名词或 to do,其句式结构:sb.+need sth.或 sb.+need to do sth.

➢ I **need** your help.
　我需要你的帮助。

➢ He **needs** to finish the work this evening.
　他需要今晚完成这项工作。

➢ He doesn't **need** to finish the work this evening.
　他今晚不需要完成这项工作。

➢ Did they **need** my help just now?
　他们刚才需要我的帮助吗?

② 主语是物时,后接 doing 或 to be done,其句式结构:sth.+need doing/to be done

➢ My bike **needs** repairing/to be repaired.
　我的自行车需要修理。

➢ These letters **need** typing/to be typed again.
　这些信需要再打一遍。

7. shall, will/would

(1) shall 表示征求对方的意见、请求,常用于第一、三人称(可以吗,好吗)。

➢ **Shall** we begin our class?
　我们开始上课好吗?

➢ What **shall** we do this weekend?
　这个周末我们做什么好呢?

(2) shall 表示说话人给对方的警告、威胁、命令或允诺,常用于第二、三人称。

➢ You **shall** be punished.
　你会受到惩罚的。

➢ He **shall** take the book when I finish reading.

当我读完这本书时,他就可以拿走这本书。

(3) will/would 表示请求、建议(可以吗,好吗)。

➢ **Will/Would** you lend me your book?

你可以把你的书借我吗?

➢ **Will/ Would** you stay for supper?

你留下来吃晚饭好吗?

【补充提示】

① would 是 will 的过去式,但表请求时 would 不是过去式,而表示比 will 的语气更为委婉。

② shall 和 will 都可以表示征求意见,但两者有区别。shall 常用于第一、三人称的疑问句,will 常用于第二人称的疑问句。

(4) will/would 表示意愿、决心、愿望(愿意,会)。

➢ I **will/would** never go back to my hometown.

我永远不会回家乡了。

➢ I **will/would** forgive you.

我会原谅你。

(5) would 表示过去反复发生的动作与倾向(习惯于)。

➢ She **would** listen to music when doing homework.

她做作业的时候会听音乐。

➢ When they were children, they **would** go swimming every summer.

当他们还是孩子的时候,每年夏天他们都会去游泳。

8.dare

dare 既可作情态动词也可作实义动词。dare 作情态动词时,没有人称和时态变化,常用于疑问句或否定句中,表示"敢于",其否定形式为 daren't (= dare not)。

➢ — **Dare** you go with me?

—Yes, I **dare**.

—No, I **dare** not.

——你敢和我去吗?

——是的,我敢。

——不,我不敢。

➢ How **dare** you do that?

你怎么敢做那件事?

➢ She **daren't** speak English in class.

她不敢在课堂上说英语。

➢ I **daren't** tell her the truth.

我不敢对她讲实话。

【补充提示】

dare 作实义动词时,表示"敢于,向……挑战",有人称和时态的变化。

➤ I **dare** to see scary movies at night.
　我敢在晚上看恐怖电影。
➤ I **dare** to swim across the river.
　我敢游过这条河。
➤ He **dares** to do things differently.
　他敢于用不同的方式做事。
➤ John doesn't **dare** to drive a car.
　John 不敢开车。

9. had better

had better 表示建议、劝告(最好做……)。常用句式结构如下:
肯定句式:sb.had better do sth. 某人最好做某事
否定句式:sb.had better not do sth. 某人最好不要做某事

➤ You**'d better** (= had better) go to hospital now.
　你最好现在去医院。
➤ You **had better** travel to Wuhan tomorrow.
　你最好明天去武汉。
➤ You**'d better** (= had better) not go out during the epidemic.
　疫情期间,你最好不要外出。
➤ We **had better** not mention it again.
　我们最好不再提起这件事。

【补充提示】

had better 的主语为人称代词时,常与人称代词缩写在一起。

➤ we had better = we'd better 　　you had better = you'd better

10. used to

used to 表示"过去常常做某事",强调过去的动作或习惯现在不再发生,常用句式结构如下:
used to do sth. 过去常常做某事

➤ She **used to** have long hair.
　她以前留着长发。
➤ He **used to** be a good man.
　他以前是个好人。

【补充提示】

① used to do sth.的否定句结构为"主语+used not to do sth."或"主语+didn't use to do sth."

➤ She used not to have long hair. = She didn't use to have long hair.
　她以前没有留长发。

> My father used not to work there. = My father didn't use to work there.
> 我爸爸以前没有在那里工作。

② used to do sth.的一般疑问句结构为"Used+主语+to do sth."或"Did+主语+use to do sth."

> Used she to have long hair? = Did she use to have long hair?
> 她过去留长发吗？

> Used he to play the violin? = Did he use to play the violin?
> 他过去常拉小提琴吗？

（二）情态动词表示推测

1. 表推测的情态动词主要有

must 表示肯定推测,语气较强,用于肯定句中,译为"一定、肯定"；

can't 表示否定推测,译为"不可能、一定不"；

may/might/can 表示不确定推测,may/might 常用于陈述句中,can 常用于疑问句中,表示"可能"；

should/ought to 表示不确定推测,译为"应该"。

2. 表示对现在或将来的推测,句式结构:主语+情态动词+动词原形+其他

> His mother **must** be cooking now.
> 他妈妈现在一定在做饭。

> His father **can't** be at home now.
> 他爸爸现在不可能在家。

> She **may/might** come tomorrow.
> 她明天可能来。

> She **should/ought to** pass her chemistry final exam.
> 她应该能通过化学期末考试。

3. 表示对过去的推测,句式结构:主语+情态动词+have done+其他

> I **must have seen** you somewhere before.
> 我之前一定在什么地方见过你。

> She was ill last week, so she **can't have gone** to work.
> 她上星期病了,所以她不可能去上班了。

> She said that he **might have missed** the plane.
> 她说他可能已经错过了飞机。

> Sonia **should have arrived** home by now.
> Sonia 现在应该已经回家了。

实 战 演 练

1. The book _____ be Mike's, for his name is on it.
   A. can　　　　　　B. should　　　　　　C. must　　　　　　D. may

2. In the summer camp, the boy learned to _____ all kinds of difficulties.
   A. overcome   B. protect   C. remain   D. control
3. —Will Bob help me look after my pet dog when I'm away?
   —Of course. He won't _____ your request. He loves animals a lot.
   A. put down   B. write down   C. turn down   D. take down
4. I'm sorry to have _____ you with so many questions on such an occasion.
   A. interfered   B. offended   C. impressed   D. interrupted
5. The football match was _____ on account of bad weather.
   A. called up   B. called on   C. called off   D. called for
6. —I left my handbag on the train, but luckily someone gave it to a railway official.
   —How unbelievable to get it back! I mean, someone _____ it.
   A. will have stolen   B. might have stolen   C. should stolen   D. must steal
7. It's impolite to _____ your teachers' office without knocking at the door.
   A. describe   B. check   C. choose   D. enter
8. My cousin volunteers in the Children's Home. His job is to _____ food and clothes.
   A. sell out   B. work out   C. hand out   D. find out
9. It _____ be the postman at the door. It's only six a.m.
   A. mustn't   B. can't   C. won't   D. needn't
10. The boy _____ an apology to the teacher for being late.
    A. made   B. asked   C. took   D. had
11. —The oil on the earth will _____ one day.
    —I think so. We should make good use of it.
    A. find out   B. work out   C. put out   D. run out
12. Harry is feeling uncomfortable. He _____ too much at the party last night.
    A. could drink   B. should drink   C. would have drunk   D. must have drunk
13. If you don't like to swim, you _____ as well stay at home.
    A. should   B. may   C. can   D. would
14. Don't forget to _____ the lights when you leave the classroom.
    A. turn on   B. turn off   C. turn down   D. turn up
15. Stephen Hawking has _____ great success as a scientist.
    A. allowed   B. achieved   C. practiced   D. promised

第四章　形容词、副词

一、形容词

形容词是指用来说明名词或代词的性质、状态与特征的词。一般在句中作表语、定语、宾语补足语或状语。

1. 作表语

说明主语的性质、状态、特征等，位于系动词之后。

➢ The boy is **shy**.
　这个男孩很害羞。

➢ The man is **tall** and **handsome**.
　那位男士又高又帅。

➢ Leaves turn **green** in spring.
　春天，树叶变绿了。

2. 作定语

修饰名词或复合不定代词，一般位于名词之前，复合不定代词之后。

➢ She is a **beautiful** girl.
　她是一个漂亮的女孩。

➢ This is an **interesting** book.
　这是一本有趣的书。

➢ This is a **wonderful** world.
　这是一个奇妙的世界。

➢ There is something **wrong** with my car.
　我的汽车出现了故障。

➢ Did you meet anyone **interesting** yesterday?
　你昨天见到什么有趣的人了吗？

【补充提示】

① 多个前置形容词修饰名词时，一般遵循以下顺序：描绘性的→表示形状的→表示年龄、新旧的→表示颜色的→表示国籍、出处的→表示材料、物质的→表示用途、类别的。

➢ My mother bought **a nice small brown leather** bag.
　我妈妈买了一个漂亮的棕色小皮包。

➢ **A beautiful short white Chinese woollen** coat sells well.
　一件漂亮的中式短装白羊毛外套十分畅销。

➢ He has **a large white German** car.
　他有一辆很大的白色的德国车。

② 一些特殊形容词修饰名词作定语时,如 alive、asleep 等,常位于名词之后。

➤ The baby **asleep** now is her son.
   那个现在熟睡着的宝宝是她的儿子。
➤ He is the only man **alive** in that accident.
   他是那场事故中唯一活着的人。

③ 部分形容词作定语时,前置和后置的意义有区别,注意识别背记一些常考形容词。

	前置		后置	
involved	an involved sentence	复杂的句子	all governments involved	各有关(的)政府
concerned	the concerned expression	忧愁的表情	the people concerned	相关(的)人员
present	the present members	现在的成员	the members present	出席的各位成员

3. 作宾语补足语

补充说明宾语的状态、特征等,位于宾语之后。

➤ I find the book **interesting**.
   我发现这本书很有趣。
➤ The story makes me **happy**.
   这个故事让我开心。

4. 作状语

表原因、伴随、方式等,通常位于句首或句末。

➤ We arrived home yesterday, **safe** and **sound**.
   我们昨天回到家了,安然无恙。(表方式)
➤ **Hungry** and **tired**, we stopped to have a rest.
   又饿又困,我们停下来休息。(表原因)
➤ He walked in the wind, **cold** and **hungry**.
   他在风中行走,又冷又饿。(表伴随)

二、副词

副词指用来修饰动词、形容词、副词或全句的词,说明时间、地点、方式、程度、状态等。按照具体功能分类如下:

副词分类	例词	例句
时间副词	today, yesterday, tomorrow, now, just now, soon, then, just, already, recently…	He has **already** come back. 他已经回来了。 My mother is cooking **now**. 我的妈妈现在正在做饭。

续表

副词分类	例词	例句
频率副词	always, usually, often, sometimes, seldom, rarely, never...	He **usually** goes to work at 8 o'clock. 他通常8点上班。 He is **sometimes** careless. 他有时会粗心大意。 I **always** drink coffee with some milk. 我总是喝咖啡的时候加一些牛奶。
地点副词	home, here, there, everywhere, nearby, downstairs...	He found his book **downstairs**. 他在楼下找到了他的书。 He will drive me **home** after work. 下班后他会开车送我回家。
地点副词	in, out, up, down, forward...	We were locked **in**. 我们被锁在里面了。 They run **forward** to welcome her. 他们跑上前去欢迎她。
方式副词	gladly, carefully, well, slowly, together, suddenly, fast, loudly, hard, quickly...	He runs **quickly**. 他跑得很快。 She read the story **loudly**. 她大声地朗读这篇故事。 We grew up **together**. 我们是在一块儿长大的。
程度副词	very, too, quite, rather, completely, a lot, almost, especially...	The movie is **quite** good. 这部电影相当好。 I've **completely** forgotten her name. 我完全把她的名字给忘了。

[补充提示]

除上述副词分类外,仍需要注意部分连接副词,例如however、besides、therefore、otherwise、though 的用法及位置。

① 常位于句首,后常用逗号与句子的其他成分隔开。

➤ It's raining now. **However**, many people are going to have a picnic.

现在正在下雨,但还是有很多人要去野餐。

➤ I don't really want to go. **Besides**, it's too late now.

我真的不想去,而且现在太晚了。

② 部分连接副词还可位于句尾或句中。
- We don't want to buy the car. We have enough money, **though**.
  我们不想买这辆车,尽管我们有足够的钱。
- They do, **however**, share a common interest in design.
  然而,他们的确对设计有共同的兴趣。

(一) 副词的句法功能

1. 作状语
修饰动词、形容词、其他副词以及全句,作时间、地点、程度、方式等状语。
- Don't drive too **fast**.
  不要开得太快。(修饰动词,作方式状语)
- Alice is **so** beautiful in red.
  Alice 穿红色的衣服非常漂亮。(修饰形容词,作程度状语)
- He ran **so** slowly in the competition.
  他在比赛中跑得很慢。(修饰副词,作程度状语)
- I met some friends in the street **yesterday**.
  我昨天在街上碰到了一些朋友。(修饰全句,作时间状语)

2. 作表语
主要指主语的方位、动作、状态等,位于系动词(尤其是 be 动词)之后。
- The lid is **on**.
  盖子是盖着的。
- He will be **back** tomorrow.
  他明天会回来。
- We are **home** now.
  我们现在在家里。

3. 作定语
主要表示时间或地点,且一般后置,位于所修饰的名词后。常用词如 today、yesterday、here、there、above、below、upstairs 等。
- The weather **today** is wonderful.
  今天的天气好极了!
- The meeting **tomorrow** is very important.
  明天的会议是非常重要的。
- The water **here** is quite clean.
  这里的水非常清澈。
- Please write your name on the sheet **below**.
  请把你的名字写在下面的这张纸上。
- The sky **above** is the home of birds.

上方的这片天空是鸟类的家园。

4. 作补足语

主要说明主语或宾语的位置、状态等。

➤ Let her **in**.

　　让她进来。

➤ Keep the light **on**.

　　让灯开着吧。

➤ The girl was seen **downstairs**.

　　有人看到这个女孩在楼下。

(二) 副词的位置

1. 程度副词的位置

程度副词常用来修饰形容词、副词、动词。修饰形容词或副词时,常位于形容词或副词之前;修饰动词时,常位于实义动词之前。

➤ The room is **very** warm.

　　这个房间很温暖。(修饰形容词)

➤ We will be here **pretty** soon.

　　我们很快就会到达。(修饰副词)

➤ I **quite** agree with you.

　　我非常同意你的观点。(修饰动词)

【补充提示】

enough 作副词时需要位于所修饰的形容词、副词、动词之后。

➤ She sings well **enough**.

　　她唱得足够好。(enough 位于副词 well 之后)

➤ This house isn't big **enough** for us.

　　这房子对我们来说不够大。(enough 位于形容词 big 之后)

➤ I have eaten **enough**.

　　我已经吃够了。(enough 位于动词 eat 之后)

2. 频率副词的位置

频率副词常用来修饰动词,常位于 be 动词、助动词之后,实义动词之前。

➤ I'm **usually** out during the day.

　　白天我通常不在家。

➤ I will **always** love you.

　　我将永远爱你。

➤ They **often** walk to school.

　　他们经常步行去学校。

> I **always** take a walk after supper.

　我总是在晚饭后散散步。

3. 方式副词的位置

方式副词常用来修饰动词,大部分由"形容词+ly"构成,常位于实义动词之后或句尾。

> In the end, the beautiful girl smiled **happily**.

　最后,那个漂亮的女孩开心地笑了。

> He read the book **quietly**.

　他安静地看这本书。

> They welcomed us **warmly**.

　他们热情地欢迎了我们。

4. 时间、地点副词的位置

时间、地点副词常用来修饰全句,一般位于句尾,有时也可放在句首表强调。

> I haven't heard from you **recently**.

　我最近没有收到你的来信。

> We will meet **upstairs**.

　我们在楼上见。

> I used to work **here**.

　我以前在这里工作。

> **Tomorrow** my parents will come to see me.

　明天我父母要来看我。

【补充提示】

若时间副词和地点副词同时出现在句中,常把地点副词放在时间副词前面,或把时间副词放在句首。

> They came **here yesterday**.

　他们昨天来了这里。

5. 多个副词的排列顺序

(1) 多个不同类的副词的排列顺序一般遵循以下顺序:程度→方式→地点→时间。

> They have been travelling **happily everywhere** in America **recently**.

　他们最近一直在美国各地开心地旅游。

(2) 多个同类的副词,一般短的在前,长的在后,用 and 或 but 连接。

> The old man walks **slowly** and **carefully**.

　这个老人走得又慢又小心。

【补充提示】

① 强调某一副词时,常将强调的副词提前。

> He **anxiously** looked at me.

　他焦急地看着我。

② 英语中有些形容词本身具备副词词性,也可在此形容词后"+ly"构成副词。两种形式的副词在意义上存在一定区别,常见的形近易混淆词如下:

most adj. 大多数的	most adv. 最;最大,最多	mostly adv. 主要地,大多地
close adj. 接近的;亲近的	close adv. (时间、空间)接近地	closely adv. 严密地;密切地
near adj. 附近的	near adv. 在附近	nearly adv. 几乎
hard adj. 坚硬的;困难的	hard adv. 努力地	hardly adv. 几乎不
late adj. 晚的,迟的	late adv. 晚,迟	lately adv. 最近,近来

三、比较级与最高级

(一) 比较级与最高级的构成

大多数形容词和副词都有三种形式,即原级、比较级和最高级。其中,原级即形容词和副词的原形,比较级和最高级的变化则可分为规则变化与不规则变化。

1. 规则变化

① 单音节词和部分双音节词,一般在词尾加 er、est 构成比较级与最高级。

➤ tall—taller—tallest   small—smaller—smallest   strong—stronger—strongest

② 以不发音的字母"e"结尾的词,在词尾加 r、st 构成比较级与最高级。

➤ nice—nicer—nicest   simple—simpler—simplest   large—larger—largest

③ 以"辅音+元音+辅音"字母结尾的重读闭音节词,先双写末尾的辅音字母,再加 er、est 构成比较级与最高级。

➤ big—bigger—biggest   thin—thinner—thinnest   hot—hotter—hottest

④ 以"辅音字母+y"结尾的词,改 y 为 i,再加 er、est 构成比较级与最高级。

➤ busy—busier—busiest   easy—easier—easiest   heavy—heavier—heaviest

⑤ 部分双音节词和多音节词直接在词前加 more、most 构成比较级与最高级。

➤ important—more important—most important
  difficult—more difficult—most difficult

【补充提示】
有些双音节词的比较级与最高级既可以在词尾加 er、est,也可以在词前加 more、most 来构成,如 clever、common、polite、pleasant、handsome 等。

2. 不规则变化

常见形容词、副词比较级和最高级的不规则变化如下:

good/well—better—best   bad/badly/ill—worse—worst
many/much—more—most   little—less—least

far—farther/further—farthest/furthest old—older/elder—oldest/eldest

（二）比较级与最高级的用法

1. 比较级的用法

(1)"A ...+比较级+than+B",用于两者进行比较,表示"A 比 B 更……"。

➤ He is **taller than** you.
　他比你更高。

➤ Children learn **faster than** adults.
　孩子比成年人学得更快。

➤ Creativity is **more important than** technical skill.
　创造力比专门技术更重要。

【补充提示】

① than 后接人称代词时,常使用人称代词的宾格形式。

➤ She looks younger than **me**.
　她看起来比我年轻。

➤ You are thinner than **him**.
　你比他瘦。

② 在对两者进行比较时,要注意前后两个比较对象的一致性。

➤ **The weather** of the south is warmer than **that** of the north.
　南方的天气比北方(的天气)更暖和。(两处天气的对比,后文用"that"指代前文已提到的"weather")

(2)"比较级+and+比较级"表示"越来越……"。

➤ I become **more and more interested** in English.
　我对英语越来越感兴趣了。

➤ It becomes **warmer and warmer** when spring comes.
　春天来了,天气变得越来越暖和了。

(3)"the+比较级…,the+比较级…"表示"越……,就越……"。

➤ **The earlier** you start, **the sooner** you will finish.
　你越早开始,就会越快完成。

➤ **The more careful** you are, **the fewer** mistakes you will make.
　你越仔细,犯的错误就越少。

(4) 比较级的修饰语。

比较级的修饰语常用 a little、a bit、a lot、much、rather、far、still、even、a great deal 等。

➤ This is **much** better than that.
　这个比那个好得多。

➤ Japanese is **far** more difficult than English.

日语比英语难多了。

➢ He knew **a great deal** more than I did.
　他知道的比我多得多。

➢ He works hard, but she works **still** harder.
　他工作很努力，但她工作更努力。

(5) 同级比较。

"A ...+as+原级+as+B"表示"A 和 B 一样……"。其否定形式为"A ...not+as/so+原级+as+B"，表示"A 不如 B……"。

➢ She looks **as young as** you.
　她看起来和你一样年轻。

➢ You're **as tall as** your father.
　你和你父亲一样高。

➢ Her English is **not as/so good as** yours.
　她的英语不如你的(英语)好。

➢ He does**n't** study **as/so hard as** Mary.
　他学习不如玛丽努力。

【补充提示】

"A ...the same(+名词)+as+B"也可用于同级比较，表示"A 和 B 一样……"。

➢ My book is **the same as** yours.
　我的书和你的一样。

➢ I bought **the same car as** you.
　我买了和你一样的车。

(6) 本身就具有比较意义的形容词。

英语中有些形容词本身就具有比较意义，不可变为比较级，如 superior"地位较高的，质量较好的"，inferior"地位较低的，质量较次的"，senior"较年长的，地位较高的"，junior"较年轻的，地位较低的"，prior"比……早的，比……重要的"等，后面常用介词 to 接比较对象。

➢ The present is **superior to** the past.
　现在胜于过去。

➢ My sister is 2 years **senior to** me.
　我姐姐比我大两岁。

➢ My brother is 5 years **junior to** me.
　我弟弟比我小五岁。

2. 最高级的用法

(1) "A ...the+最高级(+名词单数)+比较范围(in/of/among...)"，用于三者及以上进行比较，表示"A 是……中最……的"。

➢ This is **the most famous town in** London.
　这是伦敦最有名的城镇。

➢ He is **the tallest boy of/among** the three boys.

他是三个男孩中个子最高的。

➢ He runs **the fastest of/among** all the athletes.

他是所有运动员中跑得最快的。

➢ You always come **the latest in** this office.

在这个办公室里你总是最晚来。

【补充提示】

形容词最高级前需加定冠词 the,副词最高级前可不加 the。

➢ My mom is **the best** mom in the world.

我妈妈是世界上最好的妈妈。(best 为形容词)

➢ I love my mom **(the) best** in the world.

全世界我最爱我妈妈。(best 为副词)

(2) "A …+one of the+最高级+名词复数+比较范围",表示"A 是……中最……的之一"。

➢ He is **one of the most famous artists** in the world.

他是世界上最著名的艺术家之一。

➢ He is **one of the richest men** in the country.

他是全国最富有的人之一。

(3) 比较级表最高级。

英语中还可通过比较级来表示最高级的含义,常见句型如下:

① 比较级+than any other+可数名词单数,表示"比其他任何……都更……"或"最……"。

➢ He is **taller than any other student** in the class.

他比班上其他学生都高。= 他是班上最高的学生。

② 比较级+than(any of)the other+可数名词复数,表示"比其他任何……都更……"或"最……"。

➢ He is **taller than (any of) the other students** in the class.

他比班上其他学生都高。= 他是班上最高的学生。

③ 比较级还可与否定词连用,表示"最……"的含义。

➢ I have **never** read **a better story than** this one.

我从未读过比这更好的故事。= 这是我读过的最好的故事。

(4) 最高级的修饰语

最高级的修饰语常有序数词、名词所有格、形容词物主代词,此外还有(by)far、much、nearly、almost、not quite、by no means 等。

➢ The Yellow River is the **second** longest river in China.

黄河是中国第二长河。

➢ This is **(by) far** the best song that I've heard.

这是我听过的最好的歌。

➢ Jim is **by no means** the cleverest of the three boys.

在这三个男孩中，Jim 绝不是最聪明的。

【补充提示】

① 最高级前有名词所有格、物主代词、指示代词等限定词修饰时，前面不需再用定冠词 the。

➢ Today is my the happiest day.（错误）

Today is my happiest day.（正确）

今天是我最开心的一天。

② very 不能修饰比较级，但有时可置于定冠词之后修饰最高级。

➢ I think this is the **very** best dictionary.

我认为这是最好的词典。

③ 使用最高级时要注意将主语包括在比较范围内。

➢ Tom is the tallest of his three brothers.（错误）

Tom is the tallest of the three brothers.（正确）

Tom 是三个兄弟中最高的。（把 Tom 自己包含在内）

实 战 演 练

1. Every week, I write an email and tell my parents _____ that happened in our school.

   A. exciting something   B. something exciting   C. excited something   D. something excited

2. This box is _____ that one.

   A. heavy than   B. so heavy than   C. heavier as   D. as heavy as

3. The *Emperor's New Clothes* is an _____ story. All of us are _____ in it.

   A. interesting; interesting   B. interested; interested

   C. interested; interesting   D. interesting; interested

4. The poor in the country want to be treated _____ in education and employment.

   A. extremely   B. equally   C. politely   D. obviously

5. This book is _____ that one, but _____ than that one.

   A. as difficult as; expensive   B. as more difficult as; more expensive

   C. as difficult as; more expensive   D. more difficult as; as expensive

6. It's raining so _____ that we can _____ go out now.

   A. hard; hardly   B. hard; hard   C. hardly; hardly   D. hardly; hard

7. I think facts are _____ than opinions.

   A. much important   B. important

   C. much more important   D. more much important

8. —May I speak to Mr. Smith?

—I am afraid it is not _____, for he is in a meeting now.

   A. impressive   B. particular   C. convenient   D. beneficial

9. His knowledge of English literature is _____ mine.
   A. superior than   B. superior to   C. more superior to   D. as superior as
10. China is larger than _____ in Asia.
    A. any other country   B. other country   C. the other country   D. any country
11. I believe that I am _____ for the position because of my education background and work experience.
    A. qualified   B. demanded   C. applied   D. collected
12. At last, he began to cry _____.
    A. hard and hard   B. more hard and more hard
    C. harder and harder   D. less hard and less harder
13. Growing vegetables looks easy, but _____ it takes a lot of learning.
    A. mainly   B. directly   C. actually   D. immediately
14. _____ I look at the picture, _____ I like it.
    A. The best; the more   B. The more; the more
    C. The more; less   D. More; the more
15. The Yellow River is one of _____ rivers in China.
    A. long   B. longer   C. the longest   D. longest

第五章　连词、介词

一、连词

连词是一种虚词,用来连接词、短语或句子,不能独立充当句子成分。根据性质和意义,连词主要分为两类:并列连词和从属连词。

(一) 并列连词

并列连词用来连接具有相同语法功能的词、短语或句子。并列连词按照逻辑关系不同,一般分为并列关系、转折关系、因果关系和选择关系四类。

1. 表示并列关系的并列连词

(1) and "和,且;然后"。

➢ Exercise makes me relaxed **and** happy.
  锻炼让我放松、开心。
➢ There is a table **and** two chairs in the room.
  房间里有一张桌子和两把椅子。
➢ Mark is a teacher **and** writer.
  Mark 是一名老师兼作家。
➢ Tom stayed at home, watched TV **and** went to bed.
  Tom 待在家里看了电视,然后上床睡觉了。
➢ He has a little sister, **and** he likes her very much.
  他有一个小妹妹,他非常喜欢她。

(2) both...and... "……和……都……;既……又……"。

➢ **Both** Mark **and** Kerry are my brothers.
  Mark 和 Kerry 都是我的弟弟。
➢ They will **both** sing **and** dance this evening.
  今晚他们将既唱歌又跳舞。
➢ **Both** you **and** I like go swimming.
  你和我都喜欢游泳。
➢ **Both** she **and** I are good at English.
  她和我都擅长英语。

(3) not only...but (also)... "不仅……而且……;不仅……也……"。

➢ Running is **not only** good for physical health, **but** (**also**) good for mental health.
  跑步不仅有利于身体健康,而且有利于心理健康。
➢ She is **not only** beautiful **but** (**also**) friendly.
  她不仅漂亮而且友好。

➤ **Not only** his friends **but**（**also**）he likes playing basketball.
  不仅他的朋友们喜欢打篮球,他也喜欢打篮球。
➤ **Not only** the children **but**（**also**）their parents are enjoying the film.
  不仅孩子们,他们的父母也在欣赏这部电影。

（4）as well as"也,和,都"。

➤ He plays basketball **as well as** football.
  他打篮球,也踢足球。
➤ The brain needs exercise **as well as** the body.
  大脑和身体都需要锻炼。
➤ Tom **as well as** his parents is going to London next week.
  Tom 和他的父母下周要去伦敦。
➤ The students **as well as** the teacher are friendly to me.
  学生们和老师都对我很友好。

（5）neither...nor..."既不……也不……;都不……"。

➤ **Neither** you **nor** I know what happened.
  你和我都不知道发生了什么。
➤ **Neither** the students **nor** the teacher knows the news.
  学生们和老师都不知道这个消息。
➤ He seemed **neither** surprised **nor** anxious.
  他似乎既不惊讶也不焦虑。
➤ His house is **neither** big **nor** small.
  他的房子既不大也不小。

2. 表示转折关系的并列连词

（1）but"但是",注意 but 不可位于句尾。

➤ Mary did her homework very fast, **but** she made many mistakes.
  Mary 作业写得很快,但是错误很多。
➤ Jack went to bed early last night, **but** he was still sleepy this morning.
  Jack 昨晚睡得很早,但是今早仍然很困。
➤ The room is small **but** enough for us.
  房间虽小,但足够我们住了。
➤ She studied very hard, **but** she failed the final exam.
  她学习很努力,但期末考试没有及格。

（2）yet"然而,但是",常位于句中。

➤ The next class was P. E., **yet** it was going to rain.
  下节课是体育课,然而马上要下雨了。
➤ He has a good job, **yet** he always seems to have no money.
  他有一份好工作,但他似乎总是没钱。

- I failed again, **yet** I will never give up.

  我又失败了,但我永远不会放弃。

- It was dark, **yet** I slowly found my way.

  天很黑,但我还是慢慢地找到了路。

(3) while"而,然而",表前后意义上的对比或转折。

- The air in the north is dry, **while** the air in the south is wet.

  北方的空气干燥,然而南方的空气却很湿润。

- I like hot water, **while** my sister likes ice water.

  我喜欢热水,然而我姐姐喜欢冰水。

- Tom likes reading in the library, **while** I prefer playing outside with my friends.

  Tom 喜欢在图书馆看书,而我更喜欢和朋友们在外面玩。

- I went swimming, **while** the others went to play volleyball.

  我去游泳了,而其他人去打排球了。

3. 表示因果关系的并列连词

(1) for"因为,由于",常用逗号与前面分句隔开,后接句子且不能位于句首。

- You'd better put on another coat, **for** it's snowing outside.

  你最好加件外套,因为外面正在下雪。

- He didn't attend the meeting, **for** he was ill.

  他没来参加会议,因为他病了。

- He must be at home now, **for** the light in his room is on.

  他现在一定在家,因为他房间的灯是亮着的。

(2) so"因此,所以"。

- The air here is polluted, **so** the crops are dying.

  这里的空气受到了污染,所以庄稼快死了。

- My hand was still painful, **so** I went to see a doctor.

  我的手还是很疼,所以我去看了医生。

- I was tired, **so** I went to bed earlier.

  我累了,所以我早早睡了。

4. 表示选择关系的并列连词

(1) or"或者,否则"。

- To be **or** not to be, that is a question.

  生存或毁灭,这是个问题。

- Which one do you like, maths **or** English?

  你喜欢哪一个,数学还是英语?

- Come on, **or** we will be late.

  快一点,否则我们要迟到了。

- I must study hard, **or** I'll fail the exam.

  我必须要努力学习,否则我就会考试不及格。

(2) either...or..."……或者……；要么……要么……"。

➢ **Either** his father **or** his mother is picking him up today.
他爸爸或他妈妈今天会来接他。

➢ **Either** you **or** I am going to work there.
要么你要么我将去那里工作。

➢ **Either** you **or** I am right.
要么你是对的，要么我是对的。

➢ **Either** you **or** she has to finish the task today.
要么你要么她今天必须得完成这个任务。

（二）从属连词

在复合句中引导从句的连词叫作从属连词，从属连词主要用来引导名词性从句和状语从句。按照从属连词本身的词性可分为以下三类：

定义		例词	例句
简单从属连词	单个单词表示的从属连词	although(尽管)，once(一旦)，because(因为)，if(如果)，since(自……以来；由于，既然)，unless(除非)，before(在……之前)，whether(是否；不管，无论)，till/until(直到……为止)	**Although** the computer has many problems, he still insists on using it. 尽管这台电脑有很多问题，但是他仍然坚持使用。 **If** you want to pass the exam, you must study hard. 如果你想要通过考试，你必须努力学习。 I will not come to the party **unless** I'm invited. 除非我被邀请，否则我不会参加聚会。 I will wait here **until** they arrive. 我会在这里等到他们来为止。
复合从属连词	由两个或两个以上单词组成的从属连词	so that(以便；因此)，in order that(以便)，as long as(只要)，as soon as(一……就……)，as if(似乎，好像)，in case(万一，以防)，on condition that(条件是……)，even if/though(即使，尽管)	I locked the door **in order that** we might continue our discussion undisturbed. 我锁上了门，以便我们可以不受打扰继续讨论。 We will go camping **as long as** the weather is good. 只要天气好，我们就去露营。 It looks **as if** it is going to rain. 看上去似乎要下雨了。 **Even if/though** she was ill, she still went to work. 尽管她病了，她仍然去上班了。

续表

	定义	例词	例句
关联从属连词	由两个关联词组成的从属连词	so/such...that...（如此……以至于……）， whether...or...（无论……还是……）， no sooner... than...（一……就……）	I was **so** tired **that** I went to bed early. 我很累，以至于我早早睡了。 We had **no sooner** sat down at the table **than** the telephone rang. 我们刚在桌子旁坐下，电话铃就响了。

二、介词

介词用来表示名词、代词与句中其他词的关系，是一种虚词，不能独立充当句子成分，通常与名词、代词（或相当于名词的其他词类、短语或从句）搭配使用。根据意义可将介词分类如下：

分类	举例	
时间介词	at，on，in 在…… after 在……之后 since 自……以来	before 在……之前 during 在……期间 until 直到……为止
地点、方位介词	in 在……里面 under 在……下面 between 在……之间	on 在……上面 over 在……上面
方式介词	by 用……（方式）；乘坐……（交通工具） in 用……（语言、材料等）	with 用…… through 通过……
其他含义的介词	against 紧靠；反对，违反 besides 除……之外（还有）	for 为了……；对于…… except 除了……

（一）常见介词的用法

1. 表示时间的介词

（1）时间介词 at、on、in "在……"。

① at 后接具体时刻、时间点。
- at four o'clock 在四点钟
- at half past four 在四点半

② on 后接具体日期、某一天。
- on Sunday 在星期天
- on Monday 在星期一
- on October 1(st) 在10月1日
- on May 2(nd)，1998 在1998年5月2日

③ in 后接月、季节、年份、年代、世纪等。

➢ in 1998 在 1998 年　　　　in June 在六月　　　　in spring 在春天
　in the 20th century 在 20 世纪　　　in the 1980s 在 20 世纪 80 年代

【补充提示】

表达"早、中、晚"相关时间的介词用法如下：
① 表示"早、中、晚"，一般用介词 in。
➢ in the morning/in the afternoon/in the evening 在早上/在下午/在晚上
② 表示"具体某一天的早、中、晚"，一般用介词 on。
➢ on Friday morning/on the morning of Friday 在星期五早上
③ 表示"在晚上、在正午、在午夜"，一般用介词 at。
➢ at night 在晚上　　　at noon 在正午　　　at midnight 在午夜

(2) 时间介词 for、since、during。

① for 表持续时间，后接时间段，多与完成时态连用。
➢ I have studied English **for** two years.
　我学习英语已经两年了。
➢ She has been an English teacher **for** five years.
　她当英语老师已经五年了。

② since 意为"自……以来"，后接时间点，多与完成时态连用。
➢ He has worked on this book **since** last month.
　他从上个月开始写这本书。
➢ I have lived in Wuhan **since** 1999.
　我从 1999 年起就住在武汉。

③ during 意为"在……期间"。
➢ I had a good time **during** the summer vacation.
　我度过了一个愉快的暑假。
➢ They suffered a lot **during** the war.
　他们在战争期间遭受了很多苦难。

(3) 时间介词 before、by。

① before 意为"在……之前"。
➢ He arrived **before** lunch.
　他午饭前就到了。
➢ I will finish the task **before** Saturday.
　我将在星期六之前完成这项任务。

② by 意为"在……之前，到……为止"，多与完成时连用。
➢ The building will have been completed **by** the end of next year.
　到明年年底，这座大楼将会完工。
➢ I had visited ten different cities **by** the end of last year.

到去年年底,我已经参观了十个不同的城市。

(4) 时间介词 after、in。

① after 意为"在……之后"。

➢ I went home **after** three hours.
三个小时后,我回家了。

➢ We will leave **after** lunch.
我们将在午饭后离开。

② in 后接时间段可以表示将来时间,意为"在……之后"。

➢ I will come back **in** a week.
我将在一周后回来。

➢ Hurry up! The train leaves **in** five minutes.
快点!火车五分钟后就要出发了。

(5) 时间介词 until、from...to...。

① until 意为"直到……为止",还可与 not 连用,构成"not...until...",意为"直到……才……"。

➢ I read a book **until** 3 o'clock.
我看书一直看到三点。

➢ She lived in Canada **until** 2004.
到 2004 年为止,她一直住在加拿大。

➢ Jim **didn't** come back **until** 9 o'clock.
Jim 直到九点才回来。

② from...to... 意为"从……到……"。

➢ We work **from** Monday **to** Friday.
我们从星期一工作到星期五。

➢ We lived in Wuhan **from** 1998 **to** 2022.
我们从 1998 年到 2022 年都住在武汉。

2. 表示地点、方位的介词

(1) 地点介词 at、in、on。

① at 意为"在……",常接小地点,还可表示"在……旁边"。

➢ at the bus stop 在公共汽车站　　　at the door 在门口
　at the traffic lights 在红绿灯处　　at the top of... 在……的顶端
　at the bottom of... 在……的底部　　at the end of... 在……的尽头

➢ They agreed to meet **at** a restaurant.
他们约定在一家餐馆见面。

➢ He is eating **at** the table.
他正在桌子旁吃饭。

② in 意为"在……",常接大地点,还可表示"在……里面"。

➢ in a factory 在工厂里　　　in the river 在河里　　　in the south 在南方
　in town 在城里;在镇上　　in the city center 在市中心　　in Brazil 在巴西

in a shop 在商店里　　　　　in a bank 在银行　　　　　in a garden 在花园里

> Egypt is a country **in** Africa.
> 埃及是非洲的一个国家。
> She lives **in** Beijing now.
> 她现在住在北京。
> Stars sparkled **in** the sky.
> 星星在天空中闪烁。
> He was **in** his car.
> 他在他的车里。

③ on 意为"在……上(与表面接触)"。

on a shelf 在架子上　　　on the floor 在地板上　　　on a wall 在墙上
on a horse 在马上　　　　on a balcony 在阳台上　　　on the envelop 在信封上
on the ceiling 在天花板上　on a bicycle 在自行车上　　on a door 在门上

> The house lies **on** the hillside.
> 这个房子坐落在山坡上。
> There are two apples **on** the table.
> 桌上有两个苹果。
> There is a stamp **on** the envelope.
> 信封上有一张邮票。

【补充提示】

① 地点介词 at、in、on 还可构成固定用法，常见用法列举如下：

> in bed 在床上，卧床　　　　　in hospital 住院　　　　　　in the world 在世界上
> in the newspaper 在报纸上　　in a car 在车上　　　　　　in the middle of 在……中间
> at home 在家　　　　　　　　at work 在工作　　　　　　　at school 在上学
> at university 在上大学　　　　at the airport 在机场　　　　at the doctor's 在诊所
> at Jane's (house) 在 Jane 家里　at a concert 在音乐会上　　at a party 在聚会上
> on a bus 在公交车上　　　　　on a train 在火车上　　　　　on a plane 在飞机上
> on the first floor 在一楼　　　on the way 在路上　　　　　on the way home 在回家的路上

② 表示"到达"的常见用法如下：

arrive in+大地点　　　　　　arrive at+小地点　　　　　　get to+地点

> They **arrived in** England last week.
> 他们上周到达了英国。
> When did you **arrive at** the station?
> 你什么时候到车站的？
> When did you **get to** Paris?
> 你什么时候到巴黎的？
> They **got to** the hotel last night.
> 他们昨晚到了酒店。

但"到家"的用法为：arrive/get home

➢ I am always tired when I **arrive/get home**.
 我到家的时候总是很累。

(2) 方位介词 above、over、below、under。
① above 意为"在……上方",表示高于某一物体,但不一定在正上方。
➢ Our plane flew **above** the clouds.
 我们的飞机在云层上方飞行。
➢ The sun rose **above** the horizon.
 太阳从地平线上升起。
② over 意为"在……上方",强调在垂直的正上方。
➢ There is a bridge **over** the river.
 河上有座桥。
➢ There is a lamp hanging **over** the table.
 桌子上方悬挂着一盏灯。
③ below 意为"在……下面",不一定是在正下方。
➢ As the storm began, everyone disappeared **below** decks.
 暴风雨来临时,所有人都躲到甲板下面去了。
➢ The sun sank **below** the horizon.
 太阳落到了地平线以下。
④ under 意为"在……下面",强调在垂直的正下方。
➢ There is a dog **under** the table.
 桌子底下有条狗。
➢ Let's take a rest **under** that tree.
 我们在那棵树下休息一下吧。

(3) 方位介词 before、in front of、in the front of。
① before 意为"在……前面"。
➢ The mountain rose up **before** me.
 这座山耸立在我面前。
② in front of 意为"在……前面",强调在某物体外部的前面。
➢ Alice planted some trees **in front of** her house.
 Alice 在房子前面种了一些树。
③ in the front of 意为"在……前面",强调在某物体内部的前部。
➢ Victor sits **in the front of** the bus.
 Victor 坐在公交车的前排。

(4) 方位介词 after、behind。
① after 意为"在……后面"。
➢ He ran **after** her with the book.
 他拿着那本书在后面追赶她。

➢ Your name comes **after** mine in the list.

名单上你的名字在我的后面。

② behind 意为"在……后面,在……背面"。

➢ Stay close **behind** me.

紧跟在我后面。

➢ There are some trees **behind** the house.

房子后面有一些树。

(5) 方位介词 between、among。

① between 意为"在……之间(指两者)"。

➢ Lily sits **between** Jack and me.

Lily 坐在 Jack 和我中间。

② among 意为"在……之间(指三者或三者以上)"。

➢ There is a house **among** the trees.

树林中有一座房子。

(6) 方位介词 across、over、through、past。

① across 意为"横过,穿过",强调从物体表面的一边到另一边。

➢ He walked **across** the street quickly.

他快速穿过街道。

② over 意为"越过",强调从上方跨过。

➢ The plane flew **over** the mountain.

飞机越过了这座山。

③ through 意为"穿过",强调从中间、内部贯穿。

➢ A bird flew into the room **through** a window.

一只鸟从窗户飞进了房间。

④ past 意为"经过",强调从旁边经过。

➢ They drove **past** a big supermarket.

他们开车经过了一个大超市。

(7) 方位介词 along、around。

① along 意为"沿着"。

➢ Let's go for a walk **along** the river.

我们沿着河散散步吧。

➢ They walked slowly **along** the road.

他们沿公路慢慢走。

② around 意为"在……周围,围绕"。

➢ We walked **around** the town.

我们在城里走了一圈。

➢ The house is built **around** a central courtyard.

这房子是围绕着中央的庭院而建的。

(8) 方位介词 up、down、out of、into、off、next to、beside、by、opposite。

① up 意为"向上"。

➤ We walk **up** the hill to the house.
我们向山上的房子走去。

② down 意为"向下"。

➤ Be careful! Don't fall **down** the stairs.
小心！不要从楼梯上摔下来。

③ out of 意为"从……出去"。

➤ The man came **out of** the house in a hurry.
那人匆匆忙忙地从房子里出来。

④ into 意为"到……里面"。

➤ She dived **into** the water.
她潜入水中。

⑤ off 意为"离开,从……落下"。

➤ Please take your feet **off** the table.
请把你的脚从桌上拿开。

⑥ next to 意为"在……旁边"。

➤ The hospital is **next to** the bank.
这家医院在银行旁边。

⑦ beside 意为"在……旁边"。

➤ He went and sat **beside** her.
他走过去坐在她旁边。

⑧ by 意为"在……旁边"。

➤ The telephone is **by** the window.
电话在窗户旁边。

⑨ opposite 意为"在……对面"。

➤ My teacher sat **opposite** me and talked to me seriously.
老师坐在我对面,严肃地和我谈话。

(9) 方位介词 towards、to、from...to...。

① towards 意为"向……,朝……"。

➤ Mike moved **towards** the window.
Mike 朝窗户走去。

② to 意为"去……",常与表示位置移动的动词 go、get、come、return、walk 等连用。

➤ We usually go **to** school by bus.
我们通常乘公交车去学校。

➤ She returned **to** her motherland at last.
她终于回到了祖国。

③ from...to...意为"从……到……"。

➢ We walked **from** the hotel **to** the station.

我们从旅馆走到了车站。

[补充提示]

① on the left 表示方位"在左边",on the right 表示方位"在右边",in the middle 表示方位"在中间"。

➢ The bus station is **on the left**.

公共汽车站在左边。

➢ The park is **on the right**.

公园在右边。

➢ He was standing **in the middle** of the room.

他站在屋子的中间。

② 方位介词 in、on、to 可用于表示两地的相对位置,如两地分别为 A 和 B,则 in 表示 A 在 B 的范围之内,on 表示 A、B 两地接壤,to 表示 A、B 两地相隔一段距离。

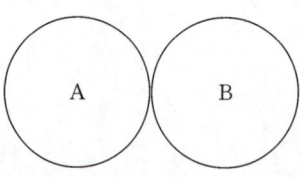
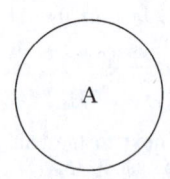
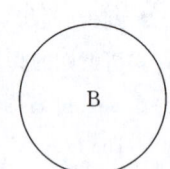

Heilongjiang Province is **in** the northeast of China.

黑龙江省在中国的东北部。

➢ China is **on** the northeast of India.

中国在印度的东北部。

➢ Japan is **to** the northeast of China.

日本在中国的东北部。

3. 表示方式的介词

(1) by 意为"通过……,以……(方式、手段);乘坐……(交通工具)",其后常接名词或动名词。

➢ They're travelling **by** car.

他们正在开车旅行。

➢ They learn English **by** watching movies.

他们通过看电影来学习英语。

(2) in 意为"以……;用……(方式、材料、语言、颜色)"。

➢ Payments can be made **in** cash.

可以用现金支付。

➢ The route has been marked **in** yellow.

这条路线已经用黄色标明了。

➢ Students are requested to answer the question **in** English.
  学生们被要求用英语回答这个问题。

(3) with 意为"用……(工具、物品或材料)"。

➢ He removes the meat **with** a fork.
  他用叉子把肉移开。

➢ I write my paper **with** a computer.
  我用电脑写论文。

(4) through 意为"通过……"。

➢ He would like to improve his physical health **through** exercise.
  他想通过锻炼来改善身体健康。

➢ You can achieve your dream **through** hard work.
  你能通过努力工作实现你的梦想。

4. 表示其他含义的介词

(1) against 意为"紧靠;反对,违反"。

➢ She leaned **against** a wall.
  她紧靠着墙。

➢ We need to unite **against** terrorism.
  我们需要团结起来反对恐怖主义。

➢ That's **against** the law.
  那是违法的。

(2) for 意为"为了……;对于……",表对象、目的或用途。

➢ The knife **for** cutting meat was in the kitchen.
  切肉用的刀在厨房里。

➢ It is a book **for** children.
  这是一本儿童读物。

➢ Can you translate this letter **for** me?
  你能为我翻译这封信吗?

(3) besides 意为"除……之外(还有)",表示将其后的宾语包括在内。

➢ She has many good qualities **besides** being very beautiful.
  除了长得漂亮之外,她还有许多优点。

➢ We have a lot of things in common **besides** music.
  除了音乐之外,我们还有很多共同之处。

(4) except 意为"除……之外",表示将其后的宾语排除在外。

➢ I won't accept anything **except** a job in Wuhan.
  除了在武汉工作之外,我不会接受其他的工作。

➢ We work every day **except** Sunday.
  除了星期天之外,我们每天都工作。

【补充提示】

① except 与 besides 的区别。

except 和 besides 都表示"除……之外",但 except 其后的宾语是被排除在外的;而 besides 其后的宾语是被包括在内的。

➢ All the students took part in the sports meeting **except** Tom.
  除了 Tom 外,其他同学都参加了运动会。(Tom 没参加)

➢ All the students took part in the sports meeting **besides** Tom.
  除了 Tom 外,其他同学也参加了运动会。(Tom 也参加了)

② except 与 except for 的区别。

except 是指在同类的人或物中除去一个部分,而 except for 是指在整体描述中除去一个细节或一个方面;且用在句首时需使用 except for。

➢ I can answer all the questions **except** the last one.
  除了最后一题外,所有的题目我都可以解答。

➢ Your composition is good **except for** a few grammar mistakes.
  除了几处语法错误外,你的作文写得很好。

➢ **Except for** traffic noise, the night passed peacefully.
  除了交通噪音外,这一夜过得很平静。

5. 时间、地点前不使用介词的情况

(1) 当时间词前被 last、this、next、every 等词修饰时,前不用介词。

➢ Let's meet at the gate **this evening**.
  我们今晚在大门口见。

➢ I go fishing **every weekend**.
  我每个周末都去钓鱼。

(2) "时间段+ago/later"作时间状语时,前不用介词。

➢ He injured himself **three days ago**.
  他三天前受伤了。

➢ I met her again **three years later**.
  三年后我又遇见她了。

(3) today、yesterday、tomorrow、tonight 等时间副词前不用介词。

➢ How are you feeling **today**?
  你今天感觉怎么样?

➢ She will have to work late **tomorrow**.
  她明天得工作到很晚。

(4) here、there、abroad 等地点副词前不用介词。

➢ I live **here**.
  我住这儿。

> I took the opportunity to work **abroad**.
> 我抓住了出国工作的机会。

（5）用于 go、come、return、get、arrive 等表示位置移动的动词之后的 home 是地点副词，不能在 home 前加介词 to、at 等；如"回家"的正确表达为 go home，"到家"的正确表达为 arrive/get home；但 home 用作名词时前可用介词，如"在家"的正确表达为 at home。

> It took him an hour to arrive **home**.
> 他花了一个小时才到家。
> Come on! It's time to go **home**.
> 快点！该回家了。
> I left my purse at **home**.
> 我的钱包落在家里了。

（二）介词短语的句法功能

介词一般不能单独使用，其后必须接宾语构成介词短语在句中作成分。介词后的宾语一般为名词（短语）、代词、动名词、从句等。介词短语一般在句中作状语、定语、表语、宾语补足语等。

1. 作状语

介词短语作状语，常位于句首或句尾，可作时间、地点、条件、目的、方式、原因、让步等状语。

> They have lived in Beijing **for 10 years**.
> 他们已经在北京生活了 10 年。（时间状语）
> They are playing football **on the playground**.
> 他们正在操场上踢足球。（地点状语）
> **Without your help**, we couldn't have finished it on time.
> 如果没有你的帮助，我们不可能按时完成。（条件状语）
> She left two hours early **for fear of missing the plane**.
> 她提前两个小时离开，以防错过飞机。（目的状语）
> They came here **by train**.
> 他们乘火车来这儿。（方式状语）
> The sports meeting was put off **because of the rain**.
> 因为下雨，运动会推迟了。（原因状语）
> **For all his faults**, we still like him.
> 尽管他有很多缺点，我们还是喜欢他。（让步状语）

2. 作定语

介词短语作定语一般位于所修饰的名词之后。

> The girl **in red** stands in front of the house.
> 那个穿红色衣服的女孩站在房子前面。
> The man **with a book** is my math teacher.
> 拿着一本书的那个人是我的数学老师。

3. 作表语

介词短语作表语位于系动词(尤其是 be 动词)之后。

➤ The dress is **out of date**.
  这条裙子过时了。
➤ My mother is **at home** now.
  我妈妈现在在家。

4. 作宾语补足语

介词短语作宾语补足语一般位于宾语之后。

➤ She found herself **at home** when she woke up.
  当她醒来的时候,她发现自己在家。
➤ Parents consider education **of great importance**.
  父母认为教育很重要。

(三)常见介词固定搭配

英语中许多名词、动词和形容词都可以与特定的介词构成固定搭配。现将部分常用介词固定搭配列举如下:

1. 名词+介词

access to 进入权,使用权
answer to ……的答案
interest in 对……的兴趣
introduction to 介绍;导论
response to 对……的反应
way to 通向……的路/……的方法
effect/impact/influence on 对……的影响

lack of 缺乏
key to ……的关键
reason for ……的原因
hunger for 对……的渴望
desire for 对……的渴望
success in 在……上的成功

charge for 对……的收费
blame for 对……的责任
respect for 对……的尊重
impression on 对……的印象
contribution to 对……的贡献

2. 动词+介词

get to 到达
get off 离开,动身
get over 克服
get through 通过;度过
cooperate with 与……合作
laugh at 嘲笑

apply for 申请
ask for 要求,请求
arrive in/at 到达
agree with 同意
graduate from 毕业于……
deal with 处理,应对

hear from 收到……的来信
pay for 支付
run across 偶然碰见
run out of 用完,耗尽
think of 想起
think about 思考

3. 形容词+介词

(be) absent from 缺席
(be) worthy of 值得
(be) fed up with 对……厌烦
(be) afraid of 对……感到害怕
(be) ready for 为……做好了准备

(be) fond of 喜欢
(be) aware of 意识到
(be) tired of 厌烦
(be) capable of 有能力做……
(be) devoted to 致力于

（be）responsible for 对……负责　　　　（be）qualified for…有资格做……
（be）famous for 以……闻名　　　　　（be）satisfied with 对……感到满意
（be）prepared for 为……做好了准备　　（be）familiar with 对……熟悉
（be）curious about 对……好奇　　　　（be）equipped with 装备

实 战 演 练

1. I always go out for a walk with my family _____ the evening.
   A. in　　　　　B. at　　　　　C. on　　　　　D. to
2. Study hard, _____ you will fail the exam.
   A. and　　　　B. for　　　　　C. but　　　　　D. or
3. When he became a famous actor, he was _____ his early twenties.
   A. in　　　　　B. at　　　　　C. after　　　　D. from
4. I'd like to go out for dinner with you, _____ I'm busy now.
   A. and　　　　B. but　　　　　C. so　　　　　D. for
5. _____ students, we should make full use of our time to study and make progress every day.
   A. On　　　　B. By　　　　　C. As　　　　　D. With
6. We didn't go to London for a trip last Sunday _____ the weather was too bad.
   A. unless　　　B. because　　　C. even if　　　D. until
7. We will go to London for a trip next month _____ we are not busy.
   A. unless　　　B. because　　　C. if　　　　　D. until
8. You can ask your teacher _____ help when you are in trouble.
   A. on　　　　　B. over　　　　C. from　　　　D. for
9. _____ my opinion, parents' care is more important than any other thing for children.
   A. On　　　　B. In　　　　　C. For　　　　　D. With
10. _____ our great surprise, he made such amazing progress last year.
    A. For　　　　B. With　　　　C. In　　　　　D. To
11. If you are interested _____ the job, you can send your resume and certifications to us.
    A. in　　　　　B. on　　　　　C. for　　　　　D. with
12. _____ my friends _____ I like running because we think it is good for our health.
    A. Both; and　　B. Neither; or　　C. Either; or　　D. Neither; nor
13. _____ she doesn't know much about Allan, they are still good friends.
    A. When　　　B. Although　　C. Because　　　D. Since
14. Great changes have taken place in China _____ reform and opening-up.
    A. before　　　B. since　　　　C. until　　　　D. although
15. The police are looking _____ the accident, hoping to find out the reason for it.
    A. into　　　　B. for　　　　　C. after　　　　D. up

第二部分　核心语法

第一章　简　单　句

　　句子是构成篇章的基本单位,由词或短语等不同句子成分构成。简单句是只含有一个主谓结构的句子,英语中的简单句包含五种基本句型,各种句子基本上是由这五种句型扩充、组合或省略而成。表达不同的句子内容需要不同类型的句式结构,这些句式结构又构成英语中的各种句子类型。掌握句子成分、简单句的五种基本句型、句子类型是学习英语句法的基础。

一、句子成分

　　句子成分由词或短语按照一定的语法规则构成。按其功能,句子成分可划分为主语、谓语、宾语、表语、宾语补足语、定语、状语和同位语。其中,主语和谓语是句子不可缺少的主要成分,宾语、表语、宾语补足语、定语、状语和同位语是可按需使用的次要成分。

(一) 主语

　　主语是谓语所表示的动作或状态的主体。可作主语的有名词(短语)、代词(短语)、数词(短语)、动名词(短语)、动词不定式(短语)和从句等。

➢ **That guy** scares me a lot.
　　那个人真的吓到我了。(名词短语作主语)
➢ **I** am very happy.
　　我很开心。(代词作主语)
➢ **Four** is the number which some Chinese people think unlucky.
　　一些中国人认为四是不吉利的数字。(数词作主语)
➢ **Swimming alone in the river** is very dangerous.
　　独自在河里游泳是很危险的。(动名词短语作主语)
➢ **To be the top one in class** is very difficult.
　　要成为班上的第一名是很困难的。(不定式短语作主语)
➢ **What I said just now** is very important.
　　我刚刚说的话非常重要。(从句作主语)

(二) 谓语

　　谓语用于说明主语的动作或所处的状态。有人称、数和时态的变化。

➢ We often **speak** English in class.
　　我们经常在课上说英语。
➢ He **wants** to be a pilot.
　　他想要成为一名飞行员。
➢ I **did** my homework yesterday.

我昨天做了作业。
- He **has lived** in Beijing for years.
  他已经在北京住了很多年了。
- She **is watching** TV at the moment.
  她现在正在看电视。

(三)宾语

宾语是谓语所表示动作的对象或承受者,一般位于及物动词或介词后。可作宾语的有名词(短语)、代词(短语)、数词(短语)、动名词(短语)、动词不定式(短语)和从句等。宾语可分为单宾语、双宾语和复合宾语。单宾语指谓语后只接一个宾语;双宾语指谓语后接两个宾语,由直接宾语和间接宾语组成;复合宾语指宾语后还需再接宾语补足语使句意完整。

- We clean **the room**.
  我们打扫房间。(名词短语作宾语)
- She looked at **me**.
  她看着我。(代词作宾语)
- Many Chinese people love **eight**.
  很多中国人喜欢数字八。(数词作宾语)
- She wants **to play basketball**.
  她想打篮球。(动词不定式短语作宾语)
- Lily enjoys **playing computer games with friends**.
  Lily 喜欢和朋友们一起玩电脑游戏。(动名词短语作宾语)
- I wonder **whether he can help me**.
  我想知道他是否能帮助我。(从句作宾语)
- She teaches **us English**.
  她教我们英语。(双宾语:us 为间接宾语,English 为直接宾语)
- You need paint **the wall white**.
  你需要把墙涂成白色。(复合宾语:the wall 为宾语,white 为宾语补足语)

(四)表语

表语用于说明主语的性质、身份、特征或状态等,一般位于系动词之后。可作表语的有名词(短语)、形容词(短语)、副词(短语)、数词(短语)、动词不定式(短语)、动名词(短语)、过去分词(短语)、介词短语和从句等。

- I am **a teacher**.
  我是一名老师。(名词短语作表语)
- She looks very **happy**.
  她看起来很开心。(形容词作表语)
- The war was **over**.
  战争结束了。(副词作表语)

- Its population is nearly **two million**.

  它的人口接近两百万。（数词短语作表语）
- Our plan is **to keep the affair secret**.

  我们的计划是对这件事保密。（动词不定式短语作表语）
- My favorite sports is **playing football**.

  我最喜欢的运动是踢足球。（动名词短语作表语）
- His heart is **broken**.

  他的心碎了。（过去分词作表语）
- Professor Wang is not **at home**.

  王教授不在家。（介词短语作表语）
- The reason why he was late for school this morning was **that he got up late**.

  他今天早上上学迟到的原因是他起床晚了。（从句作表语）

（五）宾语补足语

宾语补足语是用于补充说明宾语的动作、状态、性质等，位于宾语之后。可作宾语补足语的有名词（短语）、形容词（短语）、介词短语、非谓语动词（短语）、副词（短语）等。

- We elected him **monitor of our class**.

  我们选他为班长。（名词短语作宾语补足语）
- I find that movie **interesting**.

  我发现那部电影很有趣。（形容词作宾语补足语）
- We found her **in tears**.

  我们发现她在哭。（介词短语作宾语补足语）
- I hear a girl **singing a song**.

  我听到一个女孩正在唱歌。（非谓语动词短语作宾语补足语）
- I saw the man in black **out** just now.

  我刚才看到穿黑衣服的那位男士出去了。（副词作宾语补足语）

（六）定语

定语是对名词或代词起限定、修饰作用的成分。可作定语的有形容词（短语）、名词（短语）、代词（短语）、介词短语、非谓语动词（短语）和从句等。定语可分为前置定语和后置定语。单个单词作定语时，通常放在其修饰的词之前，作前置定语；短语和句子作定语时，常放在其修饰的词之后，作后置定语。

- It is a **difficult** problem.

  这是一个难题。（形容词作前置定语）
- She is the most famous **woman** teacher in the town.

  她是这个镇上最有名的女教师。（名词作前置定语）
- This is **my** book.

  这是我的书。（代词作前置定语）

➤ The girl **in red** is my sister.

穿红衣服的女孩是我妹妹。(介词短语作后置定语)

➤ The pollution **caused by the increasing number of the cars** is becoming more and more serious.

由日益增加的汽车所造成的污染正在变得越来越严重。(非谓语动词短语作后置定语)

➤ The man **who is talking with my teacher** is my father.

正在和我的老师谈话的那个人是我的父亲。(从句作后置定语)

(七) 状语

状语是用来修饰动词、形容词、副词或句子的一种成分。它可以表示时间、地点、方式、原因、目的、结果、条件、比较、让步、程度等。可作状语的有副词(短语)、介词短语、非谓语动词(短语)和从句等。

➤ He runs **fast**.

他跑得很快。(副词作状语)

➤ I play with my classmates **on the playground**.

我和同学们在操场上玩。(介词短语作状语)

➤ **Hearing the news**, they got very excited.

听到这个消息,他们非常兴奋。(非谓语动词短语作状语)

➤ He was watching TV **while his mother was cooking**.

他妈妈做饭的时候,他正在看电视。(从句作状语)

(八) 同位语

同位语是对句子中名词(短语)或代词作进一步解释、说明、强调的成分,常位于被解释、说明的词之后。可作同位语的有名词(短语)、代词(短语)、数词(短语)、从句等。

➤ We **Chinese** love peace.

我们中国人爱好和平。(名词作 we 的同位语)

➤ We **each** have a chance to win.

我们每个人都有机会赢。(代词作 we 的同位语)

➤ You **two** take these seats.

你们俩坐这里。(数词作 you 的同位语)

➤ The news **that we won the game** is true.

我们赢了比赛的消息是真的。(从句作 news 的同位语)

二、简单句的五种基本句型

在简单句中主谓结构是句子的主干,是句子的核心。简单句可归纳为五种基本句型,简单句使用哪个基本句型,取决于该句子中的谓语动词;也就是说不同类型的谓语动词,会构成不同类型的基本句型。

（一）主语+谓语（S+V）

该句型中的谓语动词为不及物动词,动作含义完整。

➢ The sun rises.
  太阳升起来了。
➢ The fire happened during the night.
  夜间发生了火灾。
➢ Birds fly in the sky.
  鸟儿在天上飞。
➢ The boy smiled happily.
  那个男孩笑得很开心。

（二）主语+谓语+宾语（S+V+O）

该句型中的谓语动词为及物动词,动作含义不完整,需接宾语才能表达完整含义。

➢ I borrowed four books from the library.
  我从图书馆借了四本书。
➢ She bought an English book.
  她买了一本英语书。

【补充提示】

部分不及物动词后接介词可构成及物动词词组,再接宾语。

➢ Mom shouted at me.
  妈妈冲着我喊。
➢ They looked at the blackboard carefully.
  他们认真地看着黑板。

（三）主语+谓语+间接宾语+直接宾语（S+V+Oi+Od）

该句型中的谓语动词为接双宾语的及物动词,构成双宾语结构（直接宾语+间接宾语）。直接宾语一般是指物的名词或代词,表明动作的承受者；间接宾语一般是指人的名词或代词,表明动作的方向或目标。通常间接宾语在前,直接宾语在后,但有时为了强调直接宾语,会将直接宾语提前,此时间接宾语前需要加上介词 to 或 for,构成结构：主语+谓语+直接宾语+介词（to 或 for）+间接宾语。to 侧重指动作的方向,表示"给……",for 侧重指动作的受益者,表示"为了……"。

➢ He showed the guard his passport.
  他给警卫看了他的护照。（the guard 为间接宾语,his passport 为直接宾语）
➢ Please pass me that book.
  请把那本书递给我。（me 为间接宾语,that book 为直接宾语）
➢ I sent a gift to her.
  我送给了她一个礼物。（a gift 为直接宾语,her 为间接宾语）
➢ I made a cake for him.
  我为他做了一个蛋糕。（a cake 为直接宾语,him 为间接宾语）

【补充提示】
　　直接宾语前置时,间接宾语前需加介词 to 或 for 的常见双宾语动词详见基础语法第三章动词。

(四) 主语+谓语+宾语+宾语补足语(S+V+O+C)

　　该句型中的谓语动词为及物动词,且这些及物动词接了宾语后句子意思仍不完整,在宾语后还需加上补充说明宾语的补足语。

➢ They appointed John chairman.
　他们任命 John 为主席。(chairman 为 John 的宾语补足语)
➢ You can leave the door open.
　你可以让门开着。(open 为 the door 的宾语补足语)
➢ I will invite him to deliver a speech.
　我将邀请他发表演讲。(to deliver a speech 为 him 的宾语补足语)
➢ I found a dog lying under the table.
　我发现一只狗躺在桌子下面。(lying under the table 为 a dog 的宾语补足语)

(五) 主语+系动词+表语(S+V+P)

　　该句型中的谓语动词为系动词,后接表语,用来说明主语的性质、身份、特征和状态等。

➢ She is a nurse.
　她是一名护士。
➢ He looks unhappy.
　他看起来不开心。
➢ Leaves turn yellow in autumn.
　树叶在秋天会变黄。
➢ The cake tastes delicious.
　这个蛋糕尝起来很美味。

【补充提示】
　　常见系动词详见下表:

系动词具体分类	
状态系动词	be 动词(am/is/are/was/were…)
持续系动词	keep,remain,stay
表像系动词	seem,appear
感官系动词	look,feel,smell,sound,taste
变化系动词	become,grow,turn,get,go
终止系动词	prove,turn out

三、句子类型

除了简单句的五种基本句型分类之外,英语句子按照使用目的与语用功能,还可分为以下四类:陈述句、疑问句、祈使句和感叹句。

(一)陈述句

陈述句是用来陈述某一事实或表明说话人的观点、态度的句子,句末用句点"."。陈述句包括肯定陈述句和否定陈述句。

1. 肯定陈述句

肯定陈述句的句子结构一般为"主语+谓语+其他"。

- Beijing is the capital of China.
  北京是中国的首都。
- He told the children a story.
  他给孩子们讲了一个故事。
- I have been to many cities in Japan.
  我到过日本的很多城市。
- The police are coming soon.
  警察很快就来。

2. 否定陈述句

否定陈述句通常在肯定句的基础上加否定词 not,根据陈述句的谓语构成不同,可分为以下两种情况:

(1)陈述句中谓语部分含有 be 动词/助动词/情态动词,变否定形式直接在其后加 not,其结构为"主语+be 动词/助动词/情态动词+not+其他"。

- I **am not** good at English.
  我不擅长英语。
- She **may not come** here tomorrow.
  她明天可能不会来这里。
- I **have not heard** the latest news.
  我还没听到最新的消息。
- I **will not go** to Beijing this summer.
  今年夏天我不会去北京。

(2)陈述句中谓语部分不含 be 动词/助动词/情态动词,则需借助助动词 do/does/did,再加 not,并将动词变为原形,其结构为"主语+don't/doesn't/didn't+动词原形+其他"。

- She **doesn't love** cats.
  她不喜欢猫。

> We **don't go** to school on weekends.

　　我们周末不上学。
> They **didn't know** my name and telephone number.

　　他们不知道我的姓名和电话号码。

【补充提示】

① 陈述句中谓语部分含有两个及以上 be 动词/助动词/情态动词时,变否定形式需在第一个动词后加 not。
> The work **can't be finished** within three days.

　　这项工作不可能在三天内完成。
> You **should not have told** him the news.

　　你本不应该告诉他这个消息的。

② 除 not 外,其他否定词如 no、seldom、never、hardly、few、little、nobody 等也可以构成否定陈述句。
> We **seldom** go shopping.

　　我们很少去购物。
> I have **never** been to Beijing.

　　我从未去过北京。
> He **hardly** believes her story.

　　他几乎不相信她的故事。
> There is **no** milk in the fridge.

　　冰箱里没有牛奶。
> **Few** people believe her words.

　　几乎没有人相信她的话。
> There is **little** water in the bottle. Let's go and get some.

　　瓶子里几乎没有水了,让我们去取一些来吧。

(二) 疑问句

疑问句是用来提出问题的句子,句末用问号"?"。常见的疑问句有四类:一般疑问句、特殊疑问句、选择疑问句和反义疑问句。疑问句语序为"谓语(部分谓语)+主语+其他",也称为倒装语序。

1. 一般疑问句

一般疑问句是用来询问某一事实或者状况是否属实的句子,通常用 yes 或 no 来回答,口语中也可以用 certainly (not)、of course (not)、sure、all right、I'm afraid not 等来回答。
> ——Are your parents doctors?

　　——Yes, they are.

　　——你的父母是医生吗?

　　——是的,他们是。
> ——Did you enjoy yourself in our city?

　　——No, not very well.

——你在我们市玩得开心吗?
——不,不太开心。

➢ —Would you mind my joining your talk?
——Of course not.
——你们介意我加入你们的讨论吗?
——当然不介意。

➢ —Will you please do me a favor?
——Sure.
——你可以帮我一个忙吗?
——当然可以。

陈述句改变语序可变为一般疑问句,根据陈述句的谓语构成不同,可以分为以下两种情况:

(1) 陈述句中谓语部分含有 be 动词/助动词/情态动词,直接将 be 动词/助动词/情态动词提到主语前构成一般疑问句,其结构为"be 动词/助动词/情态动词+主语+其他?"

➢ He **is** a doctor.
他是医生。
Is he a doctor?
他是医生吗?

➢ Lily **has done** her homework.
Lily 已经做了家庭作业。
Has Lily done her homework?
Lily 已经做了家庭作业吗?

➢ Everyone **can appreciate** our music.
所有人都能欣赏我们的音乐。
Can everyone appreciate your music?
所有人都能欣赏你们的音乐吗?

➢ Lucy **will go to** Wuhan tomorrow.
Lucy 明天会去武汉。
Will Lucy go to Wuhan tomorrow?
Lucy 明天会去武汉吗?

(2) 陈述句中谓语部分不含 be 动词/助动词/情态动词,则需借助助动词 do/does/did 构成一般疑问句,动词要变为原形,其结构为"Do/Does/Did+主语+动词原形+其他?"

➢ They **work** very hard.
他们工作很努力。
Do they work very hard?
他们工作很努力吗?

➢ He **likes** reading.
他喜欢读书。

> **Does he like** reading?
> 他喜欢读书吗？

> I **drank** a glass of milk yesterday.
> 我昨天喝了一杯牛奶。

> **Did you drink** a glass of milk yesterday?
> 你昨天喝了一杯牛奶吗？

【补充提示】
变一般疑问句时，陈述句中的第一人称（如 I、we、my、our）要变为第二人称（如 you、your）。

2. 特殊疑问句

由特殊疑问词引导，就句中某一部分进行提问的句子叫作特殊疑问句。特殊疑问词包括疑问代词和疑问副词（词组），常用的疑问代词有 what、who、whom、whose、which 等；常用的疑问副词（词组）有 when、where、how、why、how often、how long、how far、how much、how many 等。特殊疑问词一定位于句首，而根据被提问部分的成分不同，特殊疑问句的语序可分为以下两种情况：

（1）对主语或主语修饰语提问时，用陈述语序。

> <u>She</u> is a teacher.
> 她是教师。
> **Who** is a teacher?
> 谁是教师？

> <u>Six</u> boys are playing football.
> 六个男孩正在踢足球。
> **How many** boys are playing football?
> 有多少男孩正在踢足球？

> <u>He</u> is sweeping the floor.
> 他正在扫地。
> **Who** is sweeping the floor?
> 谁正在扫地？

（2）对主语和主语修饰语以外的成分提问时，用倒装语序，即"特殊疑问词+一般疑问句"。

> He is <u>a lawyer</u>.
> 他是一名律师。
> **What** is he?
> 他的职业是什么？

> He studies <u>English</u>.
> 他学习英语。
> What does he study?
> 他学的是什么？

> She played tennis with friends <u>last night</u>.

她昨天晚上和朋友们一起打了网球。
When did she play tennis with friends?
她什么时候和朋友们一起打网球了?

3. 选择疑问句

选择疑问句是说话者对问题提出两个或两个以上的答案,供对方选择的疑问句。它的被选择部分由 or 连接。这种疑问句有两种形式,分别是一般疑问句式的选择疑问句和特殊疑问句式的选择疑问句。

(1) 一般疑问句式的选择疑问句。

➢ Are you **a doctor or a lawyer**?
你是一名医生还是一位律师?

➢ Have you put the book **in the box or in your bag**?
你把书放在了盒子里还是放进了你包里?

➢ Do you like **English or Chinese**?
你喜欢英语还是汉语?

➢ Will you go to **Yunnan or Sanya** this summer vacation?
你这个暑假去云南还是三亚?

(2) 特殊疑问句式的选择疑问句。

➢ Which dress do you like, **the green one or the red one**?
你喜欢哪条裙子,绿色的还是红色的?

➢ Where did you go, **Beijing or Tianjin**?
你去了哪里,北京还是天津?

➢ When can you go for a trip, **this weekend or next weekend**?
你什么时候能去度假,这周末还是下周末?

➢ What did you buy for your father, **a tie or a wallet**?
你给你父亲买了什么,领带还是钱包?

4. 反义疑问句

反义疑问句又称为附加疑问句,是附加在陈述句后的简短问句。它由"陈述句+简短附加问句"两部分组成,陈述句部分提出一种看法,附加问句部分表示征询意见或证实陈述内容。前后两部分的人称、数、时态应保持一致,且遵循"前肯后否,前否后肯"的原则,即若陈述部分用肯定形式,则附加问句用否定形式;若陈述部分用否定形式,则附加问句用肯定形式。

(1) 反义疑问句的基本用法。

根据"前肯后否,前否后肯"的原则,反义疑问句句式结构可以分为以下两种情况:

① 肯定陈述句+否定附加问句(be 动词/助动词/情态动词+not+主语)+?

➢ She told you the news, **didn't she**?
她把消息告诉你了,是吗?

➢ They are students, **aren't they**?
他们是学生,是吗?

> They have finished homework, **haven't they**?
> 他们已经完成了作业,不是吗?
> They can hand in the task on time, **can't they**?
> 他们能准时提交任务,不是吗?

② 否定陈述句+肯定附加问句(be 动词/助动词/情态动词+主语)+?

> He doesn't like coffee, **does he**?
> 他不喜欢咖啡,是吗?
> She can't play the piano, **can she**?
> 她不会弹钢琴,是吗?
> They haven't been to Wuhan, **have they**?
> 他们没去过武汉,是吗?
> They aren't classmates, **are they**?
> 他们不是同学,是吗?

【补充提示】
① 反义疑问句的附加问句部分,主语常用人称代词,若陈述句的主语是名词时,附加问句的主语用相应的人称代词来代替。

> Your parents went shopping last night, **didn't they**?
> 昨晚你的父母去购物了,是吗?
> Wuhan is a beautiful city, **isn't it**?
> 武汉是一个美丽的城市,是吗?

② 反义疑问句的附加问句部分若为否定形式,be/助动词/情态动词常和 not 缩写在一起。

> Lily is very hard-working, **isn't she**?
> Lily 非常努力,不是吗?
> Tom and John are good friends, **aren't they**?
> Tom 和 John 是好朋友,不是吗?

(2) 反义疑问句的特殊用法。

① 反义疑问句的陈述部分有 seldom、hardly、never、few、little、nothing、nobody、nowhere、too...to 等否定词或否定含义的结构时,附加问句用肯定形式;但若陈述部分有带否定词缀(前缀或后缀)的派生词,如 helpless、hopeless、dislike、unable、unhappy 等时,附加问句仍用否定形式。

> There is little water left, **is there**?
> 水已经所剩无几了,是吗?
> He was too nervous to answer this question, **was he**?
> 他太紧张了回答不了这个问题,是吗?
> He was unhappy, **wasn't he**?
> 他不开心,是吗?
> They dislike the house, **don't they**?
> 他们不喜欢这个房子,是吗?

② 反义疑问句的陈述部分是 there be 句型，附加问句的主语仍用 there。
- There will be a meeting tomorrow, **won't there**?
  明天有一场会议，是吗？
- There is little money in the wallet, **is there**?
  钱包里几乎没有钱了，是吗？
- There are two glasses of milk on the table, **aren't there**?
  桌上有两杯牛奶，不是吗？
- There is no juice left in the bottle, **is there**?
  瓶子里没有果汁了，是吗？

③ 反义疑问句的陈述部分的主语是 somebody、someone、everybody、everyone、anyone、nobody 等表人的不定代词，附加问句的主语强调整体时一般用 they，强调个体时一般用 he。
- Everyone has advised you not to play computer games, **haven't they**?
  大家都建议你不要玩电脑游戏，不是吗？
- Someone is waiting for you, **isn't he**?
  有人在等你，是吗？
- Nobody knew the right answer, **did they**?
  没有人知道正确答案，是吗？
- Everybody has a chance to answer the question, **don't they**?
  大家都有一次回答这个问题的机会，是吗？

④ 反义疑问句的陈述部分的主语是 everything、nothing 等表物的不定代词或指示代词 this、that 时，附加问句的主语常用 it；当陈述部分的主语是指示代词 these、those 时，附加问句的主语常用 they。
- Everything goes well, **doesn't it**?
  一切都很顺利，不是吗？
- That is wonderful, **isn't it**?
  太棒了，不是吗？
- These are important reading materials, **aren't they**?
  这些都是很重要的阅读材料，是吗？
- Those are your workmates, **aren't they**?
  那些都是你的同事，不是吗？

⑤ 反义疑问句的陈述部分是祈使句时，附加问句有以下两种情况：

祈使句是肯定句时，附加问句一般用 will you 或 won't you；祈使句是否定句时，附加问句用 will you。

- Come in and take a seat please, **will you/won't you**?
  进来坐下，好吗？
- Put those books on the table, **will you/won't you**?
  把那些书放在桌子上，好吗？
- Don't make much noise, **will you**?

别制造太多噪音,好吗?
- Don't leave without saying goodbye, **will you**?
  别不辞而别,好吗?

以 Let's 开头的祈使句,附加问句用 shall we;以 Let us/me 开头的祈使句,附加问句一般用 will you。

- Let's go home, **shall we**?
  我们回家吧,好吗?
- Let's look at it again, **shall we**?
  我们再看一眼,好吗?
- Let us have a look at your book, **will you**?
  让我们看一看你的书,好吗?
- Let us go to the post office together, **will you**?
  我们一起去邮局,好吗?

⑥ 反义疑问句的陈述部分含有情态动词 have/has/had to 时,附加问句常用助动词 don't/doesn't/didn't。

- They have to get up early every day, **don't they**?
  他们每天不得不早起,是吗?
- Your father has to give up smoking, **doesn't he**?
  你的父亲不得不戒烟,是吗?
- She had to answer a question, **didn't she**?
  她不得不回答一个问题,是吗?

⑦ 反义疑问句的陈述部分含有情态动词 had better 时,附加问句用 hadn't 或 shouldn't。

- You'd better go now, **hadn't/shouldn't you**?
  你最好现在就走,好吗?
- You'd better give up smoking, **hadn't/shouldn't you**?
  你最好戒烟,好吗?
- You'd better hand in your homework on time, **hadn't/shouldn't you**?
  你最好按时提交作业,好吗?

⑧ 反义疑问句的陈述部分含有情态动词 used to 时,附加问句用 usedn't 或 didn't。

- He used to get up early, **usedn't/didn't he**?
  他过去常常早起,不是吗?
- Tom used to play the piano at weekends, **usedn't/didn't he**?
  Tom 过去常常在周末弹钢琴,是吗?
- Lucy used to have a walk after dinner, **usedn't/didn't she**?
  Lucy 过去常常在晚饭后散步,是吗?

⑨ 反义疑问句的陈述部分含有情态动词 ought to 时,附加问句用 oughtn't/shouldn't。

- Tom ought to be praised for his performance, **oughtn't/shouldn't he**?
  Tom 的表现应该受到表扬,不是吗?

> She ought to apologize for her being late, **oughtn't/shouldn't she**?
> 她应该为迟到而道歉,不是吗?
> You ought to get out of the house more, **oughtn't/shouldn't you**?
> 你应该多到户外去走走,不是吗?

⑩ 反义疑问句的陈述部分含有情态动词 must 时,附加问句分以下几种情况:

must 表示含义"必须"时,附加问句用 mustn't。

> He must go home now, **mustn't he**?
> 他现在必须回家,不是吗?

mustn't 表示含义"禁止,不准"时,附加问句用 must。

> You mustn't walk on the grass, **must you**?
> 禁止你们践踏草坪,知道吗?
> You mustn't smoke in a public garden, **must you**?
> 禁止你们在公园抽烟,知道吗?

must 表示推测含义"一定"时,附加问句应根据句意来选择相应的助动词。

- "must+do"表示对现在情况的推测时,附加问句由 must 后面的动词形式决定。
> He must be very happy, **isn't he**?
> 他一定很高兴,不是吗?
> The girl in red must be Lily, **isn't she**?
> 那个穿着红色衣服的女孩一定是 Lily,不是吗?
> His father must be cooking now, **isn't he**?
> 他父亲现在一定在做饭,不是吗?

- "must+have done"表示对过去情况的推测,句中使用一般过去时时间状语时,附加问句用"didn't/wasn't/weren't+主语";句中使用现在完成时时间状语时,附加问句用"haven't/hasn't+主语"。
> He must have lost his wallet yesterday, **didn't he**?
> 他昨天一定丢了钱包,不是吗?
> She must have learned English for many years, **hasn't she**?
> 她一定学英语很多年了,是吗?
> She must have finished her homework last night, **didn't she**?
> 她昨晚一定做完了作业,是吗?
> They must have known each other for a long time, **haven't they**?
> 他们一定认识很长时间了,是吗?

⑪ 反义疑问句的陈述部分含有 would rather 或 would like 时,附加问句用 wouldn't。

> He would like to go with you, **wouldn't he**?
> 他想和你一起去,是吗?
> She would like to go for a trip, **wouldn't she**?
> 她想去度假,是吗?
> Kids would rather play than study, **wouldn't they**?
> 孩子们宁愿玩也不愿学习,是吗?

⑫ 反义疑问句的陈述部分是"I am..."结构时,附加问句常用 aren't I 或 am I not。

➢ I am your best friend, **aren't I/am I not**?
　　我是你最好的朋友,是吧?
➢ I am supposed to be here, **aren't I/am I not**?
　　我应该在这里,不是吗?
➢ I'm as tall as your sister, **aren't I/am I not**?
　　我和你姐姐一样高,对吗?

⑬ 反义疑问句的陈述部分是一个主从复合句时,附加问句一般与主句的主语、谓语保持一致。

➢ She says that I did it, **doesn't she**?
　　她说那是我干的,是吗?
➢ He said that he was late for class this morning, **didn't he**?
　　他说他今天早上上课迟到了,是吗?
➢ It has been a long time since I left Wuhan, **hasn't it**?
　　我离开武汉很久了,是吗?

【补充提示】
若陈述部分是"I'm sure/I'm afraid 或 I don't think/suppose/believe 等+宾语从句"时,附加问句应与从句的主语、谓语保持一致,且要注意陈述部分的否定转移现象。

➢ I am afraid she won't come here, **will she**?
　　我恐怕她不会来这儿,是吗?
➢ I don't think she cares, **does she**?
　　我认为她不在乎,是吗?
➢ I don't believe he is a native American, **is he**?
　　我认为他不是土生土长的美国人,是吗?

(三) 祈使句

祈使句是用来发出命令或指示,提出要求或劝告等的句子。一般以动词原形开头,省略主语"you",句末用句号"."或感叹号"!"。

1. 肯定祈使句

肯定祈使句一般结构为"动词原形(be 动词或实义动词)+其他",动词没有人称、数与时态的变化,有时表请求也可在句首或句尾加上语气词 please。

➢ (Please) be quiet!
　　(请)保持安静!
➢ Clean your room!
　　打扫你的房间!
➢ Go and wash your hands please.
　　去洗你的手。
➢ Park your car here.
　　把你的车停在这儿。

2. 否定祈使句

否定祈使句一般是在肯定祈使句句首加上"Don't"或"Never",其结构为"Don't/Never+动词原形(be 动词或实义动词)+其他"。

➢ Don't be late!
  不要迟到!
➢ Don't tell others the secret!
  不要告诉别人这个秘密!
➢ Never forget me!
  别忘了我!
➢ Never say bad words about anyone.
  永远不要说任何人的坏话。

(四)感叹句

感叹句是用来表示喜、怒、哀、乐等强烈情感的句子。一般用感叹词 how 或 what 引导,句末用感叹号"!"。

1. what 引导的感叹句

what 引导的感叹句中心词为名词,常见结构如下:

(1) What+a/an+形容词+可数名词单数(+其他)+!。

➢ What a fine day it is!
  多好的天气啊!
➢ What an interesting film!
  多么有趣的一部电影!
➢ What a beautiful girl!
  多么漂亮的一个女孩!

(2) What+形容词+可数名词复数(+其他)+!。

➢ What good teachers they are!
  他们是多么好的老师啊!
➢ What beautiful flowers they are!
  多么美丽的花啊!
➢ What useful books!
  多么有用的书啊!

(3) What+形容词+不可数名词(+其他)+!。

➢ What hard work it is!
  多么困难的工作啊!
➢ What nice weather it is today!
  今天天气多好啊!
➢ What exciting news it is!
  多么激动人心的消息啊!

2. how 引导的感叹句

how 引导的感叹句中心词为形容词或副词，常见结构如下：

(1) How+形容词/副词+主语+谓语(+其他)+！。

➢ How cold it is today!
   今天好冷啊！
➢ How lovely the baby is!
   这个婴儿多么可爱啊！
➢ How funny the film is!
   这部电影多有趣啊！

(2) How+主语+谓语(+其他)+！。

➢ How time flies!
   光阴似箭！

【补充提示】

在日常实际使用过程中除 what 与 how 引导的感叹句外，也可在陈述句、疑问句、祈使句或能表达情绪的感叹词(短语)等后用感叹号，构成感叹句。

➢ Good idea!
   好主意！
➢ You are so beautiful!
   你好漂亮！
➢ Look out!
   小心！

实 战 演 练

一、判断下列句子属于哪种基本句型

1. He sent me a letter yesterday.　　　　　＿＿＿＿＿＿＿＿＿＿＿＿＿＿＿＿＿＿
2. We named our baby John.　　　　　　　　＿＿＿＿＿＿＿＿＿＿＿＿＿＿＿＿＿＿
3. She looks so beautiful today.　　　　　　＿＿＿＿＿＿＿＿＿＿＿＿＿＿＿＿＿＿
4. He looks at the beautiful girl under the tree.　＿＿＿＿＿＿＿＿＿＿＿＿＿＿＿＿＿＿
5. They often play chess in the park.　　　　＿＿＿＿＿＿＿＿＿＿＿＿＿＿＿＿＿＿

二、将下列句子转换为否定句和一般疑问句

1. She is a teacher.
   否定句：＿＿＿＿＿＿＿＿＿＿＿＿＿＿＿＿＿＿＿＿＿＿＿＿＿＿＿＿＿＿＿＿＿＿
   一般疑问句：＿＿＿＿＿＿＿＿＿＿＿＿＿＿＿＿＿＿＿＿＿＿＿＿＿＿＿＿＿＿＿
2. She has finished her work.
   否定句：＿＿＿＿＿＿＿＿＿＿＿＿＿＿＿＿＿＿＿＿＿＿＿＿＿＿＿＿＿＿＿＿＿＿
   一般疑问句：＿＿＿＿＿＿＿＿＿＿＿＿＿＿＿＿＿＿＿＿＿＿＿＿＿＿＿＿＿＿＿

3. I forgot my homework.

否定句：_____

一般疑问句：_____

4. She will finish her work soon.

否定句：_____

一般疑问句：_____

5. My friends can play basketball.

否定句：_____

一般疑问句：_____

三、单项选择

1. Lily and Cathy are good friends, _____?

   A. do they   B. don't they   C. are they   D. aren't they

2. _____ nice weather it is in Beijing today!

   A. How a   B. How   C. What a   D. What

3. —_____ do you go to the movies with your friends?

   —Twice a week.

   A. How often   B. How far   C. How long   D. How soon

4. We finally finished the work. Let's go out for a dinner, _____?

   A. shall we   B. don't we   C. do we   D. can we

5. He has to finish the task by Sunday, _____?

   A. hasn't he   B. doesn't he   C. has he   D. does he

6. Everything is ready, _____?

   A. are they   B. aren't they   C. isn't it   D. is it

7. Mary has few friends in school, _____?

   A. does she   B. is she   C. hasn't she   D. isn't she

8. _____ interesting book it is!

   A. What a   B. How   C. What an   D. How a

9. There is little milk in the fridge, _____?

   A. is there   B. isn't it   C. isn't there   D. doesn't it

10. They have already done the homework, _____?

   A. have they   B. haven't they   C. do they   D. don't they

第二章 时 态

英语中动词的时态可以用"时"和"态"分别讲述。"时"表示动作或状态所发生的"时间",可分为现在、过去、将来和过去将来四种情形。"态"表示在指定时间上动作所处的"状态",可分为一般、进行、完成和完成进行四种情形,英语中时态共有十六种。

时间 状态	现在时	过去时	将来时	过去将来时
一般	do/does	did	shall/will do	would do
进行	am/is/are doing	was/were doing	shall/will be doing	would be doing
完成	have/has done	had done	shall/will have done	would have done
完成进行	have/has been doing	had been doing	shall/will have been doing	would have been doing

一、一般时态

（一）一般现在时

1. 谓语构成

一般现在时的谓语动词主要由动词原形或第三人称单数动词形式构成,且 be 动词在一般现在时中的形式为 am、is、are。当主语为第三人称单数时,谓语动词需变化成相应的第三人称单数形式,动词第三人称单数变化规则如下表:

变化规则	例词		
一般情况下,动词末尾直接加 s	cook—cooks see—sees	smile—smiles read—reads	play—plays look—looks
以 s、x、sh、ch、o 结尾的动词,动词末尾加 es	guess—guesses watch—watches	fix—fixes go—goes	wash—washes do—does
以"辅音字母+y"结尾的动词,变 y 为 i,再加 es	study—studies try—tries	fly—flies marry—marries	carry—carries worry—worries
特例词	have—has	be—is	

➤ She usually **goes** to school by bus.
她通常坐公交车去学校。

➤ The earth **travels** around the sun.

地球绕着太阳转。

➢ She **studies** art two afternoons a week.
　她每周两个下午学习艺术。

2. 用法

（1）表示经常、习惯性动作或现在的状态，常用的时间状语有 always、often、usually、sometimes、seldom、every day、twice a week 等频率副词。

➢ I **use** the Internet almost every day.
　我几乎每天都上网。

➢ He always **goes** to work late.
　他总是上班迟到。

➢ Lily **goes** swimming twice a week.
　Lily 每周去游泳两次。

➢ He **is** a teacher.
　他是一名教师。

（2）表示客观事实、自然现象、真理等。

➢ London **lies** on the River Thames.
　伦敦位于泰晤士河畔。

➢ Knowledge **is** power.
　知识就是力量。

➢ Light **travels** faster than sound.
　光比声音传播得快。

（3）在时间、条件、让步状语从句中，主句使用一般将来时，从句使用一般现在时表将来，即遵循"主将从现"的原则。

➢ I **will discuss** this problem with you **when** we **meet** next time.
　下次见面的时候我将和你讨论这个问题。

➢ I **will stay** at home **if** it **rains** tomorrow.
　如果明天下雨，我会待在家里。

➢ I **will stay** here **in case** you **need** me.
　我会待在这里，以防你需要我。

➢ There **will be** less pollution **if** we **plant** more trees.
　如果我们种更多树，污染将会减少。

（4）表示按照时间表、计划安排好的动作，常用的动词及动词短语有 come、go、leave、arrive、start、begin、end、take place 等。

➢ The meeting **begins** at 2 p.m.
　会议下午 2 点开始。

➢ The bus **starts** at 7 a.m.

公交车早上 7 点发车。
- The plane **takes off** at 11 a. m.
  飞机上午 11 点起飞。

(二) 一般过去时

1. 谓语构成

一般过去时的谓语动词主要由动词过去式构成。be 动词在一般过去时中的形式为 was、were，动词过去式的变化可分为规则变化和不规则变化。不规则动词的过去式详见附录"不规则动词变化表"；规则动词的过去式变化规则如下表：

变化规则	例词		
一般情况下，动词末尾直接加 ed	pull—pulled play—played	cook—cooked laugh—laughed	watch—watched look—looked
以不发音的字母 e 结尾的动词，直接加 d	taste—tasted decide—decided	like—liked hope—hoped	smile—smiled raise—raised
以"辅音+元音+辅音"字母结尾的重读闭音节动词，先双写末尾的辅音字母，再加 ed	stop—stopped drop—dropped	plan—planned regret—regretted	shop—shopped fit—fitted
以"辅音字母+y"结尾的动词，变 y 为 i，再加 ed	study—studied carry—carried	try—tried hurry—hurried	marry—married worry—worried

- Tom suddenly **fell** ill yesterday and **had** to stay at home for another day.
  昨天 Tom 突然病了，不得不在家里又待了一天。
- He **played** football with his friends after school yesterday.
  他昨天放学之后和朋友们去踢足球了。

2. 用法

(1) 表示过去发生的动作或存在的状态，常用的时间状语有 yesterday、just now、last week、three days ago、in 2018、just then 等。

- He **left** ten minutes ago.
  他十分钟之前离开了。
- I **watched** the movie last week.
  我上周看了这部电影。
- She **was** born in 1998.
  她出生于 1998 年。

(2) 表示过去经常、习惯性发生的动作，可与时间状语 usually、always、often、in the past 等连用。

- Jane **went** to the park to have a walk every day in the past.

  Jane 过去每天都到公园去散步。

- When I was a boy, I often **went** to play in that park.

  当我还是个小男孩的时候,我经常去那个公园玩。

- I usually **went** to school by bus in the past.

  过去我通常坐公交车去学校。

(三) 一般将来时

1. 谓语构成

一般将来时的谓语动词主要由"will/shall(助动词)+ 动词原形"构成。will 可用于所有人称的主语,shall 只用于第一人称的主语,在现代英语中,大多数情况下采用 will。

- There **will be** less pollution in the future.

  未来污染将会变少。

- I **shall fly** to Beijing to have an important meeting tomorrow.

  明天我将乘飞机去北京参加一个重要的会议。

2. 用法

表示将要发生的动作或存在的状态,常用的时间状语有 tomorrow、next week、soon、in a few minutes、three days later、the day after tomorrow、in the future 等。

- They **will go** to a concert this evening.

  他们今晚要去听一场音乐会。

- I **will/shall see** you tomorrow to talk about the new plan.

  明天我会找你谈谈新计划。

- I **will come** back soon.

  我很快就回来。

3. 一般将来时的其他表达方式

(1) am/is/are going to do sth. 可表示说话者的主观打算,也可表示预测或客观迹象表明某事即将发生。

- We **are not going to stay** there long.

  我们不准备在那里待很久。

- The boy **is going to fall** off his bike.

  那个男孩快要从自行车上掉下来了。

- I **am going to take** the parcel to the post office this afternoon.

  我打算今天下午把这个包裹送到邮局去。

- Look! It's **going to rain**.

  看!要下雨了。

(2) am/is/are to do sth. 表示计划中约定的或按职责、义务和要求必须去做的即将发生的事。

- We **are to discuss** the report next Saturday.

我们将在下周六讨论这份报告。
- He **is to visit** Japan next year.
  明年他将访问日本。
- The boy **is to go** to school tomorrow.
  这个男孩明天要去上学。
- We **are to continue** the work next week.
  下周我们将继续这项工作。

（3）am/is/are about to do sth. 表示不久或即将要发生的动作，不强调主观，一般不能与具体的时间状语连用。

- The train **is about to leave**.
  火车即将离站。
- The jet **is about to take off**.
  那架喷气式飞机即将起飞。
- The match **is about to begin**.
  比赛即将开始。
- The device **is about to go off**.
  这个装置马上就要爆炸了。

（四）过去将来时

1. 谓语构成

过去将来时的谓语动词主要由"would（助动词）+ 动词原形"构成。

- Whenever we had trouble, he **would come** to help us.
  每当我们有困难时，他总是来帮助我们。
- He believed that he **would be** a scientist someday.
  他相信将来有一天他会成为一名科学家。

2. 用法

表示从过去某一时间看将要发生的动作或存在的状态，常用于主句是一般过去时的宾语从句中，宾语从句中常有 the next day、the following day、someday 等表将来的时间状语。

- She hoped that they **would meet** again someday.
  她希望将来有一天他们能再见面。
- He said they **would arrange** a party the next day.
  他说他们将在第二天安排一个派对。

3. 过去将来时的其他表达方式

（1）was/were going to do 表示说话者过去打算做某事或过去将要发生某事。

- She **was not going to do** anything that evening.
  那天晚上她不准备做任何事。
- I was told that he **was going to return** to Spain.

有人告诉我他准备回西班牙了。
- They thought it **was going to rain**.
  他们认为快要下雨了。
- He said that he **was going to live** in the country when he retired.
  他说他退休以后要住在农村。

（2）was/were to do 表示过去曾计划做某事，如果计划没有实现，则用不定式的完成式。

- She said she **was to take up** the position.
  她说她会担任这个职位。（计划做）
- She said she **was to have taken up** the position, but later changed her mind.
  她说她本打算担任这个职位的，但是后来改变了主意。（计划做，但最后没做）
- It was reported that another bridge **was to be built** across the Yangtze River.
  据报道，长江上将要再建一座大桥。（计划做）
- Lily said she **was to clean** the classroom after school.
  Lily 说，她放学后要打扫教室。（计划做）

（3）was/were about to do 表示过去即将发生的事情。

- She waited until he **was about to leave**.
  她一直等到他准备离开。
- I **was about to go** to bed when he came to see me.
  我正要睡觉时，他来看我了。
- I felt that something terrible **was about to happen**.
  我觉得有可怕的事要发生了。
- He **was about to start** when it suddenly began to rain.
  他刚要出发时，突然下雨了。

二、进行时态

（一）现在进行时

1. 谓语构成

现在进行时的谓语动词主要由"am/is/are（助动词）+动词现在分词"构成，动词的现在分词变化规则如下表：

变化规则	例词		
一般情况下，动词末尾直接加 ing	cook—cooking	play—playing	study—studying
	go—going	watch—watching	finish—finishing

续表

变化规则	例词		
以不发音的字母 e 结尾的动词,去 e 加 ing	make—making have—having	taste—tasting give—giving	smile—smiling raise—raising
以"辅音+元音+辅音"字母结尾的重读闭音节动词,先双写末尾的辅音字母,再加 ing	run—running cut—cutting	stop—stopping swim—swimming	shop—shopping put—putting
以 ie 结尾的动词,变 ie 为 y 再加 ing	die—dying	lie—lying	tie—tying

➤ The students **are playing** football on the playground at present.
学生们现在正在操场上踢足球。

➤ These days we **are helping** the farmers work on the farm.
这些天我们正在农场上帮农民们干活。

2. 用法

(1) 表示此刻动作正在进行或说话人说话时正在进行的动作,常用的时间状语有 now、at the moment、right now、at present 等。

➤ It **is snowing** outside.
外面正在下雪。

➤ We **are waiting** for you now.
我们现在正在等你。

➤ We **are having** English class at the moment.
我们现在正在上英语课。

(2) 表示现阶段正在进行的动作,但此刻该动作未必正在进行,常用的时间状语有 these days、this month、this term 等。

➤ I **am taking** medicine this month.
这个月我在吃药。

➤ The famous writer **is writing** another novel these days.
这位著名的作家这些天正在写另一部小说。

➤ We **are making** model planes these days.
这些天我们在做飞机模型。

(3) 表示按照计划安排即将要发生的动作,常与非延续性动词连用,如 leave、arrive、come、go、start、stop 等。

➤ Our course **is starting** at 8 o'clock.
我们的课程将在八点钟开始。

➤ I **am leaving** tonight.
我今晚就要走了。

> Hurry up! The bus **is coming**.
> 快点！公交车要来了。
> We **are arriving** on Tuesday.
> 我们将在星期二到达。

(4) 表示逐渐变化的过程,常用的动词有 become、get、go、turn 等。

> It **is getting** colder and colder in winter.
> 冬天,天气变得越来越冷了。
> I **am becoming** more and more casual.
> 我变得越来越随意了。
> Water **is becoming** an increasingly precious resource.
> 水正在成为日益珍贵的资源。

(5) 表示特定情感,如满意、赞扬、生气、不满等情绪,常与 always、constantly、forever 等副词连用。

> Mary **is always coming** late for class.
> Mary 总是上课迟到。(表示不满)
> She **is always helping** people.
> 她总是乐于帮助别人。(表示赞扬)
> The students **are making** progress **constantly**.
> 学生们在不断进步。(表示满意)
> She **is constantly interfering** in my affairs.
> 她老是干涉我的事。(表示不满)

(二) 过去进行时

1. 谓语构成

过去进行时的谓语动词主要由"was/were(助动词)+ 动词现在分词"构成。

> She **was cooking** this time yesterday.
> 昨天这个时候她正在做饭。
> Tom **was watching** TV at that time.
> Tom 那时正在看电视。

2. 用法

(1) 表示过去某一时刻或某一时间段内正在进行的动作,常用的时间状语有 then、at that moment、at that time、this time yesterday 以及"when/while+表示过去动作的时间状语从句"等。

> He **was playing** table tennis at five yesterday afternoon.
> 他昨天下午 5 点钟在打乒乓球。
> He **was reading** a book at that moment.
> 他那时正在看书。

> I **was cooking** when he came to see me.

  当他来看我的时候,我正在做饭。

(2) 表示从过去时间看将要发生的动作,常与非延续性动词 come、go、leave、arrive、start、stop 等连用。

> He told me that they **were leaving** for Beijing a few days later.

  他告诉我他们几天后要去北京了。

> He said that he **was coming** to see us the next day.

  他说他第二天要来看我们。

> He told me (that) he **was going** to London soon.

  他告诉我他很快就要去伦敦了。

【补充提示】

过去进行时与一般过去时的区别:过去进行时强调动作在过去时间点或时间段内正在进行;一般过去时则强调动作在过去时间已经完成。

> I **was reading** a book last night. I don't know if I can finish reading it today.

  我昨晚在看书。我不知道今天能不能看完。(强调昨天晚上在看书,现在书还没看完)

> I **wrote** some letters last night.

  昨晚我写了一些信。(强调昨天晚上信已经写完了)

(三) 将来进行时

1. 谓语构成

将来进行时的谓语动词主要由"**shall/will**(助动词)+ **be**(助动词)+ 动词现在分词"构成。will 可用于所有人称的主语,shall 只用于第一人称的主语。在现代英语中,大多数情况下采用 will。

> **I'll be doing** homework this time tomorrow.

  明天这个时候我将在做作业。

> She **will be watching** TV at four o'clock tomorrow.

  明天四点的时候她将在看电视。

2. 用法

(1) 表示将来某一时刻或某一时间段内正在进行的动作,常用的时间状语有 at four o'clock next week、this time tomorrow 等。

> What **will** you **be doing** this time tomorrow?

  明天这个时候你将在做什么?

> This time next week they **will be having** a meeting.

  下周的这个时候他们将在开会。

(2) 表示对即将发生动作的推测。

> They **will be having** their summer holiday in July.

  他们将在七月放暑假。

➢ We **will be spending** the winter in Hainan.
我们将在海南过冬。

➢ I'**ll be seeing** Mr. Smith tomorrow.
明天我将见史密斯先生。

三、完成时态

（一）现在完成时

1. 谓语构成

现在完成时的谓语动词主要由"have/has（助动词）+ 动词过去分词"构成，动词过去分词的变化也分为规则变化和不规则变化。规则动词的过去分词与其过去式保持一致，不规则动词的过去分词详见附录"不规则动词变化表"。

➢ We **have seen** that film before.
我们以前已经看过那部电影了。

➢ Great changes **have taken place** in China in the past few years.
在过去的几年里，中国发生了巨大的变化。

2. 用法

（1）表示过去的动作对现在产生的影响或结果，常用的时间状语有 already、just、yet、ever、never、before、lately、recently 等。

➢ My brother **has already done** his homework.
我的弟弟已经做完了他的作业。

➢ I'**ve just bought** a new house.
我刚买了一个新房子。

➢ **Have** you **used** it recently?
你最近使用过它吗？

➢ I **have watched** that film twice.
那部电影我已经看过两遍了。

（2）表示从过去开始一直持续到现在的动作或状态，用于延续性动词，常与 since+过去时间点、since+从句、for+时间段、these days、so far、up till now、up to present、in the past few years 等时间状语连用。

➢ I **have worked** here for twenty years.
我在这里工作已经二十年了。

➢ He **has lived** here since 1978.
自从1978年以来，他一直住在这里。

➢ Peter **has written** six papers so far.
到目前为止，Peter已经写了六篇论文。

(3) 用于固定句式中。

用于句式"It/This/That is the first (second/third...) time that 从句"中,意为"某人第几次做某事",that 从句用现在完成时。

➤ **It is the first time that** I **have seen** a foreigner.
　这是我第一次见到外国人。

➤ **This is the second time that** she **has been** to New York.
　这是她第二次去纽约。

【补充提示】

① have been to 与 have gone to 的区别:have/has been to 表示去过某个地方已经回来,常与 once、twice、several times 等词连用;have/has gone to 表示去了某地,现在还没有回来,可能在去的途中或已经到了目的地。

➤ He **has been to** Shanghai once.
　他去过上海一次。(去过已经回来了)

➤ The old American man **has been to** China three times.
　这位美国老人去过中国三次。(去过已经回来了)

➤ He **has gone to** London.
　他去伦敦了。(去了还没回来,可能还在路上,也可能已经到了目的地)

② 现在完成时与一般过去时的区别:两种时态都可表示过去发生的动作或存在的状态,但现在完成时侧重说明过去的动作或状态与现在有联系,可表示从过去开始持续到现在,或强调对现在造成的影响和结果;而一般过去时只表示动作或状态在过去某个时间发生,不表示和现在的联系且现在情况已经发生变化,常与表示过去时间点的时间状语连用。

➤ My brother **has been** in the army for five years.
　我的哥哥在部队服役已经五年了。(强调从五年前持续到现在,现在仍在部队)

➤ My brother **was** in the army five years ago.
　我的哥哥五年前在部队服役。(强调五年前在部队,现在已经不在部队了)

➤ She **has** just **bought** a new car.
　她刚刚买了一辆新车。(强调现在她已经拥有了一辆新车)

➤ She **bought** a new car last week.
　她上周买了一辆新车。(强调动作买车在过去发生)

(二) 过去完成时

1. 谓语构成

过去完成时的谓语动词主要由"had(助动词)+ 动词过去分词"构成。

➤ We got to the station after the train **had left**.
　火车已经离开之后,我们才到达车站。

➤ I **had flown** to Beijing by the time you called me yesterday.
　昨天你给我打电话之前我已经飞往北京了。

2. 用法

（1）表示过去某个时间或动作之前已经发生或完成的动作，即"过去的过去"，常用的时间状语有 by the end of last year/month/term、before/after+过去时间/动作等。

➢ They **had completed** the project by the end of last year.
  到去年年底，他们已经完成了这个项目。
➢ They **had got** everything ready before I came.
  在我来之前，他们已经把一切准备好了。

（2）用于固定句式中。

① 用于句式"It/This/That was the first（second/third…）time that 从句"中，意为"某人第几次做某事"，that 从句用过去完成时。

➢ **It was the second time that** I **had met** him.
  这是我第二次遇到他。
➢ **It was the third time that** I **had been** to France.
  这是我第三次去法国。

② 用于句式"no sooner…than…"与"hardly/scarcely…when…"中，意为"一……就……"，其中含 no sooner、hardly/scarcely 的主句用过去完成时，than 与 when 的从句用一般过去时，当 no sooner、hardly/scarcely 位于句首时，主句需使用部分倒装，其基本句式及倒装句式如下：

sb. +had+no sooner+done…than 从句（一般过去时）
= No sooner+had+sb. +done…than 从句（一般过去时）
sb. +had+hardly/scarcely+done…when 从句（一般过去时）
= Hardly/Scarcely+had+sb. +done…when 从句（一般过去时）

➢ I **had** no sooner **arrived** at the airport than I called him.
= No sooner **had** I **arrived** at the airport than I called him.
  我一到机场就给他打了电话。
➢ I **had** hardly/scarcely **arrived** at the airport when I called him.
= Hardly/Scarcely **had** I **arrived** at the airport when I called him.
  我一到机场就给他打了电话。

（3）表示未曾实现的愿望或打算，这类动词有 think、plan、want、hope、expect、intend 等。

➢ He **had wanted** to help you but he had no time then.
  他本来想帮助你，但是当时他没有时间。
➢ He **had intended** to speak, but time did not permit.
  他本来想发言，但是时间不允许。
➢ We **had hoped** to be able to come and see you.
  我们本来希望能来看看你。

（三）将来完成时

1. 谓语构成

将来完成时的谓语动词主要由"will/shall（助动词）+have（助动词）+ 动词过去分词"构成。

will 可用于所有人称的主语,shall 只用于第一人称的主语,在现代英语中,大多数情况下使用 will。

➢ We **shall have learned** 12 units by the end of this term.
　到这个学期末,我们将学完 12 个单元。
➢ We **will have been married** for a year by June 25th.
　到 6 月 25 日我们俩结婚就满一年了。

2. 用法

(1) 表示将来某一时刻或另一个未来的动作之前已经完成的动作,常用的时间状语有 "by+将来时间"、"by the time/when/after 等+用一般现在时表示将来动作的句子"等。

➢ We **will have finished** the project by the end of this year.
　到今年年底我们将完成这个项目。
➢ They **will have moved** to the new house when Jack comes back home from school.
　当 Jack 从学校回到家时,他们将已经搬到新房子了。
➢ I **will have had** breakfast by the time you pick me up.
　你来接我的时候,我将已经吃完早饭了。

(2) 表示持续到将来某一时刻的动作或状态,常与将来时间和"for+时间段"等时间状语连用。

➢ Next Monday, he **will have been** in Britain for three years.
　到下周一,他在英国就满三年了。
➢ By the end of this month he **will have worked** here for ten years.
　到这个月底他在这里工作就满十年了。

四、完成进行时态

这里我们主要对现在完成进行时进行介绍。

1. 谓语构成

现在完成进行时的谓语动词主要由"have/has(助动词)+ been(助动词)+ 动词现在分词"构成,当主语为第三人称单数时,助动词用 has。

➢ They **have been living** in this city for ten years.
　他们在这个城市已经住了 10 年了。
➢ We **have been waiting** for you for half an hour.
　我们已经等你半个小时了。

2. 用法

表示动作从过去某一时间开始一直延续到现在且可能继续进行下去,多使用延续性动词,如 live、learn、lie、stay、wait、stand、rest、study 等,常和 all this time、this week、this month、all night、all the morning、recently 等状语以及 since 或 for 表示的时间段连用。

➢ I **have been fixing** the fridge all the morning.
　我整个上午都在修冰箱。

➢ I **have been sitting** here for an hour.

我在这里已经坐了一个小时了。

实 战 演 练

1. John _____ over 4,000 Chinese characters before he decided to settle down in China.
   A. was learning   B. learns   C. had learned   D. has learned
2. I have known him since I _____ in the city.
   A. lived   B. have lived   C. live   D. will live
3. If I _____ on a vacation next year, I _____ part in a summer camp in Beijing.
   A. go; take   B. go; will take   C. will go; will take   D. will go; take
4. Tom _____ online when the light went out.
   A. was shopping   B. is shopping   C. shops   D. had shopping
5. Physics _____ my favorite subject when I studied in the university.
   A. were   B. was   C. is   D. are
6. By the end of next year, we _____ nearly a million cars in that auto factory.
   A. will produce   B. produce   C. will have produced   D. produced
7. He _____ on his term paper the whole morning, but he hasn't written a word.
   A. will work   B. had been working   C. has been working   D. had worked
8. They will hold a party if they _____ back on time.
   A. will come   B. come   C. came   D. had come
9. —You were out when I knocked at the door.
   —Oh, I _____ for a friend at the bus stop.
   A. was waiting   B. had waited   C. am waiting   D. have waited
10. Darwin said that natural selection _____ the chief factor in the development of species.
    A. had   B. is   C. will be   D. has
11. —What's that terrible noise?
    —The neighbors _____ their house.
    A. have decorated   B. are decorating   C. decorate   D. will decorate
12. Nowadays shopping online is an easy task because technology _____ so rapidly.
    A. is developing   B. developed   C. will develop   D. will have developed
13. He will have learned English for eight years by the time he _____ from the university.
    A. will graduate   B. will have graduated   C. graduates   D. graduated
14. I wonder why Jenny _____ to us recently. We should have heard from her by now.
    A. hadn't written   B. doesn't write   C. won't write   D. hasn't written
15. Don't lose heart. If you keep working hard, you _____ some day.
    A. have succeeded   B. succeed   C. succeeded   D. will succeed

第三章 语　态

英语中的语态通过动词的形式表现出来,用以说明主语与谓语动词之间的关系。英语中共有两种语态:主动语态和被动语态。如果主语是动作的执行者,谓语动词用主动语态;如果主语是动作的承受者,谓语动词则用被动语态。一般来说,只有及物动词(词组)才有被动语态。

一、被动语态的构成

被动语态是由"助动词 be+动词的过去分词"构成的,助动词 be 本身无词义,但有时态、人称和数的变化。以实义动词 do 为例,各种时态的被动语态形式如下:

	一般式	进行式	完成式
现在	am/is/are done	am/is/are being done	has/have been done
过去	was/were done	was/were being done	had been done
将来	shall/will be done	无	shall/will have been done

➤ The rubbish **is cleaned up** to make the table tidy.
　垃圾被清理干净来保持桌面整洁。(一般现在时的被动语态)
➤ They **were given** a warm welcome.
　他们受到了热烈的欢迎。(一般过去时的被动语态)
➤ The e-mail **will be received** by all the club members.
　所有的俱乐部成员都将收到这封电子邮件。(一般将来时的被动语态)
➤ You car **is being repaired** now.
　你的汽车现在正在维修。(现在进行时的被动语态)
➤ We had to take a detour, for the the road **was being repaired then**.
　我们不得不绕行,因为当时这条路在维修。(过去进行时的被动语态)
➤ The case **has** recently **been tried**.
　这起案子最近已审理过了。(现在完成时的被动语态)
➤ All the tickets **had been sold out** when they arrived.
　他们到达的时候,所有的票都已经售完了。(过去完成时的被动语态)
➤ The work **will have been finished** by the end of next week.
　这项工作将在下周末之前完成。(将来完成时的被动语态)

【补充提示】
过去将来时的被动语态形式为 would be done。
➤ They were told that the result **would be announced** next week.
　他们被告知,结果将在下周宣布。
➤ The teacher said that a football game **would be held** tomorrow.
　老师说一场足球比赛将在明天举行。

二、被动语态的转换

英语的五种基本句型中,只有 **S+V+O**、**S+V+Oi+Od**、**S+V+O+C** 三种句型可转换成被动语态。变被动语态时,主动语态中的谓语动词变为"助动词be动词+动词的过去分词",若强调动作的执行者,主动语态中的主语置于介词 by 之后,即"by+宾语";若不强调动作发出者,则"by+宾语"可省略。

(一) S+V+O 转换为被动语态

S+V+O 句型转换为被动语态时,将主动语态中的宾语作为被动语态中的主语,谓语动词变为相应的被动结构。

➤ I **wrote** a letter last night.
　昨晚我写了一封信。(主动语态)
➤ A letter **was written** (by me) last night.
　昨晚一封信被(我)写了。(被动语态)
➤ He **is repairing** his car now.
　他现在正在修他的车。(主动语态)
➤ His car **is being repaired** (by him) now.
　他的车现在正在被(他)修。(被动语态)

【补充提示】

① 主动语态中的宾语为从句时,变被动语态时需将宾语从句变为主语从句,但通常用形式主语 it 代替主语从句位于句首,将主语从句后置,构成"It+is/was+done(过去分词)…+that…"句型。

➤ They know that he is a famous scientist in China.
　他们知道他是中国的一位著名的科学家。(主动语态)
➤ **It is known that** he is a famous scientist in China.
　众所周知,他是中国的一位著名的科学家。(被动语态)
➤ They said that she was a popular singer in the 1990s.
　他们说她是20世纪90年代的一名流行歌手。(主动语态)
➤ **It was said that** she was a popular singer in the 1990s.
　据说她是20世纪90年代的一名流行歌手。(被动语态)

② 当谓语动词为"动词+介词""动词+副词"等构成的及物动词词组时,变被动语态时应将动词词组视为一个整体,其中的介词或副词不能省略。

➤ We **must take good care of** the baby.
　我们必须好好照顾这个婴儿。(主动语态)
➤ The baby **must be taken good care of** (by us).
　这个婴儿必须被(我们)好好照顾。(被动语态)
➤ We **put up** the tent in the field last night.
　昨天晚上我们在田野里搭起了帐篷。(主动语态)
➤ The tent **was put up** (by us) in the field last night.

昨天晚上帐篷在田野里被(我们)搭起来了。(被动语态)
- Tom **laughed at** Alice yesterday.

  Tom 昨天嘲笑了 Alice。(主动语态)
- Alice **was laughed at** by Tom yesterday.

  Alice 昨天被 Tom 嘲笑了。(被动语态)

(二) S+V+Oi+Od 转换为被动语态

S+V+Oi+Od 句型转换为被动语态,将主动语态中的间接宾语作为被动语态中的主语时,直接宾语不变;将主动语态中的直接宾语作为被动语态中的主语时,间接宾语前需要加介词 to 或 for。

- My sister **gave** me a new dress.

  我姐姐给了我一条新裙子。(主动语态)
- I **was given** a new dress (by my sister).

  我被(我姐姐)给了一条新裙子。(间接宾语作为被动语态中的主语,直接宾语不变)
- A new dress **was given** to me (by my sister).

  一条新裙子被(我姐姐)给了我。(直接宾语作为被动语态中的主语,间接宾语前加介词 to)
- My father **bought** him a computer.

  我爸爸给他买了一台电脑。(主动语态)
- He **was bought** a computer (by my father).

  他被(我爸爸)买了一台电脑。(间接宾语作为被动语态中的主语,直接宾语不变)
- A computer **was bought** for him (by my father).

  一台电脑被(我爸爸)买给了他。(直接宾语作为被动语态中的主语,间接宾语前加介词 for)

【补充提示】

间接宾语前加介词 to 或 for 的用法详见基础语法第三章动词。

(三) S+V+O+C 转换为被动语态

S+V+O+C 句型转换为被动语态时,将主动语态中的宾语作为被动语态中的主语,宾语补足语不变。

- They **elected** her chairman of the club.

  他们选她为俱乐部的主席。(主动语态)
- She **was elected** chairman of the club (by them).

  她被(他们)选为俱乐部的主席。(被动语态)
- I **consider** him a good student.

  我认为他是一个好学生。(主动语态)
- He **is considered** a good student (by me).

  他被(我)视为一个好学生。(被动语态)
- Jack **should paint** the wall white.

  Jack 应该把墙刷成白色。(主动语态)

> The wall **should be painted** white (by Jack).
> 墙应该被(Jack)刷成白色。(被动语态)

【补充提示】
　　S+V+O+C 句型中,当谓语动词为使役动词(make)或感官动词(see、hear 等)时,其后若接动词不定式(to do)作宾语补足语,主动语态中不定式需省略 to,但变为被动语态时,to 不能省略。

> The boss **made** him **work** overtime.
> 老板让他加班。(主动语态中 work 前需省略 to)
> He **was made to work** overtime (by the boss).
> 他被(老板)要求加班。(被动语态中 work 前不可省略 to)
> I **saw** a strange man **walk** into the building.
> 我看到一个陌生人走进了这栋大楼。(主动语态中 walk 前需省略 to)
> A strange man **was seen to walk** into the building (by me).
> 一个陌生人被(我)看到走进了这栋大楼。(被动语态中 walk 前不可省略 to)
> I **heard** a girl **sing** a song just now.
> 刚才我听到一个女孩唱了一首歌。(主动语态中 sing 前需省略 to)
> A girl **was heard to sing** a song just now (by me).
> 一个女孩刚才被(我)听到唱歌了。(被动语态中 sing 前不可省略 to)

三、被动语态的用法

① 不知道谁是动作的执行者,或者没有必要、不想指出谁是动作的执行者时,常淡化动作的执行者,使用被动语态。

> Some measures **have been taken** to protect the environment.
> 为了保护环境,已经采取了一些措施。(不知道动作的执行者)
> The building **was completed** last year.
> 这栋建筑是去年竣工的。(不知道动作的执行者)
> This coat **is made** of cotton.
> 这件大衣是棉制的。(没有必要指出动作的执行者)
> The cup **is used** to drink milk.
> 这个杯子是用来喝牛奶的。(没有必要指出动作的执行者)

② 为了强调或突出动作的承受者,即句子的中心是动作的承受者而非执行者时,常使用被动语态。

> Dictionaries **are** not **allowed** in the English test.
> 英语考试中不允许使用词典。(句子的中心是词典)
> He **was** warmly **welcomed** in the town.
> 他在镇上受到了热烈的欢迎。(句子的中心是他)
> These books **are written** for those children.
> 这些书是为那些孩子们写的。(句子的中心是这些书)
> The room **hasn't been cleaned** yet.

房间还没有被打扫。(句子的中心是房间)

③ 当动作的执行者是无生命的事物时,常使用被动语态。

➢ The bridge **was washed away** by the flood.
桥被洪水冲走了。(执行者是洪水)

➢ Many accidents **were caused** by careless driving.
许多事故是由粗心驾驶造成的。(执行者是粗心驾驶)

➢ The door **was opened** by wind.
门被风吹开了。(执行者是风)

④ 有些动词(词组)习惯上用被动形式,常见的此类动词(词组)有 be determined(决定)、be seated(坐)、be dressed(穿)、be born(出生)、be situated(坐落,位于)等。

➢ She **was born** in this city.
她出生在这个城市。

➢ She **is determined** to study hard.
她决定努力学习。

➢ Wuhan **is situated** in the central part of China.
武汉位于中国的中部。

➢ She **is** still **dressed** in the old-fashioned style.
她仍然穿着过时的衣服。

➢ He **is seated** on the bench.
他坐在长椅上。

四、被动语态的注意事项

(1) 系动词无被动语态,常见的系动词有 smell、taste、sound、look、feel、prove 等。

➢ The fish **tastes** delicious.
这鱼尝起来很美味。

➢ She **proves** very patient and warm-hearted.
她被证明既有耐心又很热心。

➢ The cloth **feels** soft.
这布摸起来很软。

➢ These flowers **smell** nice.
这些花儿闻起来不错。

(2) 不及物动词(词组)无被动语态,常见的有 happen(发生)、take place(发生)、break out(爆发)、take off(起飞)、belong to(属于)、come about(发生)、go up(上涨)、grow up(长大)、consist of(由……组成)、come into being(形成)、come into use(投入使用)、come true(实现)、run out(用完、耗尽)、turn up(出现)等。

➢ A fire **broke out** at midnight.
半夜发生了一场火灾。

➢ What **happened** to him last night?

他昨晚发生了什么事情？
- Great changes **have taken place** in China.
  中国发生了巨大的变化。
- The plane **takes off** at 7 p. m.
  飞机晚上七点起飞。
- This English book **belongs to** me.
  这本英语书是我的。
- The eggs in the fridge **have run out**. You need buy some.
  冰箱里的鸡蛋用完了，你需要去买一些。

（3）某些动词如 read、write、wash、clean、sell 等，当用作不及物动词，其主语是无生命的物体，且和 well、badly、easily、smoothly 等副词连用时，用来说明主语的特征、性质或状态，不用被动语态。

- This kind of book **sells** well.
  这种书很畅销。
- The pen **writes** smoothly.
  这支钢笔写起来很流畅。
- This article **reads** easily.
  这篇文章读起来很容易。
- The cloth **washes** easily.
  这布料很好洗。
- These cups **clean** easily.
  这些杯子洗起来很容易。

【补充提示】

某些及物动词，在使用习惯上无被动语态，常见的有 have(有)、own(拥有)、cost(要价，花费)、lack(缺少)、benefit(使受益)、hold(容纳，包含)、mean(意味着)、equal(等同于)、contain(包含，含有)、suit(合适)、suffer(受苦，遭受)等。

- He **lacks** self-confidence.
  他缺乏自信。
- Jack **has** a nice jacket.
  Jack 有一件漂亮的夹克。
- Lily **owns** a big house.
  Lily 有一个大房子。
- The hall **can hold** 200 people.
  这个大厅能容纳 200 个人。

实战演练

1. Mary _____ a job by a company, but she refused to take it.

  A. offered   B. was offered   C. has been offered   D. was offering

2. According to the rule, the students _____ to get enough credits before graduation.

  A. are required   B. were required   C. will require   D. have required

3. The war _____ in 1941.

  A. broke out   B. had been broken out   C. was broken out   D. had broken out

4. I believe that the environment _____ by our further efforts to reduce pollution.

  A. had been improved   B. will be improved

  C. is improved   D. was improved

5. It's said that tea _____ for the first time about 5,000 years ago.

  A. invents   B. invented   C. is invented   D. was invented

6. The little boy won't go to sleep unless his mom _____ him a story.

  A. tells   B. is told   C. is telling   D. will be told

7. I am happy that I _____ to be the monitor of our class by my classmates.

  A. choose   B. chose   C. was chosen   D. will be chosen

8. A lot of tall buildings _____ in his hometown in the last three years.

  A. have set up   B. have been set up   C. were set up   D. set up

9. It is hot and dry, so the flowers need _____.

  A. being watered   B. be watered   C. to water   D. watering

10. A strange thing _____ in our school yesterday.

  A. was happened   B. has been happened   C. happened   D. was going to happen

11. Many students _____ chances to show themselves in class because the class size is too big.

  A. don't give   B. aren't given   C. haven't given   D. won't give

12. A lecture on robots _____ in the school hall next Friday afternoon.

  A. is given   B. will be given   C. was given   D. has been given

13. Some public places, such as restaurants, _____ since COVID-19 swept the city again last month.

  A. have been closed   B. have closed   C. closed   D. was closed

14. The dish _____ terrible! I don't like it at all.

  A. tastes   B. tasted   C. will taste   D. is tasted

15. David is very productive and _____ five books in the past ten years.

  A. writes   B. wrote   C. has written   D. is writing

第四章　主谓一致

主谓一致是指主语和谓语保持一致，即谓语动词的形式必须随着主语人称和数的变化而变化。主谓一致遵循以下三个原则：语法一致原则、意义一致原则和就近一致原则。

一、语法一致原则

语法一致是指主语和谓语通常在人称和数上保持一致，即主语是单数形式，谓语动词也用单数形式；主语是复数形式，谓语动词也用复数形式。

1. 由 and、both…and 连接的两个表示不同概念的名词作主语，谓语动词用复数形式

➢ Lucy **and** I **go** to school five days a week.
　Lucy 和我每周上五天学。
➢ Her teachers **and** her mother **are** in the sitting room.
　她的老师和她的妈妈在客厅里。
➢ The dancer **and** the singer **are** performing on the stage.
　那个舞蹈演员和那个歌手正在舞台上表演。
➢ **Both** rice **and** wheat **are** grown in this area.
　这个地区种植水稻和小麦。
➢ **Both** New York **and** London **have** traffic problems.
　纽约和伦敦都有交通问题。
➢ **Both** teaching **and** research work **are** making great progress.
　教学与科研都取得了很大的进步。

【补充提示】
　由 and 连接的两个并列主语，如果指同一人或同一事物时，谓语动词用单数形式。
➢ The professor and writer **is** speaking at the meeting.
　那位教授兼作家正在会上发言。(professor 和 writer 指同一个人)
➢ A fork and knife **is** often used when eating Western food.
　吃西餐时经常使用（一副）刀叉。(fork 和 knife 被看作一个整体)
➢ War and peace **is** a constant theme in history.
　战争与和平是历史上一个永恒的主题。(war 和 peace 被看作一个整体)

2. each、every、no、many a (an)、more than one 等修饰可数名词单数，谓语动词用单数形式；即使有 and 连接多个并列主语，谓语动词仍用单数形式

➢ **Every** man and (every) woman **has** right to fight for their legal rights and interests.
　所有人都有权捍卫自己的合法权益。
➢ **Many a** boy and (many a) girl **has** made the same mistake.
　许多男孩和女孩都犯了同样的错误。
➢ **Each** student **has** to finish the homework before next Sunday.
　每个学生都得在下个星期天之前完成作业。

> **More than one** person **has** heard the story since 2018.
> 自 2018 年以来,不止一个人听过这个故事。

3. 当主语后有 with、along with、together with、as well as、accompanied by、in addition to、besides、except、but、rather than、including、such as、like 等词或短语作为修饰成分时,谓语动词不受这些修饰成分的影响,与前面主语的单复数保持一致

> **The man** together with his wife and children **is** watching TV on the sofa.
> 那个男人和他的妻子和孩子正在沙发上看电视。

> **No one** except two students **was** late for class yesterday.
> 除了两名学生之外,昨天没有人上课迟到。

> **The father**, rather than his children, **is** responsible for the accident.
> 不是孩子们,而是父亲应当为这场事故负责。

> **All of us** but Tom **were** satisfied with your idea at the meeting yesterday morning.
> 我们所有人,除了 Tom 之外,都很满意你昨天早上在会议上提出的想法。

> **The boy**, accompanied by his parents, **is** going to have a trip to London next summer.
> 明年夏天,这个男孩将在父母的陪同下去伦敦旅行。

> **He**, including his friends, **is** willing to help the poor.
> 他和他的朋友们都很乐意帮助穷人。

4. 由"a lot of、lots of、plenty of、the rest of、the majority of、a quantity of+名词"构成的短语以及由"分数/百分数+of+名词"构成的短语作主语时,谓语动词应与 of 后面名词的单复数保持一致

> A lot of **students want** to join the music club.
> 许多学生想加入音乐俱乐部。

> Plenty of **money has** been saved by my mother for me.
> 我的妈妈已经为我存了很多钱。

> A majority of **Africans are** forced to work for the Europeans.
> 大多数非洲人被迫为欧洲人工作。

> Two thirds of the **students disagree** with the plan.
> 三分之二的学生不同意这个计划。

> Three fourths of **the surface** of the earth **is** sea.
> 地球表面的四分之三是海洋。

> 80 percent of the **students** in the school usually **stay** up late.
> 学校里 80% 的学生经常熬夜到很晚。

【补充提示】
quantities of 修饰名词作主语时,谓语动词用复数。
> Large **quantities** of water **have** been polluted since the factory was built here.
> 自从这里建了工厂以来,大量的水已经被污染了。

- Large **quantities** of students **are** interested in the activity on weekends.

  许多学生对周末的活动感兴趣。

5. 非谓语动词作主语

（1）单个非谓语动词（动词不定式 to do、动名词 doing）作主语时，谓语动词一般用单数形式。

- **To see is** to believe. = **Seeing is** believing.

  眼见为实。

- **Working** overtime too much **is** bad for our health.

  过度加班对我们的健康有害。

- **Walking is** a good form of exercise for both the young and the old.

  散步对年轻人和老年人来说都是一种很好的锻炼方式。

- **Reading** newspaper **is** a way for the old to get information.

  读报纸是老年人获取信息的一种方式。

（2）由 and 连接的多个非谓语动词（动词不定式 to do、动名词 doing）作主语时，如果表达同一概念，谓语动词用单数形式；如果表达多个不同的概念，谓语动词用复数形式。

- **To go** to bed early **and to rise** early **is** a good habit.

  早睡早起是一个好习惯。（"早睡早起"表达同一概念）

- **To work and to live are** two different things but they are always together.

  工作和生活是两件不同的事情，但它们总是相伴。（"工作"和"生活"表达两个不同的概念）

- **Singing and playing** basketball **are** my favorites.

  唱歌和打篮球是我的最爱。（"唱歌"和"打篮球"表达两个不同的概念）

- **To be** strict with oneself **and to be** kind to others **are** good qualities of a person.

  严以律己、宽以待人，是一个人的优秀品质。（"严以律己"和"宽以待人"表达两个不同的概念）

6. 从句作主语时，谓语动词一般用单数形式

- How they will solve the problem **remains** to be seen.

  他们将如何解决这个问题还有待观察。

- Where we will go **has**n't been decided yet.

  我们将去哪里还尚未决定。

- Whether we will go for an outing tomorrow **remains** unknown.

  我们明天是否会外出游玩还不知道。

- What you have said **makes** a big difference to me.

  你说的话对我有很大的影响。

【补充提示】
① 在"what 引导的主语从句+be+名词"的结构中,be 动词需与其后的名词单复数保持一致。当名词为可数名词单数或不可数名词时,be 动词用单数形式(is/was);当名词为可数名词复数时,be 动词用复数形式(are/were)。
> What we badly need **is** more **time**.
  我们急需的是更多时间。(time 表"时间",为不可数名词)
> What he left me **were** only some old **books.**
  他留给我的只是一些旧书。(books 为可数名词复数)
② 定语从句中关系代词作主语时的主谓一致情况详见核心语法第五章定语从句。

7. 不定代词作主语

不定代词 one、every、each、someone、anyone、no one、everyone、something、nothing、either、neither 等作主语或修饰名词作主语时,谓语动词一般用单数形式。

> **Each** student **has** been given his or her own email address.
  每个学生都得到了一个自己的电子邮件地址。
> **Each** (one) of the houses **was** slightly different.
  每栋房子都稍有不同。
> **Something was** wrong with his bike, so he had to go to work on foot.
  他的自行车坏了,所以他不得不步行去上班。
> **No one is** allowed to enter without permission.
  未经允许,任何人不得入内。
> **Nothing is** impossible if you try your best.
  如果你竭尽全力,一切皆有可能。
> **Neither** of my sisters **likes** watching TV.
  我的两个妹妹都不喜欢看电视。
> **Either** of the two clothes **is** suitable for you.
  这两件衣服中的任何一件都很适合你。

【补充提示】
① 不定代词 both 作主语或修饰名词作主语时,谓语动词用复数形式。
> **Both** of her children **are** girls.
  她的两个孩子都是女孩。
> **Both** of my sisters **have** great interest in reading books.
  我的两个姐姐都对读书很感兴趣。
② 不定代词 all 作主语时,谓语动词形式根据 all 的意义而定。all 指人时,谓语动词通常用复数形式;all 指物时,谓语动词通常用单数形式。
> **All are** present at the meeting except Lily.
  除了 Lily 之外,所有人都出席了会议。
> **All is** silent on the island now.
  现在岛上一片寂静。

二、意义一致原则

意义一致是指谓语动词的单复数形式需与主语所表达的单复数概念保持一致。

1. "the+形容词"表示一类人，作主语时，谓语动词用复数形式

➢ **The rich are** not always happy.
　富人并不总是开心的。

➢ **The young** always **help** the old.
　年轻人总是帮助老年人。

➢ **The Chinese are** very friendly to the foreign people.
　中国人对外国人很友好。

➢ **The disabled stay** at home for most of the time because they don't want to trouble others.
　残疾人因为不想麻烦别人，大部分时间待在家里。

2. "a number of+复数名词"作主语时，谓语动词用复数形式，意为"许多的，大量的"；"the number of+复数名词"作主语时，谓语动词用单数形式，意为"……的数量"

➢ **A number of** trees **were** planted on that day.
　那天种了很多树。

➢ **A number of** students **want** to join the music club.
　许多学生想加入音乐俱乐部。

➢ **The number of** books in the library **is** larger than ever before.
　图书馆的图书数量比以往任何时候都多。

➢ **The number of** employees **was** reduced from 40 to 25.
　员工人数从40人减少到了25人。

3. 集合名词作主语

（1）有些集合名词只有复数含义，常见的此类集合名词有 people、police、cattle 等。它们作主语时，谓语动词用复数形式。

➢ **People** often **watch** movies for pleasure during their spare time.
　人们经常在空闲时间看电影取乐。

➢ The **police are** looking for the suspect.
　警方正在寻找嫌疑犯。

➢ The **cattle are** rounded up in the evening.
　到了晚上，牛都要圈起来。

（2）有些集合名词既有单数含义也有复数含义，常见的此类集合名词有 class、crew、crowd、audience、family、team、group 等。它们作主语时，若视作一个整体，则表示单数含义，谓语动词用单数形式；若着眼于该集体的每个成员，则表示复数含义，谓语动词用复数形式。

➢ **Our class has** 20 girls and 20 boys.
　我们班有20个女生和20个男生。（强调班级这个整体）

- **Our class are** watching a movie.

  我们班的同学们正在看电影。(强调班上的每位同学)

- **A family is** a basic unit of the society.

  家庭是社会的基本单位。(强调整个家庭)

- The whole **family are** ill.

  全家人都病了。(强调家庭的每位成员)

- The **team was** defeated by the younger team yesterday evening.

  昨天晚上,这个队被更年轻的队击败了。(强调整个团队)

- The **team are** all friendly to the new comer and **are** willing to help him.

  队员们对这个新来的人都很友好,都愿意帮助他。(强调团队的每位成员)

4. 表示"时间、距离、金额、温度、重量"等名词的复数形式作主语时,一般把它们看作一个整体,用来表示一定的量,此时谓语动词用单数形式

- **Thirteen miles is** really a long walk for me.

  对我来说,步行13英里真的是很长的一段路程。

- **Ten years is** a long time for us.

  十年对我们来说是很长的一段时间。

- **One hundred yuan is** enough to buy a meal.

  一百块钱足够买一顿饭了。

- **Ten tons is** too heavy for him.

  十吨对他来说太重了。

5. 以复数形式结尾的名词作主语

(1) 有些表示学科的名词,如 physics、mathematics/maths、economics、politics 等,它们作主语时,谓语动词要用单数形式。

- **Mathematics is** a required course for middle and high school students.

  数学是初高中生的必修课。

- **Maths is** my favorite subject.

  数学是我最喜欢的科目。

- **Politics does**n't interest me.

  我对政治不感兴趣。

- **Economics is** an inexact science.

  经济学是一门不精确的科学。

(2) 有些以 s 结尾的名词,如 earnings、surroundings、savings、belongings 等,它们作主语时,谓语动词用复数形式。

- All my **belongings were** stolen.

  我所有的财产都被偷了。

- **Surroundings are** covered with flowers and plants.

  周围全是花花草草。

- Her **savings were** in the First National Bank.

她的积蓄存在第一国民银行。

➢ **Earnings are** averaged over the whole period.
收入是整个时期的平均值。

(3) 有些名词的单复数同形,如 means(方法)、works(工厂)、crossroads(十字路口)等,需要根据其表达的是单数概念还是复数概念来确定谓语动词的单复数。

➢ **This means** of transport **has** been tried.
这种运输方式已经尝试过了。

➢ **All possible means** have been tried.
所有可能的方法都试过了。

➢ **A crossroads is** a place where two roads meet and cross each other.
十字路口是两条道路相交的地方。

➢ There **are** many **crossroads** in this area.
这个区域有很多十字路口。

(4) 有些名词总是以复数形式出现,如 trousers、glasses、clothes、shoes、scissors 等,它们作主语时,谓语动词用复数形式。

➢ My new **shoes are** too small.
我的新鞋子太小了。

➢ My **trousers are** white and **shoes are** black.
我的裤子是白色的,鞋子是黑色的。

➢ Your **glasses are** on the table.
你的眼镜在桌上。

➢ His **clothes were** all mussed up.
他的衣服都弄乱了。

【补充提示】

当单位量词(pair、suit、piece、kind 等)限定、修饰名词作主语时,谓语动词的单复数取决于单位量词的单复数。

➢ **A pair of** scissors **is** lying in that drawer.
那个抽屉里有一把剪刀。

➢ **These kinds of** glasses **are** popular this summer.
今年夏天这些款式的眼镜很流行。

(5) 表示人名、书名、国家、机构、组织等的专有名词作主语时,即使形式上以 s 结尾,谓语动词也应使用单数形式。

➢ **The United States is** a developed country.
美国是一个发达国家。

➢ **The Arabian Nights tells** us lots of mysterious folklore.

《一千零一夜》向我们讲述了许多神秘的民间传说。

➤ **The Little Prince is** a worthwhile book for everyone to read.

《小王子》是一本值得人人阅读的书。

➤ **The United Nations is** an association of many countries to help to solve problems in the world in a peaceful way.

联合国是一个由许多国家组成的协会,以和平的方式帮助解决世界上的问题。

(6) 以 s 结尾的表示群岛、山脉、海峡、瀑布等的专有名词作主语时,谓语动词用复数形式。

➤ **The Himalayas have** a magnificent variety of plants.

喜马拉雅山脉上的植物种类繁多。

➤ **The Niagara Falls are** splendid waterfalls.

尼亚加拉大瀑布是壮观的瀑布。

三、就近一致原则

就近一致是指谓语动词的单复数与离它最近的主语保持一致。

① there be 句型结构为"There be+名词(短语)+其他……",主语为 be 动词之后的名词(短语),be 动词的单复数与其保持一致。若 be 动词后有 and 连接的多个并列主语时,be 动词的单复数要与与其最邻近的主语保持一致,即就近一致原则。

➤ There **are two desks** and a bench in the office.

办公室有两张桌子、一条长凳。

➤ There **are thousands of books** and a blackboard in the library.

图书馆里有成千上万的书和一个黑板。

➤ There **is a book** and some pens in the teacher's hand.

老师手里有一本书和一些笔。

➤ There **is a university** and many students in this city.

这个城市有一所大学和许多学生。

② 由连词 either...or、or、neither...nor、not only...but also、not...but 等连接两个名词作主语时,使用就近一致原则。

➤ You or **he is** to blame.

你或他有一人要受责备。

➤ Either you or **she is** going to be fired.

不是你就是她将被辞退。

➤ Neither he nor his **parents are** bank clerks.

他和他父母都不是银行职员。

➤ Not only his family but also **he likes** funny movies.

他的家人和他都喜欢搞笑电影。

实战演练

1. More than one person _____ been infected with the disease.
   A. has   B. have   C. having   D. to have
2. The injured in the earthquake _____ good care of by some medical teams.
   A. is taking   B. are being taken C. are taking   D. has taken
3. The professor and writer _____ speaking at the meeting.
   A. is   B. are   C. am   D. be
4. The man together with his wife and children _____ TV on the sofa every evening.
   A. is watched   B. watches   C. watch   D. watching
5. The number of students in our class _____ 25 this term.
   A. is   B. was   C. are   D. were
6. There _____ many trees in front of my house three years ago.
   A. is   B. are   C. was   D. were
7. One hundred years _____ not a very long period of time in history.
   A. is   B. are   C. has been   D. have been
8. Neither I nor he _____ to go shopping with Tom.
   A. wants   B. want   C. have want   D. wanting
9. Every boy and girl _____ reading this interesting story book.
   A. like   B. have liked   C. likes   D. liking
10. Not only my friends but also I _____ interested in football and Messi is our favorite star.
    A. be   B. am   C. is   D. are
11. Either he or his sons _____ responsible for this accident which happened yesterday.
    A. is   B. are   C. have   D. has
12. Mathematics _____ one of the most difficult subjects for me.
    A. are   B. is   C. have been   D. were
13. Many a student _____ the importance of learning a foreign language.
    A. have realized   B. has realized
    C. have been realized   D. has been realized
14. John as well as Jack _____ just been back from an important meeting.
    A. have   B. are   C. has   D. is
15. Half of his goods _____ stolen last month.
    A. are   B. were   C. is   D. was

第五章 从　　句

当一个句子充当另外一个句子中的主语、宾语、表语、同位语、定语、状语等成分时,这个句子就被称为从句,其所在的句子被称为主句,而这种包含主句和从句的句子则被称为复合句。根据从句在句中所充当的成分与语法功能,从句可分为三大类:名词性从句、定语从句和状语从句。

一、名词性从句

在主句中起到名词作用的从句叫名词性从句,在复合句中充当主语、宾语、表语和同位语,根据其所充当的成分与语法功能,名词性从句可分为主语从句、宾语从句、表语从句和同位语从句。

(一) 名词性从句的引导词

名词性从句的引导词位于从句句首,一般可以分为三类:从属连词、连接代词和连接副词。

引导词分类	引导词	含义	在从句中充当的成分
从属连词	that	无含义	无
	whether (if)	是否	无
连接代词	what	什么	主语/宾语/表语
	who	谁	主语/宾语/表语
	whom	谁	宾语
	which	哪个	主语/定语(+n.)
	whose	谁的	定语(+n.)
	whatever	无论什么,任何事	主语/宾语/表语
	whoever	无论谁,任何人	主语/宾语/表语
	whomever	无论谁,任何人	宾语
	whichever	无论哪个	主语/定语(+n.)
连接副词	how	如何,怎样	状语
	when	什么时候	状语
	where	在哪里	状语
	why	为什么	状语
	whenever	无论何时	状语
	wherever	无论哪里	状语
	however	无论怎样	状语

- He said **that he had already known the truth**.
  他说他已经知道了真相。
- There is some doubt **whether he will keep his promise**.
  他是否会信守承诺还存在疑问。
- I wonder **if/whether I can get some advice from you**.
  我想知道我是否能从你那里得到一些建议。
- I don't know **what he said**.
  我不知道他说了些什么。
- **How and when he will solve the problem** is more important than anything else.
  他将如何以及何时解决这个问题比什么都重要。

【补充提示】

① 引导名词性从句的从属连词还有because,但because只能引导表语从句,意为"因为",且在从句中不充当成分。

- This is **because they keep working every day**.
  这是因为他们每天都在工作。

② 名词性从句的引导词中,"whether/if"表示疑问含义,意为"是否"。此外,大多数连接代词和连接副词也表示疑问含义。

- **Who will win the match** is still unknown.
  谁能赢得这场比赛还不得而知。
- **Where the English Speech Contest will be held** has not yet been announced.
  英语演讲比赛将在哪里举行还没有宣布。

③ 名词性从句的语序为陈述语序,不受what、who(m)、whose、when、where、how、whether等表示疑问含义的引导词的影响。

- We don't know **when he will come**.
  我们不知道他什么时候会来。
- **Where we can find the book** is still a problem.
  我们在哪儿能找到这本书还是一个问题。

④ whether和if均有"是否"的含义,但在下列情况中,只能用whether不能用if。

- 引导主语从句且置于句首时。
- **Whether he can come to the party on time** depends on the traffic.
  他是否能准时来参加聚会取决于交通状况。

- 引导表语从句、同位语从句时。
- The question is **whether we can contact her**.
  问题是我们是否能和她取得联系。
- He must answer the question **whether he will leave**.
  他必须回答他是否会离开这一问题。

- 引导介词后的宾语从句时。
- I am thinking about **whether I should quit my present job**.
  我正在考虑是否要辞掉现在的工作。

- 与 or not 连用时。
> I don't know **whether or not my parents agree with me**.
  我不知道我的父母是否同意我的意见。

(二) 名词性从句的类别

1. 主语从句

在复合句中充当主语的从句叫主语从句。主语从句通常置于句首且位于主句的谓语动词之前，或 it 作为形式主语置于句首，主语从句则后置。主语从句的引导词主要有从属连词 that、whether，连接代词 what、who，连接副词 when、where、how 等。

(1) that 引导的主语从句。

that 引导主语从句时，在从句中不作任何成分，也没有含义，不能省略。

① that 引导的主语从句置于句首。
> **That light travels in straight lines** is known to all.
  众所周知，光沿直线传播。
> **That the earth moves around the sun** is a common sense.
  地球绕着太阳转是常识。

② it 作为形式主语置于句首，that 引导的主语从句后置，常见结构为"It+be+形容词/名词/过去分词+that 从句"。
> It is likely **that he can't come to the meeting**.
  有可能他不能来参加会议了。
> It is no wonder **that you've failed again**.
  难怪你又失败了。
> It is announced **that the plan has been successfully carried out**.
  据宣布，计划已顺利实施。

(2) whether 引导的主语从句。

whether 引导主语从句时，在从句中不作任何成分，但表示疑问含义，意为"是否"。whether 引导的主语从句可置于句首；但 if 引导主语从句时，it 作为形式主语置于句首，而主语从句则后置。

> **Whether he can finish his task on time** is of great importance.
  他是否能按时完成任务非常重要。
> It is doubtful **whether/if they are coming**.
  他们是否会来还不确定。

(3) 连接代词和连接副词引导的主语从句。

连接代词和连接副词引导主语从句时，要在从句中作一定的成分，且表示一定的含义，连接代词和连接副词常在从句中作主语、宾语、表语、定语或状语等。

> **What we should do next** remains unknown.
  我们接下来应该做什么还不知道。(what 在从句中作宾语，意为"什么")
> **Where we can look up his address** is still a problem.
  我们在哪里可以查到他的地址还是个问题。(where 在从句中作地点状语，意为"在哪里")

➢ **How they will solve the serious problem** has not been decided yet.

他们将如何解决这个严重的问题还没决定。(how 在从句中作方式状语,意为"如何,怎样")

2. 宾语从句

在复合句中充当宾语的从句叫宾语从句。宾语从句通常位于动词(词组)、介词或形容词后。宾语从句的引导词主要有从属连词 that、whether、if,连接代词 what、who、whom、which、whose 和连接副词 when、where、how、why 等。

(1) 位于动词(词组)后的宾语从句。

① 位于接单宾语的动词(词组)后。

➢ I hope **that everything is all right**.
我希望一切都好。

➢ I doubt **whether/if he will succeed**.
我怀疑他是否会成功。

➢ Joe wanted to know **who bought him the gift**.
Joe 想知道谁给他买了这个礼物。

② 位于接双宾语的动词(词组)后。

➢ Go and ask William **whether/if he's coming tonight**.
去问问 William,看他今晚是否会来。

➢ I'll tell you **why I ask you to come**.
我会告诉你我为什么要你来。

(2) 位于介词后的宾语从句。

➢ Our success depends on **whether everyone works hard or not**.
我们的成功取决于每个人是否努力工作。

➢ My teacher was satisfied with **what I did**.
我的老师对我所做的很满意。

➢ He was astonished at **what he found**.
他对自己的发现感到很惊讶。

(3) 位于形容词后的宾语从句。

sure、certain、pleased、glad、happy、afraid、worried、sorry、confident、aware、satisfied、proud 等表示"情感、态度"的形容词后也可接宾语从句。

➢ We're all pleased **that we have once again overcome the difficulty**.
我们所有人都很高兴我们再一次克服了困难。

➢ I'm extremely sorry **that I have troubled you so much**.
非常抱歉,我给您添了这么多麻烦。

➢ I'm not sure **whether they'll make it**.
我不确定他们是否能成功。

➢ I was afraid **that nobody would believe me**.
我害怕没有人会相信我。

➢ I am confident **that everything will come out right in time**.
我相信最终一切都会好起来的。

【补充提示】

宾语从句的时态常与主句时态保持一致,一般遵循以下原则:

① 主句如果是现在时或将来时,从句可根据需要使用任何适当的时态。

➢ I know **that he studies English every day**.

我知道他每天学习英语。(宾语从句用一般现在时)

➢ I know **that he studied English last term**.

我知道他上学期学了英语。(宾语从句用一般过去时)

➢ I know **that he will study English next year**.

我知道他明年将学习英语。(宾语从句用一般将来时)

② 主句如果是过去时,从句需要使用相应的过去时态。

➢ He said **that they were having a meeting at that time yesterday**.

他说昨天那个时候他们正在开会。

③ 当宾语从句表达客观事实、真理时,无论主句使用何种时态,从句都用一般现在时。

➢ The teacher told us **that the sun rises in the east**.

老师告诉我们太阳从东方升起。

3. 表语从句

在复合句中充当表语的从句叫表语从句。表语从句通常位于系动词(尤其是 be 动词)之后,表语从句的引导词主要有从属连词 that、whether、because、as if/though,连接代词 what、who、whom、which、whose 和连接副词 when、where、how、why 等。

➢ My opinion is **that it is worth trying**.

我的意见是这值得一试。

➢ The question is **whether we can reduce the cost of the product**.

问题是我们是否能降低产品的成本。

➢ This is **what I am interested in**.

这就是我所感兴趣的。

➢ This is **because I don't care about you**.

这是因为我不在乎你。

【补充提示】

① 除 be 动词之外,系动词 seem、appear、look、sound 等后也常接 as if/though 引导的表语从句。

➢ It looks **as if it is going to rain**.

看起来好像要下雨了。

➢ You sound **as if you are in a hurry**.

听起来你好像很着急。

② 当主句的主语为名词 reason 时,后接的表语从句的引导词要用 that 而不用 because 或 why。because 或 why 引导的表语从句常用于结构"It/This/That+be+because/why+…"中。

➢ The reason for the accident was **that the driver was too careless**.

这场交通事故的原因是司机太过粗心。

> That's **why I want you to work here**.
> 那就是我想让你在这里工作的原因。

> It's just **because he doesn't know her**.
> 这仅仅只是因为他不认识她。

4. 同位语从句

在复合句中充当某一抽象名词的同位语的从句叫同位语从句,用于解释说明该抽象名词的具体内容。同位语从句的引导词主要有从属连词 that、whether,连接代词 what、who 和连接副词 when、where、how、why 等,且同位语从句的连接词一般不可省略。

> Give me your promise **that you will come to our party tonight**.
> 答应我你今天晚上会来参加我们的聚会。

> We have some doubt **whether they can complete the task on time**.
> 我们怀疑他们是否能按时完成任务。

> The question **who should do the work** requires consideration.
> 谁该做这项工作,这个问题需要考虑。

【补充提示】

常接同位语从句的抽象名词列举如下:

advice 建议	opinion 看法	conclusion 结论	demand 要求	doubt 怀疑
evidence 证据	fact 事实	message 信息	idea 想法	information 信息
news 消息	order 命令	possibility 可能性	problem 问题	promise 承诺
proposal 建议	question 问题	request 要求	suggestion 建议	word 消息
chance 可能性	thought 想法	belief 看法;信念		

二、定语从句

在复合句中用来修饰名词、代词或整个主句的从句叫定语从句。定语从句包括限制性定语从句和非限制性定语从句。被修饰的名词、代词或整个主句叫先行词。用来引导定语从句的词叫关系词,包括关系代词和关系副词。

(一) 定语从句的先行词

定语从句的先行词,可以是指人、物、时间、地点、原因等的名词或代词,也可以是整个主句。

> **The boys** who are playing basketball on the playground are from Class One.
> 正在操场上打篮球的那些男孩是一班的。

> **Time is precious,** which is known to us all.
> 众所周知,时间是宝贵的。

> I still remember **the day** when I first met him.
> 我还记得我第一次遇到他的那一天。

> **The man** who is standing at the gate is my teacher.
> 站在门口的那个人是我的老师。

(二) 定语从句的关系词

1. 关系词的分类

定语从句由关系词引导,关系词不仅指代先行词,还在定语从句中充当一定的成分,关系词主要分为关系代词与关系副词。关系词的分类及其句法功能详见下表。

关系词		所修饰的先行词	在从句中充当的成分
关系代词	who	人	主语、宾语
	whom	人	宾语
	which	物	主语、宾语
	that	人/物	主语、宾语、表语
	whose	人/物	定语
关系副词	when	表示时间的名词	时间状语
	where	表示地点的名词	地点状语
	why	表示原因的名词	原因状语

【补充提示】
as 也可作关系代词,但通常只用于固定结构或非限制性定语从句中,故不包含在本表格内。

2. 关系代词的用法

(1) who/whom 的用法。

who 和 whom 都用于指人,who 在定语从句中作主语、宾语,whom 在定语从句中只能作宾语。who 和 whom 在定语从句中都可以作宾语,且作宾语时一般可以省略;但作介词的宾语且介词提前时只能用 whom,whom 不能省略。

➤ He is the man **who lives next door**.
他是住在隔壁的那个男人。

➤ I happened to meet the professor **(who/whom) I got to know at a party**.
我碰巧遇见了在一次聚会上认识的那位教授。(who/whom 作宾语,可省略)

➤ The girl **who is cleaning the floor** is a student.
正在扫地的那个女孩是一名学生。

➤ The man **(who/whom) my father is talking with** is my teacher.
正在和我父亲谈话的那个人是我的老师。(who/whom 作宾语,可省略)

➤ The man **with whom my father is talking** is my teacher.
正在和我父亲谈话的那个人是我的老师。(whom 作介词 with 的宾语且介词提前,不可省略)

(2) which 的用法。

which 用于指物,在定语从句中作主语、宾语。which 在定语从句中作宾语时一般可以省略,但作介词的宾语且介词提前时不能省略。
- The train **which has just left** is for Beijing.
  刚刚开走的火车是开往北京的。
- The package（**which**）**you are carrying** belongs to my friend.
  你正拿着的这个包裹是我朋友的。(which 作宾语,可省略)
- This is the camera **with which he often takes photos**.
  这就是他经常用来拍照的相机。(which 作介词 with 的宾语且介词提前,不可省略)
- The house（**which**）**I used to live in** has become a shopping mall.
  我过去住的房子现在变成一家购物中心。(which 作介词 with 的宾语且介词未提前,可省略)
- The house **in which I used to live** has become a shopping mall.
  我过去住的房子现在变成一家购物中心。(which 作介词 in 的宾语且介词提前,不可省略)

(3) that 的用法。

that 用于指人或物,指人时可与 who、whom 互换,指物时可与 which 互换。that 在定语从句中作主语、宾语、表语。that 在定语从句中作宾语、表语时,一般可以省略。但是关系代词作介词的宾语且介词提前时,不能用 that,这时关系代词指人用 whom,指物用 which。

- This is the book **that/which has been translated recently by the young man**.
  这就是那个年轻人最近翻译的那本书。(先行词指物,关系代词可用 that 或 which)
- This is the man **that/who wants to see you**.
  这就是要见你的那个人。(先行词指人且作主语,关系代词可用 that 或 who)
- The man（**that/who/whom**）**you met at the airpor**t is a famous actor.
  你在机场遇见的那个人是一个著名的演员。
  (先行词指人且作宾语,关系代词可用 that、who 或 whom,可省略)
- He is not the man（**that**）**he used to be**.
  他不是过去的那个他了。(先行词指人且作表语,关系代词用 that,可省略)
- The gentleman **about whom you talked yesterday** turned out to be a thief.
  你昨天谈到的那位绅士原来是个小偷。(关系代词作介词的宾语且介词提前,不能用 that)
- Here is the money **with which you can buy the phone**.
  这是你可以用来买手机的钱。(关系代词作介词的宾语且介词提前,不能用 that)

(4) whose 的用法。

whose 既可指人,也可指物,在定语从句中作定语,表示先行词的所属关系,用法为"whose+名词"。

- This is the student **whose handwriting is the best in our school**.
  这就是我们学校书法最好的那个学生。
- Do you know the girl **whose skirt is white**?
  你认识那个穿白色裙子的女孩吗?
- Please pass me the book **whose cover is green**.
  请递给我那本绿色封面的书。
- We live in a house **whose windows face south**.
  我们住在一所窗户朝南的房子里。

（5）as 的用法。

as 既可指人，也可指物，常用于先行词被 the same、such 等修饰的限制性定语从句中，在定语从句中作主语、宾语、表语。

➢ We have found such materials **as are used in our factory**.
　我们找到了我们工厂用的这种材料。

➢ This is not the same result **as we had expected**.
　这和我们所预期的结果不一样。

➢ This is the same instrument **as I used yesterday**.
　这台仪器跟我昨天用过的那台一样。

➢ He is such a boy **as he used to be**.
　他还是和从前一样。

3. 关系副词的用法

（1）when 的用法。

when 用于指代表示时间的先行词，在定语从句中作时间状语。

➢ I will always remember the moment **when we met each other for the first time**.
　我将永远记得我们第一次见面的那一刻。

➢ Do you know the date **when Lincoln was born**?
　你知道林肯的出生日期吗？

➢ We will never forget the days **when we stayed with Mr. Smith**.
　我们永远不会忘记和 Smith 先生待在一起的那些日子。

➢ Can you tell me the time **when the film will start**?
　你能告诉我电影什么时候开始吗？

（2）where 的用法。

where 用于指代表示地点的先行词，在定语从句中作地点状语。

➢ Keep the books in a place **where you can find them easily**.
　请把书放在一个你容易找到的地方。

➢ He did all his research in the room **where he lived**.
　他在他自己的房间里做了所有的研究。

➢ This is the classroom **where we study**.
　这就是我们学习的教室。

➢ This is the school **where I studied a few years ago**.
　这就是我几年前就读的学校。

➢ I like watching TV shows **where people show their hidden talents**.
　我喜欢观看人们展示他们隐藏的才能的电视节目。（先行词 TV shows 可看作表示抽象地点的名词）

（3）why 的用法。

why 用于指代表示原因的先行词，在定语从句中作原因状语，通常情况下其先行词只能用 reason。

- Is this the reason why she refused our offer?
  这就是她拒绝我们提议的原因吗？
- The reason why he did that is quite clear.
  他那样做的原因很清楚。
- I don't know the reason why he was late.
  我不知道他迟到的原因。
- This is the reason why I didn't attend the meeting yesterday.
  这就是我昨天没有参加会议的原因。

（三）介词+关系代词

定语从句中的介词可置于关系代词之前，形成"介词+关系代词"结构。该结构中的关系代词可用whom、which、whose，不可用that与who。

1. "介词+关系代词"结构中关系代词的确定

(1) 关系代词指人时用whom。

- The man with whom I communicated just now is my cousin.
  刚才和我交谈的那个人是我的堂兄。
- The man with whom you shook hands is our Chinese teacher.
  你和他握手的那个人是我们的语文老师。
- The man to whom my father is talking is our English teacher.
  正在和我父亲谈话的那个人是我们的英语老师。

(2) 关系代词指物时用which。

- Here is the money with which I can buy a piano.
  这是我可以用来买一架钢琴的钱。
- This is a topic about which we talked many times.
  这是一个我们谈过很多次的话题。
- This is the school in which I studied three years ago.
  这是我三年前就读的那所学校。

【补充提示】

当先行词是表示时间、地点、原因的名词且在定语从句中作状语时，可用"介词+which"替换关系副词when/where/why。

- I'll never forget the days on which (= when) we studied together.
  我永远忘不了我们一起学习的日子。
- This is the town in which (= where) Shakespeare was born.
  这是莎士比亚出生的小镇。
- I'd like you to explain the reason for which (= why) you were absent.
  我想让你解释一下你缺席的原因。

(3) 表示所属关系时用 whose。

➤ I am grateful to my headteacher with whose help I have managed to pass the exam.
　我非常感谢我的班主任,在他的帮助下我成功通过了考试。

➤ I threw away the chair, one of whose legs was broken.
　我扔掉了那把椅子,它的一条腿断了。

2. "介词+关系代词"结构中介词的确定

(1) 根据定语从句中动词的固定搭配来确定。

➤ Yesterday, I came across the man about whom you talked last time.
　昨天我偶然遇到了你上次提到过的那个人。(talk about sb./sth.)

➤ Is this the car for which you paid a high price?
　这是你花大价钱买的那辆车吗？(pay sth. for sth.)

➤ In the dark street, there wasn't a single person to whom she could turn for help.
　在黑暗的街道上,没有一个她可以求助的人。(turn to sb. for help)

【补充提示】
　　定语从句中的动词如果是"动词+介词"构成的短语,如 look for、look after、call on 等,不可将其拆开而把介词置于关系代词前。

➤ She is the baby who I should look after.
　她是我应该照顾的婴儿。(不可把 after 提前)

➤ This is the novel which Lily is looking for.
　这是 Lily 正在找的那本小说。(不可把 for 提前)

➤ The old woman who he is taking care of is my grandmother.
　他正在照顾的那位老人是我的外婆。(不可把 of 提前)

(2) 根据先行词的搭配习惯来确定。

➤ Here is the money with which I go for a trip.
　这是我用来旅游的钱。

➤ I still remember the day on which I graduated from university.
　我仍然记得我大学毕业的那一天。

➤ This is the drawer in which they often put postcards.
　这是他们常放明信片的抽屉。

(3) 根据句子所表达的含义来确定。

➤ The colorless gas without which we can't live is called oxygen.
　这种无色的、没有了它我们就无法生存的气体叫作氧气。

➤ He came back at ten o'clock, by which all the guests had already left.
　他十点钟回来的,在那之前所有的客人已经走了。

➤ She studied in a local high school, after which she was admitted to Wuhan University.
　她在当地一所高中读书,在那之后她被武汉大学录取了。

（四）非限制性定语从句

1. 定义和特征

根据从句与先行词之间关系的紧密程度，可将定语从句分为限制性定语从句和非限制性定语从句。

定语从句分类	特点及句法功能
限制性定语从句	从句常紧跟在先行词之后，是对先行词起限定、修饰作用的不可缺少的部分，去掉它主句的意思往往不明确；翻译时常译为"……的"，位于先行词之前。
非限制性定语从句	从句与先行词常用逗号隔开，是对先行词起补充说明作用的附加部分，去掉它也不影响主句的意思；翻译时通常不译为"……的"，而是将主句和从句译为两个并列的句子。

➢ This is the house **which we bought last month**.
这是我们上个月买的房子。（限制性定语从句）
➢ A doctor is a person **who is trained to treat people who are ill**.
医生是经过训练来治疗病人的人。（限制性定语从句）
➢ Helen was kinder to her youngest son than to the others, **which made the others envy him**.
Helen 对她最小的儿子比对其他孩子好，这使得其他孩子都嫉妒他。（非限制性定语从句）
➢ Jane, **who was my former English teacher**, retired last year.
Jane 去年退休了，她以前是我的英语老师。（非限制性定语从句）

【补充提示】
that 不能引导非限制性定语从句，whom 在非限制性定语从句中作宾语时不可用 who 替代，且非限定性定语从句的关系代词不可省略。

2. 使用非限制性定语从句的情况

（1）关系代词指代整个主句的内容时，用非限制性定语从句。

➢ My parents bought me a big present for my birthday, **which made me very happy**.
我的父母在我生日的时候给我买了一个大礼物，这让我非常开心。
➢ Jim passed the driving test, **which surprised everybody in the office**.
Jim 通过了驾照考试，这让办公室里的所有人都很惊讶。
➢ **As is often the case**, boys tend to be more active than girls.
通常情况下，男孩往往比女孩更活跃。

【补充提示】
关系代词指代整个主句的内容时，which 和 as 均可引导非限制性定语从句，在从句中作主语、宾语。which 和 as 有时可以互换，但二者的用法也有不同。首先，as 引导从句时位置比较灵活，可位于主句之前、之中（通常位于主句的主语和谓语之间）、之后；而 which 引导从句时一般位于主句之后。其次，which 引导从句时通常是对主句所叙述的事情进行补充说明，意为"这，这一点"，而 as

引导从句时通常表示说话人的看法、态度、解释或评论，意为"正如，像"，且常用于一些固定结构中，比如 as is known to all、as is reported、as is expected、as is often the case 等。

➤ You pretended not to know me, **which I didn't understand**.
你假装不认识我，这令我不明白。（which 从句位于主句之后）

➤ Shanghai is a big city in China, **as we all know**. （as 从句位于主句之后）
= Shanghai, **as we all know**, is a big city in China. （as 从句位于主句的主语和谓语之间）
= **As we all know**, Shanghai is a big city in China. （as 从句位于主句之前）
众所周知，上海是中国的一个大城市。

（2）先行词是专有名词或其他具有独一无二性的普通名词时，用非限制性定语从句。

➤ They have been to Beijing, **which is an attractive city**.
他们去过北京，那是一个迷人的城市。

➤ We all honor and respect Albert Einstein, **who is the greatest physicist in the world**.
我们都敬重阿尔伯特·爱因斯坦，他是世界上最伟大的物理学家。

➤ He has just come back from New York, **which is a very big city in the United States**.
他刚从纽约回来，那是美国的一个非常大的城市。

➤ Our guide, **who was a French Canadian**, was an excellent cook.
我们的导游，一个法裔加拿大人，是一位优秀的厨师。

（3）"代词/数词/形容词最高级+of+关系代词（which/whom）"结构中，用非限制性定语从句。

➤ The committee consists of 20 members, **five of whom are women**.
该委员会由 20 名成员组成，其中 5 名为女性。

➤ There are 120 students in the class, **some of whom have learned English before**.
班上有 120 位同学，其中有一些之前学习过英语。

➤ Here are the questions, **some of which I thought difficult for you**.
问题都在这儿，其中一些我认为对你来说很困难。

➤ I bought some books from the bookstore, **three of which were English novels**.
我从书店买了一些书，其中三本是英文小说。

➤ He has six daughters, **the tallest of whom is Lily**.
他有六个女儿，其中最高的是 Lily。

【补充提示】
在"代词/数词/形容词最高级+of+关系代词（which/whom）"结构中，当先行词是人时，关系代词用 whom；当先行词是物时，关系代词用 which。

（五）定语从句的特殊情况

1. 引导词只能用 that 的情况

（1）当先行词是 all、little、few、much、none、some、everything、something 等不定代词时，只能用 that。

➤ **Everything that can be done** has been done.

一切能做的都已经做了。
- In this factory I found **little that was different from ours**.
  在这家工厂，我几乎没有发现和我们的工厂不同的地方。
- This is **all that I can do for you**.
  这是我能为你做的一切。
- He did **everything that he could** to help us.
  他做了一切他能做的来帮助我们。

（2）当先行词被 all、every、no、little、few、some、any、the only、the very、the last、the next 等修饰时，只能用 that。

- Music is **the only thing that interests me**.
  音乐是唯一令我感兴趣的东西。
- This is **the very book that I want**.
  这正是我想要的那本书。
- I have done **all the work that you have told me to do**.
  我已经把你让我干的活都干完了。
- There is **little water that is left in the bottle**.
  瓶子里的水所剩无几了。

（3）当先行词是序数词、形容词最高级，或被序数词、形容词最高级修饰时，只能用 that。

- **The first thing that we should do now** is to find a local guide.
  我们现在应该做的第一件事是找一个当地的导游。
- That hotel is **the most expensive that I've ever stayed in**.
  那家宾馆是我住过的最贵的宾馆。
- Jane is **the tallest girl that I have seen**.
  Jane 是我见过的个子最高的女孩。

（4）当先行词既有人又有物时，只能用 that。

- The guests spoke highly of **the children and their performances that they saw at the Children's Palace**.
  客人们高度赞扬了他们在少年宫看到的这些孩子们和他们的表演。
- She described in her composition **the people and places that impressed her most**.
  她在作文中描述了让她印象最深刻的一些人和地方。
- **The singer and her song that you told me about** are both very nice.
  你告诉我的那位歌手和她的歌曲都很棒。

（5）当先行词在从句中作表语时，只能用 that，且可以省略。

- He is not the man（that）he used to be.
  他不再是过去的那个他了。
- The city is no longer the place（that）it used to be.
  这个城市不再是过去的面貌了。

(6) 在 there be 句型中,句子主语是先行词且是指物的名词时,只能用 that。

➤ There are two letters **that I have to reply to**.
  我有两封必须回复的信件。

➤ There is much work **that I have done today**.
  我今天做了很多工作。

2. 引导词只能用 which 的情况

(1) 引导非限制性定语从句且先行词是物时,只能用 which。

➤ These trees, **which were planted by my father three year ago**, have grown up.
  这些树是我父亲三年前种的,现在已经长大了。

➤ She achieved the first prize, **which I have never got**.
  她获得了一等奖,而我从来没有获得过。

(2) 引导限制性定语从句,先行词为物且关系代词前有介词时,只能用 which。

➤ The house **in which I used to live** has become a shopping mall.
  我曾经住过的房子现在已经变成一家购物中心。

➤ The pen **with which you are writing** is mine.
  你正在用来写字的那支钢笔是我的。

3. 只能用 who 的情况

(1) 当先行词是指人的代词 one、ones、anyone 或 those 时,只能用 who。

➤ The ones **who flatter me** don't please me.
  那些奉承我的人并不能取悦我。

➤ We don't want anyone **who can't afford the tuition fee** to drop out of school.
  我们不想让任何交不起学费的人辍学。

➤ Those **who are not fit for their work** should leave office at once.
  那些不能胜任工作的人应该立刻离职。

(2) 在 there be 句型中,句子主语是先行词且是指人的名词时,只能用 who。

➤ There is a gentleman **who wants to see you**.
  有位先生想要见你。

➤ There is a girl **who is playing the guitar**.
  有一个正在弹吉他的女孩。

➤ There are lots of boys **who like playing football**.
  有很多喜欢踢足球的男生。

4. 定语从句中的主谓一致问题

(1) 定语从句中的关系代词作主语时,一般情况下,从句的谓语动词要与先行词的人称、数保持一致。

➤ Is he **the man** who **wants** to see you?
  他就是想见你的那个人吗?

➤ This is **the girl** that **wants** to attend the meeting.

这就是想参加会议的那个女孩。
- **The two boys** who **are** playing on the playground are my sons.
  那两个在操场上玩的男孩是我的儿子。

(2) 当先行词为"one of the+复数名词"时,从句的谓语动词用复数形式。先行词为"the only one of the+复数名词"时,从句的谓语动词用单数形式。

- Freddy is **one of the students** who **want** to be diplomats in our class.
  Freddy 是我们班上想当外交官的学生之一。
- This is **one of the rooms** that **were damaged** in the fire.
  这是在火灾中受损的房间之一。
- He is **the only one of the students** who **has been** a winner of scholarship for three years.
  他是唯一一个连续三年获得奖学金的学生。
- Mary is **the only one of the youngest girls** who **attends** the meeting.
  Mary 是参加此次会议的最年轻的女孩。

三、状语从句

在复合句中作状语的从句叫状语从句,状语从句可以修饰谓语、非谓语动词、定语、状语或整个句子。根据其作用与功能,状语从句可分为时间状语从句、地点状语从句、目的状语从句、结果状语从句、方式状语从句、条件状语从句、原因状语从句、让步状语从句和比较状语从句。

(一) 时间状语从句

时间状语从句常用的引导词有 when、while、as、before、after、until/till、since、as soon as、hardly/scarcely...when、no sooner...than、the moment、immediately、by the time 等,根据含义可以大致分为以下几类。

1. when、while、as 引导的时间状语从句

when 和 while 引导时间状语从句,意为"当……的时候"。when 引导的从句通常既可用延续性动词也可用非延续性动词;while 引导的从句一般只用延续性动词,且 while 引导的从句和主句可同时使用进行时,强调动作同时发生,但 when 一般不这么用;as 引导时间状语从句时,既可以表示主句和从句的动作同时发生,意为"当……的时候",也可以表示动作紧接其后发生,表示"随着……"。

- Mary was shopping **when I saw her**.
  我看到 Mary 的时候,她正在购物。
- **When I was having a walk with my parents**, I met an old friend.
  当我和父母散步的时候,我遇到了一位老朋友。
- My sister was preparing a report **while I was playing games**.
  当我在玩游戏的时候,我的姐姐正在准备一份报告。
- **While we were having a party**, the light suddenly went out.
  当我们正在聚会的时候,灯突然熄灭了。
- **As you grow older**, you'll know yourself better.
  随着年龄的增长,你会更加了解你自己。

> **As he finished the speech**, the audience burst into applause.

当他结束演讲的时候，听众爆发出热烈的掌声。

2. as soon as、hardly/scarcely...when、no sooner...than 引导的时间状语从句

as soon as、hardly/scarcely...when、no sooner...than 引导时间状语从句，意为"一……就……"，其他表示相同含义的连词还有 the minute、the moment、the instant、immediately 等。

> **As soon as he gets to Beijing**, I'll call you.

他一到北京我就给你打电话。

> He had **hardly** sat down to supper **when the telephone rang**.

我们刚坐下用晚餐，电话就响了。

> They had **no sooner** arrived at the airport **than the plane took off**.

他们刚到机场，飞机就起飞了。

> **The moment you feel ill**, you must go to see the doctor.

你一感觉不适就得去看医生。

> **The instant I arrive there**, I will call you.

我一到那儿就给你打电话。

3. before、after 引导的时间状语从句

before 意为"在……之前"，表示主句的动作发生在从句动作之前；after 意为"在……之后"，表示主句的动作发生在从句动作之后。

> Check your homework carefully **before you hand it in**.

你在交作业前仔细检查一下。

> The students had gone out of the classroom **before the bell rang**.

下课铃响之前，同学们就走出了教室。

> They went home **after they had done the shopping**.

他们买完东西之后就回家了。

> Jill lost his job **after he had injured his eyes**.

Jill 眼睛受伤后丢了工作。

4. till、until 引导的时间状语从句

till、until 意为"到……为止，直到……才"，表示主句的动作持续到从句动作的时间为止。

> He lived in Texas **until he was twenty**.

他在得克萨斯州一直住到了二十岁。

> She watched her children **till they turned the corner**.

她看着她的孩子们，直到他们转过了拐角。

5. by the time 引导的时间状语从句

by the time 意为"到……的时候，在……之前"，表示主句的动作在从句动作之前就已经完成。

> The victim had died **by the time the ambulance arrived**.

救护车到达时，受害者已经死亡了。

> **By the time we came here**, they had already left for Shanghai.

我们到这里的时候，他们已经出发去上海了。

6. since、ever since 引导的时间状语从句

since、ever since 意为"自……以后,从……以来",表示主句的动作自从句的动作时间起延续到现在且可能继续延续下去。

➤ She has lived a hard life **since his parents died**.
　自从父母去世后,她一直过着艰苦的生活。

➤ He's been avoiding me **ever since I asked him to return my money**.
　从我要求他还钱以来,他一直在躲我。

(二)地点状语从句

地点状语从句的常用引导词有 where(……的地方)、wherever(无论哪里)、everywhere(所有地方)、anywhere(任何地方)等。

➤ I found all the missing things **where I lived before**.
　我在以前住过的地方找到了所有丢失的东西。

➤ Let's go **wherever this path will take us**.
　我们就顺着这条小路走,走到哪里算哪里。

(三)目的状语从句

目的状语从句的常用引导词有 so that/in order that(为了,以便于)、in case(以防,万一)、for fear(that)(唯恐,生怕)、lest(以免,免得)等,且从句中常有情态动词 can、could、may、might、should 等。

➤ We climbed very high **so that we could get a better view**.
　我们爬得很高,以便于能看到更好的风景。

➤ I often open the window **in order that fresh air can come in**.
　我经常把窗户打开,以便于新鲜空气可以进来。

➤ He takes a torch **in case it gets dark** before he returns home.
　他带着手电筒,以防回家前天黑了。

➤ He worked hard **for fear that he might be fired by the boss**.
　他工作很努力,生怕被老板解雇了。

➤ They spoke in whispers **lest they should be heard**.
　他们低声说话,以免被人听见。

(四)结果状语从句

结果状语从句的引导词主要有 so that(所以,因此), so...that.../such...that...(如此……以至于……)等。

1. so that 引导的结果状语从句

so that 既可以引导目的状语从句也可以引导结果状语从句,在引导目的状语从句时,从句中往往含有 can/could/may/might/should 等情态动词;而引导结果状语从句时类似的情态动词则很少出现。

➤ We moved to the country **so that we were away from the noisy and dull city**.
　我们搬到了乡下,从而远离了喧闹、沉闷的城市。

> They brought her a lot of meat **so that she never went hungry**.
> 他们给她带了很多肉,因此她就不会挨饿了。

2. so...that 引导的结果状语从句结构

so...that 引导的结果状语从句,可构成如下结构:

$$so+\begin{cases}形容词/副词\\many/few+可数名词复数\\much/little+不可数名词\\形容词+a/an+可数名词单数\end{cases}+that+从句$$

> Kathy is **so lovely that we all like to play with her**.
> Kathy 是如此可爱,所以我们都喜欢和她玩。
> There were **so few mistakes** in his composition **that the teacher praised him**.
> 他的作文错误很少,所以老师表扬了他。
> There's **so little time** left **that we have to speed up**.
> 剩下的时间不多了,所以我们不得不加快速度。
> Tom is **so kind a boy that they all like to make friends with him**.
> Tom 是一个非常善良的男孩,所以他们都喜欢和他交朋友。

3. such...that 引导的结果状语从句

such...that 引导的结果状语从句,可构成如下结构:

$$such+\begin{cases}a/an+形容词+可数名词单数\\形容词+可数名词复数\\形容词+不可数名词\end{cases}+that+从句$$

> He is **such a good teacher that we all respect him**.
> 他是一位如此好的老师,我们大家都尊敬他。
> These were **such difficult questions that none of us could answer**.
> 这些问题如此难,以至于我们没人能回答。
> We had **such terrible weather that we couldn't finish the work on time**.
> 天气太糟糕了,以至于我们没能按时完成工作。

(五) 方式状语从句

方式状语从句的引导词主要有 as(按照)、as if/as though(似乎,好像)。

> You ought to do **as Mike tells you**.
> 你应该按照 Mike 告诉你的去做。
> It looks **as if /though the weather may pick up very soon**.
> 看来天气似乎很快就会好起来。

【补充提示】

as if/as though 引导的方式状语从句除表示真实情况外,也可用虚拟语气,表示与事实相反的情况。

> His mother stared at him **as if/though she had seen him for the first time**.
> 他的妈妈目不转睛地看着他,就好像第一次看见他似的。

（六）条件状语从句

条件状语从句的常用引导词有 if(如果)、unless(除非,如果不)、as long as/so long as(只要)、on condition that(条件是,如果)、in case(万一,假如)、suppose/supposing that、provided/providing that(假如,如果)等。

- ➢ I will buy a computer **if I am able to save up enough money**.
  如果我能存下足够的钱,我就去买一台电脑。
- ➢ You will fail the exam **unless you study hard**.
  除非你努力学习,否则你将会考试不及格。
- ➢ I'm happy **as long as you are happy**.
  只要你快乐,我就会快乐。
- ➢ I can tell you the truth **on condition that you promise to keep a secret**.
  我可以告诉你真相,条件是你答应保守秘密。
- ➢ **In case she comes back**, let me know immediately.
  假如她回来了,请马上告诉我。
- ➢ He won't be against us in the meeting **provided that we ask for his advice in advance**.
  如果我们提前征求他的意见,他就不会在会议上反对我们。
- ➢ **Supposing that you are wrong**, what will you do next?
  假如你错了,接下来你会做什么?

（七）原因状语从句

原因状语从句的常用引导词有 because(因为)、as(因为)、since(既然,由于)、now that(既然,由于)、in that(因为,由于)、seeing that(既然,鉴于)、considering that(考虑到)、given that(考虑到)等。

- ➢ He failed the exam **because he didn't work hard**.
  因为学习不努力,他考试没及格。
- ➢ **Since Monday is Bob's birthday**, let's give him a party.
  既然星期一是 Bob 的生日,我们给他办个派对吧。
- ➢ I prefer the country to the city **in that there's fresher air**.
  相比城市我更喜欢乡村,因为那里有更清新的空气。
- ➢ **Now that all of us are part of the global village**, everyone should protect it.
  既然我们都是地球村的一部分,每个人都应该保护它。
- ➢ **Considering that he is just a kid**, she is not very strict with him.
  考虑到他只是个孩子,她对他不是很严格。

【补充提示】

for 也可以表示原因,但它是并列连词,一般起附加说明的作用,不可位于句首。

- ➢ We should be more careful, **for it was dark outside**.
  我们应该更加小心,因为外面天黑了。

（八）让步状语从句

让步状语从句的常用引导词有 though/although/while/as(尽管,即使,虽然)、whereas(然而,但是)、even if/even though(尽管,即使,虽然)、疑问词+ever(无论……)、no matter+疑问词(无论……)等。

➢ **Although it's raining**, they are still working in the field.
虽然在下雨,但他们仍在地里干活。

➢ We won't be discouraged **even if/though we fail again**.
即使再次失败,我们也不会气馁。

➢ **While I am willing to help you**, I do not have enough time.
尽管我愿意帮助你,但我没有足够的时间。

➢ You should persist in your dream **no matter what difficulties you meet**.
无论遇到什么困难,你都应该坚持你的梦想。

➢ **Child as he is**, he knows a lot.
虽然他是个孩子,但他懂得很多。

➢ **No matter where we go**, we should return home to accompany our parents during the Spring Festival.
无论我们去哪里,春节期间我们都应该回家陪伴父母。

【补充提示】

① 疑问词-ever引导的让步状语从句。

疑问词-ever既可引导名词性从句,也可引导让步状语从句,在引导让步状语从句时可与no matter+疑问词互换。

➢ **Whatever(=No matter what) happened**, he would not mind.
无论发生什么,他都不会介意的。(让步状语从句)

➢ I'll wait for you **however(=no matter how) late it is**.
无论有多晚我都会等着你。(让步状语从句)

➢ **Whoever(=No matter who) you are**, you must obey the law.
无论你是谁,你都要遵纪守法。(让步状语从句)

➢ **Whoever comes** will be welcome.
无论谁来都欢迎。(名词性从句)

➢ Do **whatever she tells you**.
她说什么你就做什么。(名词性从句)

② as引导让步状语从句时,从句需使用部分倒装,详见核心语法第七章倒装句。

(九) 比较状语从句

比较状语从句的常用引导词有as(和……一样)、than(比……),其常见句式如下:

1. "A+谓语动词+形容词/副词比较级+than+B" 表示 "A 比 B 更……"

➢ His brother is **taller than** me.
他哥哥比我高。

➢ She speaks English **better than** me.
她英语讲得比我好。

2. "A+谓语动词+as+形容词/副词原级+as+B"表示"A 和 B 一样……"

➢ My dog is **as old as** that one.
  我的狗和那条狗一样大。

➢ Lily is **as tall as** Tom.
  Lily 和 Tom 一样高。

3. "A+谓语动词+倍数+as+形容词/副词原级+as+B"表示"A 是 B 的……倍"

➢ This garden is **ten times as large as** that one.
  这个花园是那个花园的十倍大。

➢ The house is **three times as big as ours**(is).
  这个房子是我们的房子的三倍大。

4. "A+谓语动词+倍数+形容词/副词比较级+than+B"表示"A 比 B 大/长/多……倍"

➢ Our room is **twice larger than theirs**(is).
  我们的房间比他们的房间大两倍。

5. "the+比较级…,the+比较级…"表示"越……就越……"

➢ **The sooner** you get here,**the better** it is.
  你越早到越好。

➢ **The earlier** you start,**the sooner** you come back.
  你越早出发,回来得就越早。

6. "A+谓语动词+形容词/副词比较级+than any other+可数名词单数"表示"A 是最……"

➢ Susan is **taller than any other girl** in her class.
  Susan 是她们班上最高的女生。

➢ He is **younger than any other student** in his class.
  他是班上最小的学生。

7. "A+谓语动词+形容词/副词比较级+than the other+可数名词复数"表示"A 是最……"

➢ The city has a **larger** population **than the other cities** of this province.
  这个城市的人口是这个省里最多的。

➢ He is **younger than the other students** in his class.
  他是班上最小的学生。

【补充提示】

① what 引导的句子也可以表示对比关系,其基本句式为"A is/are to B what C is/are to D",表示"A 对 B 而言就如 C 对 D 一样"。

➢ Food is to men what oil is to machine.
  食物之于人,犹如油之于机器。

➢ Engines are to machines what hearts are to animals.
  引擎对于机器而言就好比心脏对于动物一样。

② 比较级还可用在否定句中表示最高级含义。

➤ I have never read a better book than this.
我从未读过比这更好的故事。(这是我读过的最好的故事)
➤ I think nothing is more pleasant than travelling.
我认为没有什么比旅行更令人愉快。(我认为旅行是最令人愉快的)

实 战 演 练

1. See the flags on top of the building? That was _____ we did this morning.
   A. when　　　　　　B. which　　　　　　C. where　　　　　　D. what
2. Bill left word with my secretary _____ he would call again in the afternoon.
   A. who　　　　　　 B. that　　　　　　 C. as　　　　　　　 D. which
3. He talked a lot about things and persons _____ he remembered in the school.
   A. which　　　　　 B. that　　　　　　 C. whom　　　　　　D. what
4. Someone called me up at midnight, but he hung up _____ I could answer the phone.
   A. as　　　　　　　B. since　　　　　　C. until　　　　　　D. before
5. Mother asked me to take more money _____ something unexpected would happen.
   A. in case　　　　　B. so that　　　　　C. in order that　　 D. when
6. I can never forget the day _____ we worked together and the day _____ we spent together.
   A. when; which　　 B. which; when　　C. what; that　　　 D. on which; when
7. I hope that _____ I have done will be good for all of them.
   A. which　　　　　 B. what　　　　　　C. that　　　　　　 D. when
8. You aren't allowed to get in _____ you have the ticket.
   A. as if　　　　　　B. as though　　　　C. as long as　　　　D. unless
9. _____ she couldn't understand was _____ fewer and fewer students showed interest in her lessons.
   A. That; what　　　B. What; why　　　 C. What; because　　D. Why; that
10. _____ is mentioned above, the number of the students in senior school is increasing.
    A. Which　　　　　B. As　　　　　　　C. That　　　　　　D. It
11. David is such a good boy _____ all the teachers like him.
    A. that　　　　　　B. who　　　　　　 C. as　　　　　　　 D. whom
12. He had thousands of students, many of _____ gained great success in their own field.
    A. whom　　　　　B. them　　　　　　C. which　　　　　　D. who
13. Our company will move to a tall building _____ we worked two years ago.
    A. where　　　　　B. when　　　　　　C. that　　　　　　 D. which
14. He asked _____ for the violin.
    A. did I pay how much　　　　　　　　B. I paid how much
    C. how much did I pay　　　　　　　　D. how much I paid
15. Sarah hopes to become a friend of _____ shares her interests.
    A. anyone　　　　 B. whomever　　　　C. whoever　　　　　D. no matter who

第六章 非谓语动词

非谓语动词指句中不充当谓语的动词,非谓语动词分为三种基本形式:to do(不定式)、doing(现在分词/动名词)和done(过去分词)。除了不能独立作谓语之外,非谓语动词可充当其他各种句子成分。非谓语动词仍保留动词的某些特点,可以带有自己的宾语和状语,即以非谓语动词词组的形式来充当相应的句子成分。

一、非谓语动词的形式

(一) to do 形式

to do 形式指不定式,具有名词、代词、形容词、副词的特征,在句中可作主语、宾语、表语、补足语、定语、状语等。

一般式	to do
	to be done
进行式	to be doing
完成式	to have done
	to have been done
完成进行式	to have been doing

➢ The teacher told us **to do morning exercises**.
老师让我们做早操。
➢ The car **to be bought** is for his sister.
要买的这辆车是给他姐姐的。
➢ She pretended **to be reading** when the teacher came into the classroom.
老师进入教室时,她假装正在读书。
➢ The thief is said **to have escaped**.
据说小偷已经逃跑了。
➢ The thief is said **to have been arrested**.
据说小偷已经被抓住了。
➢ She is said **to have been working in the factory** over the last 20 years.
据说,在过去的20年里,她一直在这家工厂工作。

(二) doing 形式

doing 形式指现在分词和动名词,具有名词、代词、形容词、副词的特征,在句中可作主语、宾语、表语、补足语、定语、状语等。

一般式	doing
	being done
完成式	having done
	having been done

- **Travelling in space** will be common in the future.
  在未来,太空旅行将会是普遍的。
- **Being scolded by the teacher in front of the whole class** embarrassed Tom.
  在全班同学面前被老师训斥让 Tom 很尴尬。
- I have no idea of **having done such a thing against you**.
  我不知道做过这样对你不利的事情。
- Many customers complain of **having been given short weight at that shop**.
  很多顾客抱怨在那家店被缺斤少两过。

(三) done 形式

done 形式指过去分词,具有形容词、副词的特征,在句中可作表语、补足语、定语、状语等。

一般式	done

- **Seen in the distance**, the building looks more magnificent.
  从远处看,这栋建筑看起来更加宏伟。
- They found the door **locked**.
  他们发现门锁着。
- **Followed by the girl**, he came in.
  他被那个女孩跟着,走了进来。

【补充提示】

非谓语动词的否定式通常是在非谓语动词之前加否定词 not 或 never。

- He felt regretful about **never being** at home.
  他后悔从未待在家里。
- She regretted **not having told** him the truth.
  她后悔没有告诉他真相。
- Please do not pretend **not to know** what I am talking about.
  请不要假装不知道我在说什么。
- We decided **never to buy** that house.
  我们决定永远不买那所房子。
- **Not having finished** his work, he had to stay at home at weekends.
  由于工作没有完成,他周末不得不待在家里。

> **Not treated** in time, the injured dog died soon.
> 由于没有及时治疗,受伤的狗很快就死了。

(四) 非谓语动词的语态和时态意义

非谓语动词与谓语动词一样有其动作的发出者或承受者,在逻辑意义上为非谓语动词的主语。为了加以区别,我们称非谓语动词动作的发出者或承受者为逻辑主语,逻辑主语与非谓语动词之间存在主动或被动关系。非谓语动词的逻辑主语有时候与句中谓语动词的主语一致,但有时候非谓语动词也会自带逻辑主语,与句中谓语动词的主语不一致。

非谓语动词本身不能直接表示现在、将来和过去,在表示时态意义时是以句中谓语动词发生的时间为参照的"相对时间"概念:非谓语动词动作在谓语动词之前发生表示"完成";非谓语动词动作和谓语动词同时发生表示"进行";非谓语动词动作在谓语动词之后发生表示"将来";非谓语动词动作在谓语动词之前发生且一直持续到谓语动作的时间表示"完成进行"。

		主动	被动	时态
to do	一般式	to do	to be done	将来
	进行式	to be doing	/	进行
	完成式	to have done	to have been done	完成
	完成进行式	to have been doing	/	完成进行
doing	一般式	doing	being done	进行
	完成式	having done	having been done	完成
done	/	/	done	完成

> I'm glad **to see** you.
> 很高兴见到你。
> **Praised** by everybody, he became the pride of his family.
> 被所有人赞扬,他成了家里的骄傲。
> More time **given**, we can do the work better.
> 如果给更多时间的话,我们就能把工作做得更好。
> He regretted **having worked** for them.
> 他后悔曾为他们工作。
> She is going to the conference **to be held** next week.
> 她将去参加下周举行的会议。
> **Seen** from the hill, the garden is nice.
> 从山上看,花园很漂亮。
> He was happy **to have been staying** with his brother.
> 他很开心一直和他哥哥住在一起。
> All flight **canceled** because of the snowstorm, we decided **to take** the train.
> 由于暴风雪,所有的航班都被取消了,我们决定去坐火车。

【补充提示】
一般来说,非谓语动词的逻辑主语在句中可以找到,但在有些情况下逻辑主语会被省略。另外,除相对于谓语动词可表示进行、将来、完成等时态之外,非谓语动词有时也可不强调时间意义。
➢ **Making** a film takes time.
   拍电影需要时间。(逻辑主语被省略,且 doing 形式不强调时间意义)

二、非谓语动词的句法功能

(一)非谓语动词作主语

动词原形不能在句中直接作主语,将其转化为非谓语动词 to do/doing 形式后用法类似于名词,可以在句中充当主语。to do 侧重于表示一次性具体的动作;doing 则侧重于表示经常、习惯性动作。

➢ **To win** the first prize in the game is difficult.
   在比赛中赢得第一名是很困难的。(一次性具体的动作)
➢ **Swimming** is my favorite sport.
   游泳是我最喜欢的运动。(经常、习惯性动作)

但 to do/doing 作主语时,常使用 it 作形式主语位于句首,而把真正的主语 to do/doing 后置。

1. to do 作真正主语的常见句型

- It+be+*adj.*/*n.*+(for/of sb.)+to do sth. (对于某人来说)/(某人)做某事是……
- It take (sb.)+时间+to do sth. 做某事花费(某人)……时间

➢ **It** is important for us **to express** our opinions.
   对我们来说,表达我们的意见很重要。
➢ **It** is not easy **to acquire** English.
   学会英语不容易。
➢ **It** was polite of the child **to give** his seat to the elderly woman.
   这个孩子把自己的座位让给那个老妇人,是很有礼貌的。
➢ **It** is my honor **to be invited** to this party.
   我很荣幸被邀请参加这个聚会。
➢ **It** is our duty **to keep** the classroom clean.
   保持教室干净是我们的责任。
➢ **It** took her two days **to finish** her homework.
   完成家庭作业花费了她两天时间。

【补充提示】
在 It+be+*adj.*/*n.*+(for/of sb.)+to do sth. 句型中,for sb. 句型常用于表示事物的特征、客观情况的形容词,如 dangerous、difficult、hard、easy、impossible、important、necessary、possible 等;of sb. 句型常用于表示人的性格、品质,表示主观感情或态度的形容词,如 brave、careful、clever、cruel、honest、polite、impolite、kind、nice、rude、selfish、wise 等。

➢ It is **difficult for us** to learn English well in a short time.
　对于我们来说，在短时间内学好英语很难。

➢ It is **wise of your father** to have invested in property years ago.
　你父亲许多年前投资房地产是很明智的。

2. doing 作真正主语的常见句型

- It is/was no/not any/of little good+doing sth. 做某事没有好处
- It is/was useless/of little use+doing sth. 做某事没有用处
- It is/was a waste of time+doing sth. 做某事浪费时间

➢ **It** is no use **crying** over spilt milk.
　覆水难收。

➢ **It** is no good **talking** with him.
　和他谈话没有什么好处。

➢ **It** is of little good **putting** your trust in him.
　你信任他没有好处。

➢ **It** is of little good **staying** up too late every day.
　每天熬夜太晚没有什么好处。

➢ **It** is a waste of time **trying** to change his mind.
　试图改变他的想法是浪费时间。

（二）非谓语动词作宾语

动词原形不能在句中直接作宾语，将其转化为非谓语动词 to do/doing 形式后用法类似于名词，可以在句中充当宾语。

1. 只能用 to do 作宾语

有些动词(词组)只能用 to do 形式作宾语，如 agree、aim、arrange、afford、ask、beg、choose、claim、decide、demand、desire、hesitate、dare、determine、expect、fail、hope、help、learn、manage、offer、plan、prepare、pretend、promise、refuse、volunteer、want、wish、would like、would love 等。

➢ He decided **to work** harder this year.
　他决定今年更加努力地工作。

➢ She pretended **not to see** me when I passed by.
　当我路过的时候，她假装没看见我。

➢ He managed **to save** the little girl in time.
　他设法及时挽救了那个小女孩。

➢ Most teachers couldn't refuse **to help** the poor students.
　大多数老师无法拒绝帮助贫困学生。

➢ His friends promise **not to let** him alone.
　他的朋友们承诺不会让他孤身一人。

➢ If you have any problems, don't hesitate **to ask** for advice.
　如果你有任何问题，要毫不犹豫向人请教。

【补充提示】

① to do 形式作主语或宾语时,前面可带有疑问词,构成"疑问词+to do"结构,即"what(什么)/who(谁)/when(什么时候)/where(在哪里)/how(如何,怎样)/whether(是否)/which(哪个)+to do",但需要注意特殊情况"why(为什么)+do"。

➢ Please ask him **when to pay** the bill.
请问问他什么时候支付账单。

➢ She doesn't explain **how to do** the work.
她没有解释如何做这项工作。

➢ I don't understand **why leave** now.
我不明白为什么要现在离开。

➢ **Where to build** the new library hasn't been decided.
在哪里建新的图书馆还没有决定。

② to do 形式可跟在意为"除了"的介词 but 或 other than 后作宾语,如果介词之前有实义动词 do 的某种形式,那么介词后用不带 to 的不定式,否则就用 to do 形式。另外在 can't choose but、can't help but、can't but 后面也要用不带 to 的不定式,例如:

• have nothing to do but+do... 除了……无事可做
• have no choice but+to do... 除了……别无选择

➢ We could **do** nothing but **wait**.
我们除了等,无事可做。

➢ We had nothing **to do** other than **wait**.
我们除了等,无事可做。

➢ We **have no choice** but **to wait**.
我们除了等,别无选择。

➢ I **can't choose** but **laugh**.
除了笑,我别无选择。

2. 只能用 doing 作宾语

有些动词(词组)只能用 doing 形式作宾语,如 advise、suggest、discuss、practice、allow、permit、appreciate、enjoy、finish、burst out、can't resist、can't stand、can't help、consider、deny、avoid、miss、escape、forbid、imagine、mind、delay、postpone、risk、bear、tolerate、ban 等。

有些以介词结尾的动词词组也只能用 doing 形式作宾语,如 admit to、be accustomed to、be used to、contribute to、devote to、confess to、get down to、look forward to、stick to、object to、pay attention to、when it comes to、submit to、accuse sb. of、aim at、apologize to sb. for、be fond of、be responsible for、believe in、depend on、dream of、feel like、give up、keep on、insist on、persist in、prevent from、put off、succeed in、think of、thank sb. for、worry about、be busy (in)、have difficulty/trouble (in)、have a good/wonderful/hard time (in) 等。

➢ Nobody will risk **being killed**.
没有人会冒被杀的风险。

➢ I can hardly imagine **spending** so much money on a coat like that.
我很难想象花费那么多钱买一件那样的外套。

➢ No one can avoid **being influenced** by advertisements.
　没有人能够避免受到广告的影响。
➢ I don't mind your **smoking** here.
　我不介意你在这里抽烟。
➢ I am accustomed to **drinking** a cup of coffee every morning.
　我习惯每天早晨喝一杯咖啡。
➢ She apologized for **having made** such a mistake.
　她为犯了这样的错误而道歉。
➢ When it comes to **evaluating** homework, the professor will treat his students equally.
　在评估家庭作业时,教授将会一视同仁地对待他的学生。

[补充提示]

① doing 形式作主语或宾语时,通常情况下 doing 形式的逻辑主语与句子的主语一致,但有时 doing 形式有与句子的主语不一致的逻辑主语,此时可在 doing 形式前使用人称代词宾格、形容词性物主代词或名词所有格来体现逻辑主语。

➢ Do you mind **him smoking** here?
　你介意他在这里抽烟吗?
➢ I would appreciate **your keeping** it a secret.
　我会感激你保守秘密。
➢ **Jackie's disappearing** made them worried.
　Jackie 的失踪让他们很担心。
➢ I really appreciate **your offering** to help me, but I am sure that I will be able to manage it by myself.
　我真的很感激你向我提供帮助,但是我确信我自己可以做到。

② 动词 allow、permit、advise、forbid 后直接跟 doing 形式作宾语;如果这些动词后有表示人的名词或代词作宾语时,则跟 to do 形式作宾语补足语。

• allow/permit/advise/forbid doing sth. 允许/建议/禁止做某事
• allow/permit/advise/forbid sb. to do sth. 允许/建议/禁止某人做某事

➢ We don't allow **smoking** here.
　我们不允许在这里吸烟。
➢ We don't allow students **to smoke**.
　我们不允许学生吸烟。

③ 形容词 worth、worthy、worthwhile 的固定用法中,也可用 doing 和 to do 形式作宾语或主语。

• be+worth+doing sth. 值得(被)……
• be+worthy+of+doing sth. 值得(被)……
  be+worthy+to be done. 值得(被)……
• It+be worthwhile to do sth.…… 是值得的

➢ The book is worth **reading**.
　这本书值得一读。

- The museum is worthy of **visiting**.
  这个博物馆值得一去。
- The museum is worthy **to be visited**.
  这个博物馆值得一去。
- It is worthwhile to ask him **to join** the club.
  邀请他加入俱乐部是值得的。

3. 既可用 to do 作宾语又可用 doing 作宾语

有些动词(词组)既可用 to do 形式作宾语,也可用 doing 形式作宾语,但表达的含义不同。常见的这类动词(词组)如下:

forget to do sth.	忘记去做某事	forget doing sth.	忘记做过某事
remember to do sth.	记得去做某事	remember doing sth.	记得做过某事
regret to do sth.	遗憾去做某事	regret doing sth.	后悔做过某事
stop to do sth.	停下来去做另一件事	stop doing sth.	停止正在做的事
go on to do sth.	(做完某事)继续做另一件事	go on doing sth.	继续做同一件事
try to do sth.	尽力做某事	try doing sth.	尝试做某事
mean to do sth.	打算做某事	mean doing sth.	意味着做某事
can't help to do sth.	不能帮助做某事	can't help doing sth.	情不自禁做某事

- Don't forget **to turn** off the lights before you leave.
  在你离开之前不要忘记关灯。
- I forget **seeing** him at the park last week.
  我忘记上个星期在公园见过他了。
- I'm sorry that I can't help **to clean** the room.
  很抱歉我不能帮忙打扫房间。
- I can't help **laughing** out loud.
  我情不自禁大笑出声。
- The old woman means **to go** to the market alone.
  这个老妇人打算自己去市场。
- Sometimes love means **taking** a step back.
  有时候爱意味着做出让步。

【补充提示】

① 在 forget、remember、regret 后接 having done 相当于 doing,表示"忘记/记得/后悔(已经)做过某事"。

- I forget **seeing/having seen** him at the park last week.
  我忘记上个星期在公园(已经)见过他了。

> I remember **spending/having spent** the summer vacation with them three years ago.

我记得三年前(已经)和他们一起度过暑假了。

② 当句子主语是物,谓语动词使用 need、require、want 表示"需要(被)"时,其后必须用 doing 或 to be done 作宾语,且动名词 doing 的主动形式表示被动含义。当句子主语是人,动词 need 表"需要"、require 表"要求"、want 表"想要"时,其后须先接表示人的名词或代词作宾语,然后接 to do 作宾语补足语。

- sth. +need/require/want+doing/to be done 某物需要(被)……
- need/require/want sb. to do sth. 需要/要求/想要某人做……

> The window needs **cleaning/to be cleaned**.

窗户需要(被)擦一下。

> Your hair wants **cutting/to be cut**.

你的头发需要(被)剪一下。

> The bike requires **repairing/to be repaired**.

这辆自行车需要(被)修一下。

> I try not to bother you but I do need you **to help** me.

我尽量不打扰你,但是我确实需要你来帮助我。

(三) 非谓语动词作表语

1. to do 作表语

to do 形式作表语时,常用来表示具体的动作、将来要做的事,主语通常是"目的、计划、需求、愿望、梦想、职责"等。

> My aim is **to learn** English well in a short time.

我的目标是短时间内学好英语。

> Our duty is **to make** our country a better place.

我们的责任是让我们的国家变得更好。

> Her plan is **to travel** around the world.

她的计划是环游世界。

2. doing/done 作表语

doing 形式作表语时,常用来表示抽象的动作,主语通常是"身份、职业"等。此外,doing 形式和 done 形式作表语时,基本已形容词化。部分与人的情绪相关的及物动词的 doing 形式和 done 形式常作为形容词使用,且 doing 形式表示"令人……的",done 形式表示"感到……的",作表语时用来表示说明主语的特征、性质、状态和感受等。

> My job is **teaching** English.

我的工作是教英语。

> The lecture is **interesting**.

这个讲座很有趣。

> I am **interested** in the lecture.

我对这个讲座很感兴趣。

> They were **disappointed** at the result of the game.
> 他们对比赛结果感到失望。
> The conclusion of the book was **disappointing**.
> 这本书的结尾令人失望。

【补充提示】
① 常见的与人的情绪相关的及物动词的 doing 形式和 done 形式用作形容词的列举如下：

amazing	令人惊叹的	amazed	感到惊叹的
boring	令人厌烦的	bored	感到厌烦的
confusing	令人困惑的	confused	感到困惑的
convincing	令人信服的	convinced	感到信服的
disappointing	令人失望的	disappointed	感到失望的
embarrassing	令人尴尬的	embarrassed	感到尴尬的
encouraging	令人鼓舞的	encouraged	感到鼓舞的
exciting	令人兴奋的	excited	感到兴奋的
frustrating	令人沮丧的	frustrated	感到沮丧的
interesting	有趣的	interested	感兴趣的
satisfying	令人满意的	satisfied	感到满意的
shocking	令人震惊的	shocked	感到震惊的
surprising	令人惊讶的	surprised	感到惊讶的

② get+done 形式可构成系表结构，其中的 done 形式也已形容词化，常用在一些固定词组中，来表示人的某种状态、动作、心理或情感的变化等，常见的列举如下：

get drunk	喝醉	get dressed	穿衣服
get lost	迷路	get undressed	脱衣服
get started	开始	get changed	换衣服
get married	结婚	get shaved	刮脸,刮胡子
get engaged	订婚	get tired of	厌倦
get divorced	离婚	get used to	习惯

> He went out and **got drunk**.
> 他出去喝醉了酒。
> You will soon **get used to** this kind of work.
> 你很快就会习惯这种工作。

(四)非谓语动词作宾语补足语

非谓语动词 to do/doing/done 形式均可作宾语补足语,其中 to do 作宾语补足语时可分为带 to 的不定式和不带 to 的不定式。非谓语动词作宾语补足语结构,往往与感官动词、使役动词和一些其他动词的固定用法及搭配有关。

1. 感官动词后接非谓语动词作宾语补足语

感官动词 see、watch、notice、observe、hear、feel 等后接的宾语补足语有四种形式,即 do(不带 to 的不定式)形式、doing 形式、being done 形式和 done 形式。do 表示主动且完成,doing 表示主动且进行,being done 表示被动且进行,done 表示被动且完成。

➢ I heard her **sing** an English song just now.
  我刚才听见她唱了一首英文歌。
➢ I heard her **singing** an English song when I passed by her room yesterday.
  昨天我经过她的房间的时候,我听见她正在唱英文歌。
➢ I heard the English song **being sung** by a little girl when I passed by her room yesterday.
  昨天我经过一个小女孩的房间的时候,我听见她正在唱英文歌。
➢ I heard the English song **sung** many times.
  我听见这首英文歌被唱了许多次了。
➢ I saw a girl **close** the window.
  我看到一个女孩关了窗户。
➢ I saw a boy **playing** football on the ground when we passed by the playground.
  当我们经过操场的时候,我看到一个男孩正在操场上踢足球。
➢ I saw him **being taken** away by the police.
  我看到他正在被警察带走。
➢ I saw a boy **bitten** by a dog just now.
  我刚才看到一个男孩被狗咬了。

2. 使役动词后接非谓语动词作宾语补足语

使役动词 make、have、let、get、keep、leave 后接非谓语动词作宾语补足语时,常用句型如下:

- make/have/let+宾语+do   让……做……(不带 to 的不定式作宾语补足语,表主动)
- make/have/get+宾语+done   让……被做(done 作宾语补足语,表被动)
- get+宾语+to do   让……做……(to do 作宾语补足语,表主动且将来)
- leave/keep+宾语+doing   让……一直做……(doing 作宾语补足语,表主动且进行)
- keep+宾语+done   让……被做(done 作宾语补足语,表被动)
- catch+宾语+doing   抓住……正在做……(doing 作宾语补足语,表主动且进行)

➢ My mother **makes** me **drink** milk every day.
  我妈妈让我每天喝牛奶。
➢ The boss **had** his secretary **wait** for an hour outside the door.
  老板让他的秘书在门外等了一个小时。

> He raised his voice to **make** himself **heard**.
> 他提高了声音以便让别人听见他的话。
> My boss asked me to **have** all these tasks **done** as soon as possible.
> 我的老板要求我尽快完成这些任务。
> You shouldn't **leave** the water **running** when you brush your teeth.
> 你刷牙的时候不应该让水一直流着。
> She still couldn't **make** herself **understood** in English.
> 她仍然不能用英语表达自己的意思。
> I'll **get** my bike **repaired** tomorrow.
> 明天我要修一下我的自行车。
> You should **keep** me **informed** of his final decision.
> 你应该让我知道他的最终决定。
> The teacher **caught** him **cheating** in the exam.
> 老师抓到他在考试中作弊。

【补充提示】

感官动词 see、hear 和使役动词 make 接不带 to 的不定式作宾语补足语时,若句子变为被动语态,则需要使用带 to 的不定式。

> I **am made to drink** milk every day.
> 我被要求每天喝牛奶。
> A girl **is seen to close** the window.
> 有人看见一个女孩把窗户关上了。
> The woman **was seen to enter** the bank.
> 有人看见那个女人走进了银行。

3. 一些其他动词接 to do 形式作宾语补足语

一些其他动词,如 warn、advise、allow、ask、encourage、expect、force、forbid、permit、invite、order、persuade、require、want、need、wish 等,常用 to do 形式作宾语补足语。

> We don't allow students **to smoke**.
> 我们不允许学生吸烟。
> Our teacher asked us **to hand** in our homework.
> 老师要求我们交家庭作业。
> We persuaded him **to go** to school with us.
> 我们说服了他和我们一起去上学。
> I advised him **to go** home at once.
> 我建议他立刻回家。
> They have invited me **to go** to Paris with them.
> 他们邀请我和他们一起去巴黎。
> The teacher asked us **not to make** so much noise.
> 老师要求我们不要发出太多噪音。

- We expect our goal **to be achieved** next year.
  我们期望我们的目标明年能被实现。

（五）非谓语动词作定语

1. to do 作定语

to do 形式作定语时修饰名词或代词，且必须位于被修饰词后作后置定语，to do 与被修饰词之间关系复杂，存在逻辑上的主谓、动宾、同位、动状等关系。

（1）被修饰词前有序数词、形容词最高级、the only/the very/the next/the last 等限定时，常用 to do 形式作定语。

- This is the best way **to work** out the problem.
  这是解决问题的最好的方法。
- She was the first woman **to win** the gold medal in the Olympic Games.
  她是第一位在奥运会上获得金牌的女性。
- He is the only person **to think** of the idea.
  他是唯一一个想到这个主意的人。
- The next thing **to do** is to relax yourself completely.
  下一步要做的事情是完全放松你自己。

（2）一些抽象名词，如 ability、promise、way、reason、time、plan、order、intention、need、necessity、courage、chance、opportunity、decision、right、wish 等，后常接 to do 形式作定语。

- I have a chance **to go** sightseeing.
  我有一个观光旅行的机会。
- They have made a plan **to learn** from Lei Feng.
  他们制订了一个向雷锋学习的计划。
- The army got an order **to leave** the city.
  军队接到了离开这座城市的命令。

（3）不定代词 something、nothing、little、much、a lot 等后常接 to do 形式作定语。

- I have something **to tell** you.
  我有事要告诉你。
- Do you have anything **to say**?
  你有什么要说的吗？
- I have a lot **to do**.
  我有许多事要做。

【补充提示】

① to do 形式作定语时，如果 to do 中的动词是不及物动词，to do 形式后可添加适当的介词。

- Sally has no friends **to depend on**.
  Sally 没有可以依靠的朋友。
- This is a comfortable room **to live in**.
  这是一间舒适可住的房间。

② to do 形式作定语时，如果 to do 所表示的动作不是由主语发出，可使用 to do 的被动式 to be done。

➤ Here are the questions **to be discussed** tomorrow.
这些是明天要讨论的问题。

➤ The test **to be held** in our school tomorrow is helpful for us.
我们学校明天将要举行的考试对我们很有帮助。

➤ The airport **to be completed** next year will help promote tourism in this area.
明年建成的飞机场将有助于促进这一地区的旅游业。

2. doing/done 作定语

（1）doing/done 作前置定语。

单个词的 doing 形式和 done 形式可作前置定语，位于被修饰词前，doing 表主动、进行，done 表被动、完成，但不及物动词的 done 形式不表示语态意义上的被动，仅表示时态意义上的完成。

➤ The **sleeping** baby is so cute.
这个正在睡觉的宝宝是如此的可爱。

➤ The **broken** vase is very expensive.
这个碎掉的花瓶非常昂贵。

➤ She gathered **fallen** flowers and buried them.
她收集了落花并把它们埋了。

【补充提示】

一些动词的 doing 形式和 done 形式均可作前置定语，且基本已形容词化，其中 doing 形式意为"正在……的"，done 形式意为"已经……的"，常见的一些列举如下：

falling leaves	正在下落的树叶	fallen leaves	已经落在地上的树叶
changing world	正在变化的世界	changed world	已经变化了的世界
boiling water	正在沸腾的水	boiled water	已经煮沸过的水
developing country	发展中国家	developed country	发达国家

➤ We are living in a **changing world**.
我们生活在一个不断变化中的世界。

➤ There are many **developed countries** in the world.
世界上有许多发达国家。

（2）doing/being done/done 作后置定语。

doing 形式、being done 形式和 done 形式可作后置定语修饰名词或代词，以词组的形式位于被修饰词后，doing 表主动、进行，being done 表被动、进行，done 表被动、完成。

➤ The young man **sitting behind me** is our monitor.
正坐在我后面的年轻人是我们的班长。

- The houses **being built now** are for the teachers.
  现在正在建造的房子是给教师们的。
- The novel **written by Dickens** is very popular.
  狄更斯写的这本小说很受欢迎。
- The meeting **held in our school yesterday** is very important for all students.
  昨天在我们学校举行的会议对所有学生都很重要。

(六) 非谓语动词作状语

1. to do 作状语

to do 形式作状语时,可以表示目的、结果或原因,前面不能带从属连词。to do 形式表示主动、将来,to be done 形式表示被动、将来。

(1) 作目的状语。

- **To see** the whole city, I climbed to the top of the mountain.
  为了看到整座城市,我爬上了山顶。
- He opened the window **to get** some fresh air.
  他打开窗户去呼吸些新鲜空气。

【补充提示】

① to do 形式作状语时,逻辑主语通常与句子的主语一致,如果逻辑主语与句子的主语不一致,则需要用介词 for 接逻辑主语,置于 to do 形式之前。

- He stood aside **for them to enter**.
  他站到一边让他们进去。

② 表示目的时,也可用 in order to/so as to do,意为"以便,为了……",注意 so as to 不用于句首。

- My father got up early **in order to have** enough time to pack.
  我的父亲起得很早,以便有足够的时间收拾行李。
- He left early **so as not to miss** the last train.
  为了不错过最后一班火车,他早早离开了。

(2) 作结果状语,常表示出乎意料、令人失望的结果,且 to do 形式前常有 only、just。

- He hurried home **only to find** that his father was dead.
  他匆忙回到家,却发现他父亲已经去世了。
- They got to the station **only to be told** that the train had left.
  他们到了车站,却被告知火车已经开走了。
- He returned home after the war, **just to be informed** his wife had left.
  战争结束后他回到家,却被告知他的妻子已经离开了。

【补充提示】

表示结果时,也可用 so...as to do,such...as to do,too...to do,enough...to do 等结构。

- His work was **so good as to make** him well-known in the city.
  他的工作如此出色,因此他在这个城市很知名。

- It was **such a loud noise as to wake** everybody in the house.

  声音如此之大,以致屋里的所有人都被吵醒了。

- The coffee is **too hot to drink**.

  这咖啡太烫了,不能喝。

- She plays the violin well **enough to perform** at a concert.

  她的小提琴拉得很好,足以在音乐会上演奏。

(3) 作原因状语。

- I'm delighted **to know** that you have a job.

  知道你有工作了,我很开心。

- We regret **to tell you** that we won't be able to attend the ceremony.

  我们很遗憾地告诉你,我们不能参加典礼了。

【补充提示】

表示原因时,to do 形式通常与表示喜怒哀乐、运气好坏的形容词或动词连用。

- I'm sorry **to hear** this news.

  听到这个消息,我很难过。

- We are glad **to see** you.

  见到你真高兴。

2. doing/done 作状语

doing 形式和 done 形式作状语时,可以表示时间、条件、结果、原因、让步和伴随,分为带从属连词和不带从属连词两种情况。doing 形式表示主动、进行,having done 形式表示主动、完成,done 形式表示被动、完成(或进行),having been done 形式表示被动、完成。

(1) 作时间状语。

- **When heated by the sun**, the ice began to melt.

  受到太阳的照耀时,冰开始融化了。

- **Hearing the news**, they got very excited.

  听到这个消息,他们很兴奋。

- **Seen from the top of the Mount Tai**, the building is small.

  从泰山顶上看过去,这栋楼很小。

(2) 作条件状语。

- **Keeping on learning English**, you will eventually make progress.

  (如果)坚持学习英语,你最终会取得进步。

- **Grown in rich soil**, these seeds can grow faster.

  (如果)种在肥沃的土壤里,这些种子能长得更快。

- **If asked to speak**, he has no problem expressing himself.

  如果要求他发言,他能毫不费力地表达自己的意思。

（3）作结果状语。

- The cup dropped to the ground, **breaking into pieces**.
  杯子掉到地上，摔成了碎片。
- It rained heavily, **causing serious flooding in that area**.
  雨下得很大，在那个地区造成了严重的洪水。

【补充提示】

表示结果时，通常只用 doing 形式而不用 done 形式。

（4）作原因状语。

- **Living far from the school**, I have to get up early every morning.
  由于住得离学校很远，我不得不每天早起。
- **Having finished their homework**, the kids wanted to hang out.
  已经做完了作业，孩子们想出去玩。

（5）作让步状语。

- **Though understanding no Italian**, Charlie was able to communicate with them.
  虽然 Charlie 不懂意大利语，但他能和他们交流。
- **Having been told many times**, he still repeated the same mistake.
  虽然已经被告知了很多次，他仍然重复着同样的错误。

（6）作伴随状语。

- The old man was fast asleep, **holding a book in his hand**.
  老人手里拿着一本书，睡得很熟。
- The teacher came into the lab, **followed by some students**.
  老师走进实验室，后面跟着一些学生。

【补充提示】

有些 to do 形式和 doing 形式的固定结构也可作状语，称作独立成分，常见的列举如下：

generally speaking... 一般说来　　　frankly speaking... 坦白地说
judging from... 根据……来判断　　　to be frank... 坦白地说
to tell you the truth... 说实话　　　to be honest... 说实话

- **Frankly speaking/To be frank**, the book is worth reading.
  坦白地说，这本书值得一读。
- **Judging from the weather**, the sports meeting will be put off.
  根据天气来判断，运动会将会推迟。
- **To tell you the truth/To be honest**, I have passed the CET4.
  说实话，我已经通过了大学英语四级考试。

（七）非谓语动词的独立主格

"名词/代词+非谓语动词"构成的结构称为非谓语动词的独立主格，通常作状语用于修饰整个句子,常位于句首、句尾,用逗号与句子的其他成分隔开。此结构中,非谓语动词前的名词或代词即为非谓语动词的逻辑主语。

1. 常见形式

(1) 逻辑主语+to do。

to do 形式表示逻辑主语和非谓语动词为主动关系,且往往表示还未发生的动作或者状态,在句中常作原因、条件状语。

➢ No one **to wake me up**, I might be late for the first class.
   如果没人叫醒我,我第一节课可能会迟到。

(2) 逻辑主语+doing/having done。

doing 形式和 having done 形式都表示逻辑主语和非谓语动词为主动关系,但 having done 形式强调非谓语动词动作在谓语动词之前发生,doing 形式和 having done 形式在句中常作时间、原因、条件、伴随等状语。

➢ All the students **having sat down**, the lecture began.
   所有的学生坐下来之后,讲座便开始了。

➢ Time **permitting**, we will answer your questions after the discussion.
   如果时间允许的话,讨论之后我们会回答你的问题。

(3) 逻辑主语+done。

done 形式表示逻辑主语和非谓语动词为被动关系,在句中常作时间、方式、伴随、原因、条件等状语。

➢ The problems **solved**, the quality has been improved.
   问题解决了,质量也提高了。

2. with 的复合结构

with 的复合结构,相当于在独立主格结构前加上 with,常构成"with+名词/代词+to do/doing/done"结构,在句中常作伴随、方式、原因、条件等状语。

➢ **With so much work to do**, I can't spare a minute.
   有这么多工作要做,我一分钟也挤不出来。

➢ **With so many children talking and laughing**, I couldn't settle down to my work.
   这么多孩子又说又笑,我无法静下心来工作。

➢ The murder was brought in, **with his hands tied**.
   凶手被带了进来,手被绑着。

➢ **With more time given**, I will visit you.
   再给我点时间,我会去看你的。

实 战 演 练

1. The teacher doesn't allow his students _____ on the exam.
   A. cheated   B. cheating   C. cheat   D. to cheat

2. _____ from the hill, the garden is nice.
   A. Seeing   B. Seen   C. Sees   D. Be seen
3. The story is so _____ that I'm so _____ in it.
   A. interesting; interested   B. interesting; interesting
   C. interested; interested   D. interested; interesting
4. He is said _____ two trips to China in the last two years.
   A. to be making   B. to make   C. to have made   D. to have been making
5. With lots of trees and flowers _____ here and there, the city looks very beautiful.
   A. having planted   B. planted
   C. have been planted   D. to be planted
6. _____ finished his work, he had to stay at home at weekends.
   A. Having not been   B. Being not   C. Not having   D. Having not
7. All flights _____ because of the snowstorm, we decided to take the train.
   A. having canceled   B. had been canceled
   C. were canceled   D. having been canceled
8. He hurried to the hospital, only _____ his father had just died.
   A. to tell   B. to be told   C. telling   D. told
9. I couldn't understand why he pretended _____ in the garden.
   A. not to see me   B. not see me   C. to see me not   D. to see not me
10. I can hardly imagine _____ so much money on a coat like that.
    A. spending   B. spend   C. to spend   D. spent
11. The room is so dirty that it wants _____.
    A. cleaning   B. being cleaning   C. to clean   D. cleaned
12. You're going to the United States next year. You should now practice _____ English as much as possible.
    A. speak   B. to speak   C. speaking   D. spoke
13. My children are looking forward to _____ a trip to Paris.
    A. make   B. making   C. be making   D. have made
14. The bank is reported _____ last night.
    A. to rob   B. to be robbed   C. to have robbed   D. to have been robbed
15. He studies so hard to avoid _____ at the bottom of the class.
    A. finishing   B. to finish   C. finished   D. finish

第七章 特殊句型

一、强调句

强调是一种修辞,是为了突出在一定语境中的部分内容而采用的一种形式。在英语中,表示强调有多种方式,如口语中可通过重读某一部分来起强调作用,而在书面语中可通过表示强调意义的词、短语或句式来加强语势、突出信息。

(一) 强调句的基本句型

强调句型为"It is/was+被强调部分+that/who(当强调主语且主语指人时)/whom(当强调宾语且宾语指人时)+其他"。这种句型可以强调句子的主语、宾语和状语,一般不能用来强调谓语、表语、补足语等。

➢ It was **I** that/who met him in the park this morning.
  今天早上正是我在公园里遇见了他。(强调主语)

➢ It was **him** that/whom I met in the park this morning.
  今天早上我在公园里遇见的正是他。(强调宾语)

➢ It was **in the park** that I met him this morning.
  今天早上我正是在公园里遇见了他。(强调地点状语)

(二) 强调句的疑问形式

1. 强调句的一般疑问句式

强调句型的一般疑问句结构是"Is/Was it+被强调部分+that/who+其他?"。

➢ Is it **your mom** that/who cooks dinner every day?
  是你的妈妈每天做晚饭吗?

➢ Was it **Julie** that/who phoned just now?
  刚才打电话的是Julie吗?

2. 强调句的特殊疑问句式

强调句型的特殊疑问句结构是"特殊疑问词+is/was it+that+其他?",意为"究竟……,到底……",特殊疑问句结构中特殊疑问词所表示的成分即为被强调部分。

➢ **Who** was it that phoned just now?
  刚才打电话的究竟是谁?

➢ **When** was it that you went back?
  你究竟什么时候回来的?

➢ **Where** was it that Shakespeare was born?
  莎士比亚出生的地方到底是在哪里呢?

（三）强调句的几点注意

1. 强调句中的"it is/was"和"that/who/whom"

（1）强调句中的 it is/was 本身没有词义，只起引出被强调部分的作用。

（2）当被强调部分是指人的主语时，强调句中的连接词可用 that/who。

➤ It was **my manager that/who** met a superstar at the airport yesterday.
　　昨天正是我的经理在机场遇到了一位超级巨星。（被强调部分 my manager 是指人的主语）

（3）当被强调部分是指人的宾语时，强调句中的连接词可用 that/whom。

➤ It was **him that/whom** I met in the street yesterday.
　　我昨天在街上遇到的正是他。（被强调部分 him 是指人的宾语）

2. 强调句的时态

如果原句中谓语动词使用的是一般现在时、现在进行时、现在完成时、现在完成进行时、一般将来时、将来进行时、将来完成时等，强调句用"It is...that..."结构；如果原句中谓语动词使用的是过去范畴的时态（一般过去时、过去进行时、过去完成时、过去将来时等），则用"It was...that..."结构。被强调部分无论是单数还是复数，it 后的 be 动词均用单数形式，即 is 或 was。

➤ It **is** music that I **hate** most.
　　我最不喜欢的就是音乐。（is 与 hate 时态范畴保持一致）

➤ It **is** with foreign companies that we **are competing**.
　　我们正在与之竞争的是外国公司。（is 与 are competing 时态范畴保持一致）

➤ It **was** because I was stuck in the traffic jam that I **came** late.
　　我来晚了正是因为交通堵塞。（was 与 came 时态范畴保持一致）

➤ It **was** this novel that they **were talking** about.
　　他们讨论的就是这部小说。（was 与 were talking 时态范畴保持一致）

3. 强调句的主谓一致

强调句中被强调的部分如果是句子的主语，that/who 之后的谓语动词在人称和数上应与被强调的主语保持一致。

➤ It is **she** that/who **is** to blame for the fault.
　　正是她应该为这个过失受责备。

➤ It is **you** that/who **are** likely to win the contest.
　　有可能赢得这场比赛的正是你。

➤ It is **your parents** that/who **are** going to see you.
　　正是你的父母要去见你。

4. not...until...的强调句

"not...until..."结构的强调句型为"It is/was not until＋被强调部分（从句）＋that＋其他部分（主句）"，until 后接的从句为被强调部分，that 后接主句，并且主句应由否定句变为肯定句。

➤ He didn't go to bed until his wife came back.
　　直到他的妻子回来，他才上床睡觉。（原句）

> **It was not until** his wife came back **that** he went to bed.

　　直到他的妻子回来,他才上床睡觉。(强调句)

5. "do/does/did+动词原形"强调谓语

强调句型不可强调谓语动词,若强调谓语动词应用"do/does/did+动词原形",但这种强调只能用于一般现在时和一般过去时的肯定句式中,且谓语动词一般不能是 be 动词,do/does/did 和原句中的谓语动词时态和数保持一致。

> I like the book.

　　我喜欢这本书。(原句)

> I **do like** the book.

　　我真的喜欢这本书。(强调句)

> He looks tired.

　　他看上去很累。(原句)

> He **does look** tired.

　　他真的看上去很累。(强调句)

> I called you in the morning.

　　我早上给你打过电话。(原句)

> I **did call** you in the morning.

　　我早上的确给你打过电话。(强调句)

【补充提示】

一般来说,如果把强调句中的"It is/was...that/who/whom..."去掉后,剩余部分仍能组成一个完整的句子则为强调句型,如果不能组成一个完整的句子,则为其他句型。

> It was at eight o'clock that I got home last night.

　　我正是在昨天晚上八点钟到家的。

　　(去掉 It was...that...后,剩余部分仍能组成一个完整的句子(〈I got home at eight o'clock last night.〉,是强调句)

> It was him that I met in the street this morning.

　　今天早上我在街上遇到的正是他。

　　(去掉 It was...that...后,剩余部分仍能组成一个完整的句子〈I met him in the street this morning.〉,是强调句)

> It was said that he met her in the street this morning.

　　据说他今天早上在街上碰见了她。

　　(去掉"It was...that..."后,剩余部分不能组成一个完整的句子,不是强调句)

> It is obvious that he has lost the game.

　　很显然他输掉了这场比赛。

　　(去掉"It is...that..."后,剩余部分不能组成一个完整的句子,不是强调句)

二、虚拟语气

虚拟语气指说话人所说的话不是一个事实,而是一种愿望、假设或建议等。在表示虚假的、与事实相反的或难以实现的情况时用虚拟语气。在表示主观愿望或某种强烈情感时,也用虚拟语气。

(一) if 虚拟条件句

英语中的条件句分为两种:真实条件句和非真实条件句。真实条件句表示提出的假设可实现,而非真实条件句表示提出的假设实现的可能性很小或不可能实现,在非真实条件句中需要使用虚拟语气。

1. if 引导的虚拟条件句

虚拟语气在 if 引导的虚拟条件句中,描述与现在、过去或将来事实相反的情况。在表示对不同的时间进行假设时,主句与 if 从句的谓语动词形式不同,详见下表:

虚拟情况	if 从句	主句
现在	did/were (be 动词过去式一律用 were)	would/should/could/might+do
过去	had done	would/should/could/might+have done
将来	① did/were ② were to do ③ should do	would/should/could/might+do

(1) 表示与现在事实相反的虚拟条件句。

- If+主语+did/were(be 动词过去式一律用 were),主语+would/should/could/might+do。

➢ If I **had** time, I **would** certainly **accompany** you to the hospital.
　　如果我有时间,我肯定会陪你去医院。

➢ If I **knew** the answer to all your questions, I **would be** a genius.
　　如果我知道你所有问题的答案,我就是个天才了。

➢ If I **were** a boy, I **would join** the army.
　　如果我是一个男孩,我就参军去。

(2) 表示与过去事实相反的虚拟条件句。

- If+主语+had done,主语+would/should/could/might+have done。

➢ If she **hadn't been** busy last week, she **would have come** here earlier.
　　上周如果不是太忙,她早就来这儿了。

➢ If we **hadn't built** so many Hope Primary Schools, a lots of kids **would have dropped** out of school.
如果我们没有建这么多希望小学,很多孩子就会辍学。

(3) 表示与将来事实相反的虚拟条件句。

- If+主语+did/were
- If+主语+were to do ⎫, 主语+would/should/could/might+do
- If+主语+should do ⎭

➢ If he **came** tomorrow, he **might find** me in the company.
如果他明天来,他可能会在公司找到我。

➢ If she **were to marry** Jack, she **would be** happy.
如果她嫁给Jack,她会幸福的。

➢ If it **should rain**, the crops **could be saved**.
如果下雨,庄稼就能得救。

2. 混合虚拟语气——错综时间条件句

在错综时间虚拟语气结构中,虚拟条件句与主句动作发生的时间不一致,因此主句和从句的谓语动词需根据各自的不同时间使用对应的虚拟语气形式。

➢ If I **had listened** to you yesterday, I **wouldn't be** in this situation now.
如果我昨天听了你的话,我现在就不会处于这种境地了。(从句是对过去的虚拟,主句是对现在的虚拟)

➢ If I **were** you, I **wouldn't have missed** the birthday party last night.
如果我是你,我就不会错过昨晚的生日聚会。(从句是对现在的虚拟,主句是对过去的虚拟)

3. 含蓄虚拟条件句

有些句子不是以 if 引导的虚拟条件句形式出现,而是通过某些单词或短语来暗示虚拟语气的存在,这样的句子称为含蓄虚拟条件句。常用在含蓄虚拟条件句中的单词或短语有 without、otherwise、but for、or 等。

➢ She came to town yesterday, **or** I would not have met her.
= If she hadn't come to town yesterday, I would not have met her.
昨天她到城里来了,不然我就不会遇见她了。

➢ **Without** air, there would be no living things on the earth.
= If there were no air, there would be no living things on the earth.
如果没有空气,地球上就没有生物。

➢ **But for** your help, I wouldn't have finished the work in time.
= If you had not helped me, I wouldn't have finished the work in time.
要不是你帮我,我就不能按时完成工作了。

➢ We didn't know his telephone number, **otherwise** we would have telephoned him.
= If we had known his telephone number, we would have telephoned him.
我们不知道他的电话号码,否则就给他打电话了。

（二）从句中的虚拟语气

① 表示"命令、要求、建议"等含义的动词后所接的宾语从句需用虚拟语气，从句中谓语动词的形式为"should+动词原形"，且 should 可以省略。常见的动词有 insist、require、order、command、advise、suggest、recommend、propose、demand、request 等。

> She **suggested** that I (**should**) **have** breakfast every morning.
> 她建议我每天早上吃早餐。

> He **insisted** that the meeting (**should**) **be put** off.
> 他坚持要求推迟会议。

> The general **ordered** that all the soldiers (**should**) **leave**.
> 将军命令所有士兵离开。

【补充提示】

当 suggest 表示"暗示，表明"而不表示"建议"，insist 表示"坚持认为，坚持说"而不表示"坚持要求"时，后接的宾语从句用陈述语气，而不用虚拟语气。

> The smile on his face **suggested** that he **was satisfied** with our work.
> 他脸上的笑容表明他对我们的工作很满意。

> The man **insisted** that he **had never stolen** the money.
> 那人坚持说他从未偷过那笔钱。

② 表示"命令、要求、建议"等含义的名词所接的主语从句、表语从句或同位语从句中需用虚拟语气，从句中谓语动词的形式为"should+动词原形"，且 should 可以省略。常见的名词有 order、requirement、demand、request、suggestion、advice、proposal、recommendation、desire、necessity、plan、idea 等。

> My **advice** is that we (**should**) **take** an umbrella with us every day.
> 我的建议是我们每天都要带把伞。

> It is my **plan** that my family (**should**) **travel** every year.
> 我的计划是我们全家每年都要去旅游。

> His **demand** is that all sentences (**should**) **be written** out in English.
> 他的要求是所有的句子都要用英语写出来。

③ "It is(was)+形容词(或过去分词)+that 从句…"结构中，若形容词是 advisable、appropriate、desirable、necessary、important、vital、essential、natural、urgent、possible、strange 等或过去分词是表示"命令、要求、建议"等含义的动词，从句需用虚拟语气，从句中谓语动词的形式为"should+动词原形"，且 should 可以省略。

> It's **essential** that we (**should**) **learn** some knowledge about first aid.
> 我们学习一些关于急救的知识是很有必要的。

> It is **demanded** that we (**should**) **work out** a plan.
> 我们被要求制订出一个计划。

> It is **vital** that he (**should**) **be warned** in time.
> 及时警告他是至关重要的。

（三）其他虚拟情况

1. wish 后所接的宾语从句常用虚拟语气

（1）表示与现在事实相反的情况，从句谓语动词用 did/were。

➢ I **wish**（that）I **were** a bird.
　我希望我是一只鸟。

（2）表示与过去事实相反的情况，从句谓语动词用 had done。

➢ I **wish**（that）she **had taken** my advice then.
　那时她要是听了我的建议就好了。

（3）表示将来没有把握或不太可能实现的愿望，从句谓语动词用"would/could+do"。

➢ I **wish**（that）I **would/could go** soon.
　我希望我很快就能走。

2. "It's（high/about）time that 从句…"句式中从句需用虚拟语气，从句谓语动词用过去式或者"should+动词原形"，且 should 不能省略，意为"到该做……的时候了"

➢ **It is high time that** we **left/should leave**.
　到我们该离开的时候了。

➢ **It is about time that** you **had/should have** breakfast.
　到你该吃早饭的时候了。

3. as if/as though（似乎，好像，仿佛）、if only（要是……就好了）引导的方式状语从句或表语从句常用虚拟语气

从句引导词	虚拟语气的时间	从句谓语动词形式
as if/as though, if only	表现在（与现在事实相反）	did/were
	表过去（与过去事实相反）	had done
	表将来（与将来事实相反）	would/could+do

➢ It seems **as if** he **knew** all.
　他似乎什么都知道。（与现在事实相反）

➢ He looks **as though** he **hadn't slept** yesterday.
　他看起来好像昨天没睡觉一样。（与过去事实相反）

➢ He speaks **as if** no one **would see** him tomorrow.
　他说得好像明天没有人会看见他似的。（与将来事实相反）

➢ **If only** he **were** here now.
　要是他现在在这儿就好了。（与现在事实相反）

> **If only** I **had gone** to bed earlier yesterday.

　要是我昨天早点睡就好了。（与过去事实相反）

4. would rather（宁愿）后所接的宾语从句常用虚拟语气

（1）表示现在或将来的愿望时，从句谓语动词用 did/were。

> I **would rather** you **came** next week.

　我宁愿你下周来。

（2）表示过去的愿望时，从句谓语动词用 had done。

> I **would rather** you **hadn't let** out the secret.

　我宁愿你没有把这个秘密泄露出去。

5. "情态动词+have done"表示虚拟语气

（1）could have done 表示本能够做某事，但实际上没做。

couldn't have done 表示本不能做某事，但实际上做到了。

> He **could have finished** the task on time, but the heavy snow came.

　他本可以按时完成任务，但是暴雪来了。

> She **could not have covered** the whole distance, but in fact she arrived ahead of time.

　她本不能走完全程，但实际上她提前到了。

（2）needn't have done 表示本不必做某事，但实际上却做了。

> She **needn't have attended** the meeting yesterday but she did.

　她本不必参加昨天的会议，但她参加了。

（3）should/ought to have done 表示本应该做某事，但实际上没做。

shouldn't/oughtn't to have done 表示本不应该做某事，但实际上却做了。

> The plant was dead. I **should/ought to have given** it more water.

　那盆植物死了，我本应该多给它浇点水的。

> I **shouldn't/oughtn't to have watched** that movie because it gave me horrible dreams.

　我本不应该去看那场电影，因为它让我做了噩梦。

（4）might have done 表示本可能做某事，但实际上没做到。

> What a pity! Considering his ability and experience, he **might have done** better.

　真可惜！考虑到他的能力和经验，他本可能做得更好。

三、倒装句

英语中有两种句子语序：陈述语序和倒装语序。陈述语序为"主语+谓语+……"，倒装语序为"谓语（或部分谓语）+主语+……"。倒装句可分为全部倒装和部分倒装。全部倒装是将整个谓语提到主语前面，部分倒装是将谓语的一部分（助动词或情态动词）提到主语前面。

（一）全部倒装

全部倒装是指将句子中的谓语动词全部置于主语之前，此结构通常用于一般现在时和一般过去时。常见用法如下：

① 在 there be 或者 there live（stand, appear, seem, remain, exist…）句型中，用全部倒装。

➢ **There are** many forms of energy.

　　有很多种能量形式。

➢ **There stands** a stone bridge over the river.

　　河上有一座石桥。

➢ **There exists** some misunderstanding between them.

　　他们之间有点儿误会。

② 表示时间、地点、方位的副词或介词短语位于句首时，用全部倒装。

以 now、then、here、there、down、up、in、out、off、away、in the distance、on the hill 等表示时间、地点、方位的副词或介词短语位于句首，且主语为名词时，要用全部倒装。

➢ **Here** is the book you want.

　　你要的书在这里。

➢ **In front of the house** stood a tree.

　　房子前面有一棵树。

➢ **Under the tree** sat a little girl.

　　树下坐着一个小女孩。

➢ **In** came a man with an umbrella.

　　一个拿着伞的男人进来了。

【补充提示】

① 上述全部倒装的句型结构中的主语必须是名词，如果主语是人称代词则不能使用倒装。

➢ Here **he** comes.

　　他来了。（主语是人称代词，不能使用倒装）

② 全部倒装中谓语动词的数由动词后面的主语决定，与动词后面主语的单复数保持一致。

➢ On the wall **hang** two maps.

　　墙上挂着两张地图。（hang 与 two maps 的数保持一致）

➢ On the wall **hangs** a world map.

　　墙上挂着一张世界地图。（hangs 与 a world map 的数保持一致）

③ 在主系表结构中，有时为了强调表语，可将表语提前构成倒装句式，即"表语+系动词+主语"。

➢ **Gone** are the days when we were students.（倒装语序）

= The days when we were students are gone.（正常语序）

　　我们当学生的日子一去不复返了。（表语 gone 提前）

> **Present** at the meeting were a group of young people.（倒装语序）

= A group of young people were present at the meeting.（正常语序）

出席会议的是一群年轻人。（表语 present 提前）

④ 在某些表示祝愿的句型中。

> Long live the People's Republic of China!

中华人民共和国万岁！

（二）部分倒装

部分倒装是指将谓语动词的一部分如助动词或情态动词置于主语之前，如果句子的谓语动词中没有助动词或情态动词，则需要添加助动词 do、does、did 并将其置于主语之前。

(1) 否定或半否定意义的词或词组，如 no、not、never、seldom、little、hardly、scarcely、at no time、by no means、on no account、in no case、under no circumstances、in no way、not until 等位于句首时，句子要用部分倒装。

> **Seldom do I go** out alone in the evening.

晚上我很少一个人出去。

> **Never have I seen** such a performance.

我从来没有看过这样的表演。

> **Not** often **do they meet**.

他们不常见面。

> **Not until** the child fell asleep **did the mother leave** the room.

直到孩子入睡后母亲才离开房间。

【补充提示】

当 not until 引导主从复合句且 not until 位于句首时，从句不倒装，主句使用部分倒装。

> **Not until** they pointed out my fault to me **did I realize** it.

直到他们指出了我的错误，我才意识到这一点。（主句 did I realize 使用部分倒装）

(2) 以否定连词，如 not only...but also、hardly/scarcely...when、no sooner...than 等开头的句型中，前面的分句使用部分倒装，后面的分句不倒装，即前倒后不倒。

> **Not only did he refuse** the gift, he also severely criticized the sender.

他不仅没有收下礼物，而且还狠狠地批评了送礼的人。

> **Hardly/Scarcely had she gone** out when a student came to visit her.

她刚出门，就有一个学生来访。

> **No sooner had he arrived** than we wanted to leave.

他刚到，我们就想离开了。

【补充提示】

以 not only...but also 开头的句型中，只有当 not only...but also 连接两个分句时，才在前面的分句中使用部分倒装。当 not only...but also 连接两个并列单词或词组作句子的主语时,不用倒装结构。

> **Not only you but also I** am fond of music。

　不仅你喜欢音乐,我也喜欢音乐。

> **Not only he but also I** dislike the cake.

　不仅他不喜欢这个蛋糕,我也不喜欢这个蛋糕。

(3) only+状语或状语从句位于句首时,句子用部分倒装。

① only+状语位于句首,句子部分倒装。

> **Only in this way can you learn** English well.

　只有这样,你才能学好英语。

> **Only after the accident did he become** careful.

　只有在那次事故之后,他才小心了起来。

② only+状语从句位于句首,主句使用部分倒装,从句不倒装。

> **Only when one falls in love can one understand** the meaning of it.

　人只有恋爱了才能理解爱的真谛。

> **Only when he received the email did he realize** what had happened.

　只有当他收到邮件的时候,他才意识到发生了什么。

(4) 在 so…that 和 such…that 句型中,如果"so+形容词/副词"和"such+名词"置于句首,主句使用部分倒装。

> **So carelessly did he drive** that he almost killed himself.

　他开车如此粗心,差点把他自己害死。

> **Such a nice man does he seem** that we all like him.

　他看上去是个很和蔼的人,所以我们都喜欢他。

(5) so 用在句首,表示另一主语"也……"时,用"so+be 动词/助动词/情态动词+主语"结构;而表示另一主语"也不……"时,用"nor/neither+be 动词/助动词/情态动词+主语"结构。

> Tom can speak French, **so can Jack**.

　Tom 会讲法语,Jack 也会。

> He didn't see the film last night, **nor/neither did she**.

　他昨晚没看电影,她也没看。

【补充提示】

　如果是对上文同一主语的情况进行肯定,意为"的确,确实"讲时,不使用倒装。句型为"so+主语+be 动词/助动词/情态动词"。

> I promised to buy you a gift, and **so I did**.

　我答应给你买个礼物,我确实买了。

(6) as/though 引导让步状语从句时,从句使用部分倒装。

将表语(形容词或不加冠词的名词)、状语(副词)、动词原形或分词短语置于句首,后接"as/though+主语+谓语",as/though 意为"尽管,即使,虽然"。在此结构中,当形容词最高级和单数可数名词置于句首倒装时,前面均不用冠词。

➢ Shortest **as** she is, she is the richest.
  尽管她最矮,但她最富有。

➢ Child **as** he is, he knows a lot.
  尽管他还是个孩子,但他懂的东西很多。

➢ Hard **as** he tried, he didn't pass the exam.
  尽管他努力了,但他没有通过考试。

➢ Fail **as** I did, I would try again.
  尽管我失败了,我还会再尝试一次。

(7) if 虚拟条件句的部分倒装。

当 if 虚拟条件句中的从句谓语动词含有 were、had 或 should 时,可省略 if,并将 were、had、should 置于句首,构成部分倒装。

➢ **Were** he here, we would have no difficulty with this matter.
  他要是在这里的话,我们在这件事上就不会有难处了。

➢ **Had** I left a little earlier, I would have caught the train.
  我要是早一点出发,我就赶上火车了。

➢ **Should** he act like that again, he would be punished.
  他要是再那样做,就要受到惩罚了。

实战演练

1. The teacher insisted that we _____ our homework before 9 o'clock.
   A. finished   B. had finished   C. finish   D. was finishing

2. It was not until 1920 _____ regular radio broadcasts started.
   A. which   B. that   C. when   D. since

3. It was a good education _____ made him a successful teacher.
   A. when   B. what   C. that   D. which

4. The order was that the troops _____ to the front immediately.
   A. went   B. had gone   C. would go   D. go

5. He is a poorly learned man. But he acts as though he _____ a lot.
   A. knows   B. knew   C. should know   D. know

6. It _____ Mike and Mary who helped the old man several days ago.
   A. was   B. are   C. were   D. had been

7. If I _____ in charge of the project now, I'd make better use of the money.
   A. am B. was C. were D. have been

8. It's essential that every child _____ the same educational opportunities.
   A. has B. have C. having D. had

9. Frankly speaking, I'd rather you _____ anything about it for the moment.
   A. do B. don't do C. didn't do D. will not do

10. Not until that day _____ the importance of good manners in the interpersonal relationship.
    A. I realized B. I have realized C. did I realize D. will I realize

11. _____ tomorrow, he would be able to see the opening ceremony.
    A. Would he come B. If he comes
    C. Was he coming D. Were he to come

12. Only after the revolution _____ to be treated as human beings.
    A. did they begin B. they had begun C. they did begin D. had they began

13. Not only _____ polluted but _____ crowded.
    A. was the city; were the streets B. the city was; were the streets
    C. was the city; the streets were D. the city was; the streets were

14. She wanted to go fishing, _____.
    A. so her sister did B. so did her sister
    C. too her sister D. did her sister too

15. _____, he knows a lot.
    A. Child as he is B. Child as is he
    C. A child as he is D. A child as is he

第八章 其他结构

一、割裂

在英语中,句子成分按照相对固定且有规律的次序排列,其中修饰语通常位于所修饰的中心词后作后置定语。但有时会在中心词与修饰语之间插入成分,使其分隔开来,因而形成了割裂的结构。

(一) 定语从句与先行词的割裂

定语从句一般直接置于先行词之后,但有时为了强调或为了整个句子的平衡,会将定语从句与先行词分隔形成割裂。

➤ A new teacher will come tomorrow who will teach you physics.
明天会有一位新老师来教你物理。
(who 引导的定语从句和先行词 teacher 被 will come tomorrow 分隔)

➤ Computers have already been widely used and the time has come when ordinary people can use them as well.
计算机已经被广泛使用,普通人也可以使用计算机的时代已经到来。
(when 引导的定语从句和先行词 time 被 has come 分隔)

(二) 同位语从句与先行词的割裂

同位语从句一般直接置于先行词之后,但有时为了强调或使整个句子平衡,会将同位语从句与先行词分隔形成割裂。

➤ Word came that a snowstorm would take place here.
有消息说这里将要发生暴风雪。
(that 引导的同位语从句和先行词 word 被 came 分隔)

(三) 介词短语、分词短语、不定式短语与所修饰的名词割裂

为了强调或使整个句子平衡,介词短语、分词短语、不定式短语有时与所修饰的名词割裂。

➤ One day a young man was brought to his tent with a badly burnt arm.
一天,一位手臂严重烧伤的年轻人被带到他的帐篷里。
(介词短语 with a badly burnt arm 和中心词 a young man 被 was brought to his tent 分隔)

➤ A decision was made at the meeting to resume the project.
在会上做出了恢复这个项目的决定。
(不定式短语 to resume the project 和中心词 A decision 被 was made at the meeting 分隔)

二、插入语

插入语指对一句话作附加说明的部分,常常用逗号或破折号与其他成分隔开,并且在语法上不影响其他成分。就作用而言,插入语一般用于对主句的补充、说明、解释,表明说话人的观点或想法,强调或突出主句意思或进行逻辑上的承接和过渡。插入语的类型较多,常见的有以下几种:

（一）形容词（短语）作插入语

能用作插入语的形容词（短语）常见的有 true、wonderful、excellent、strange to say、most important of all、sure enough 等。

- **True**, it would be too bad.
  真的，太糟了。
- **Wonderful**, we have won again.
  太好了，我们又赢了。
- **Strange to say**, he hasn't got my letter up to now.
  说来也奇怪，他到现在还没有收到我的信。
- **Most important of all**, we must learn all the skills.
  最重要的是，我们必须掌握所有的技巧。

（二）副词（短语）作插入语

能用作插入语的副词（短语）常见的有 indeed、surely、still、otherwise、certainly、however、generally、personally、honestly、fortunately、luckily、though、besides、exactly、perhaps、maybe、probably、frankly 等。

- When he got there, he found, **however**, that the weather was too bad.
  可是到了那儿之后他发现，那儿的天气太糟糕了。
- **Otherwise**, he would still be at home.
  不然的话，他还会在家的。
- **Fortunately**, you have the power to change all that.
  幸运的是，你有能力去改变所有的一切。

（三）介词短语作插入语

能用作插入语的介词短语常见的有 in fact、in one's opinion、in general、in a word、in other words、in a few words、of course、by the way、as a result、for example、on the contrary、on the other hand、to one's surprise、in short、as a matter of fact、in conclusion、in brief 等。

- You can't wait anymore; **in other words**, you should start at once.
  你不能再等了，换句话说，你应该立刻出发。
- **On the contrary**, we should strengthen our corporation with them.
  相反，我们应该加强和他们的合作。
- **For example**, singers should avoid aspirin.
  例如，歌手应该避免服用阿司匹林。

（四）分词短语作插入语

能用作插入语的分词短语常见的有 generally speaking、judging from/by、talking of、compared with 等。

- **Generally speaking**, the weather there is neither too cold in winter nor too hot in summer.
  一般来说，那儿的气候冬天不太冷，夏天也不太热。
- **Judging by** his clothes, he may be an artist.

从衣着来判断,他可能是个艺术家。
- **Compared with** women, men are stronger.
  与女人相比,男人更加强壮。

(五) 不定式短语作插入语

能用作插入语的不定式短语常见的有 to be frank、to be honest、to be sure、to tell you the truth、to make matters worse、to sum up、to start with、to begin with 等。
- **To be frank**, I don't quite agree with you.
  坦率地说,我不太同意你的观点。
- **To tell you the truth**, I'm not so interested in the matter.
  说实话,我对这件事情的兴趣不大。
- **To sum up**, success results from hard work.
  总而言之,成功是艰苦努力的结果。

(六) 句子作插入语

能用作插入语的句子常见的有 I am sure、I believe、I think、I know、I suppose、I hope、I'm afraid、you see、what's more、that is to say、as we know、as I see、believe it or not 等。
- Some animals only half-hibernate, **that is to say**, their sleep is not such a deep one.
  有些动物只是半冬眠,也就是说,它们的睡眠并不是深度睡眠。
- **I believe**, China will catch up with the developed countries sooner or later.
  我确信,中国迟早会赶上发达国家。
- He can't pass the exam, because he doesn't study hard. **What's more**, he isn't so clever.
  他考试不及格,因为他没有努力学习。更何况,他也不是那么聪明。

三、否定

(一) 全部否定

① 英语中表示三者以上的"全不"时,常用否定词 no one、none、nothing、nobody、never、nowhere、not...any 以及"no+名词"等,表示全部否定。
- **No one** knew how to treat this terrible disease.
  没人知道如何治疗这种可怕的疾病。
- **None of these people** will admit responsibility for their actions.
  这些人都不愿意为自己的行为负责。

② 表示两者的全部否定,用 neither;either 与 not 连用时也可表示两者的全部否定。
- **Neither of us** is a doctor.
= **Either of us** isn't a doctor.
  我们俩都不是医生。

(二) 部分否定

① 三者或三者以上的部分否定,常用表示全部肯定含义的不定代词 all、every、everyone、

everybody、everything 或总括性副词 everywhere、wholly、always、altogether 等与 not 连用，意为"不是所有都……，并非全部都……"。

> **Not all** birds can fly.
> 不是所有的鸟儿都能飞。

> **Not everyone** thinks that the government is being particularly generous.
> 并非所有人都认为政府特别慷慨。

> I **don't wholly** understand him.
> 我并不完全了解他。

② 两者的部分否定，由 not+both 构成，意为"并非两者都"。

> **Not both** the artists have a keen eye for beauty.
> 两位艺术家并非都有敏锐的审美眼光。

> **Not both** of them are fit for the job.
> 他们两个人不是都适合这份工作。

> **Not both** horses can run fast.
> 两匹马并非都能跑得快。

（三）双重否定

简单来说，双重否定就是在同一个句子里出现两次否定。其主要作用是加强语气或表示委婉的说法，双重否定句通常有两种译法，即译为委婉的肯定句或译为加强版的否定句。

① 否定代词（nothing、none、neither）+带有否定前缀或后缀的词，这类句子通常译为肯定形式。

> **Nothing** is **impossible**.
> 一切皆有可能。

> **Nothing** is **changeless**.
> 万物皆在变化之中。

> **Nothing** is **unexpected**.
> 一切都在预料之中。

② "否定词+without+名词/动名词"，既可以译成肯定形式，也可以译成双重否定的形式。

> **No** machine can run **without** some friction.
> 没有任何机器能在没有摩擦的情况下运转。

> There was **never** a great genius **without** a little madness.
> 任何伟大的天才都有一点疯狂。

> The cleverest housewife **can't** cook a meal **without** rice.
> 巧妇难为无米之炊。

③ no/not+带有否定意义的词（包括形容词、副词、动词、名词等）或带有否定前缀或后缀的词，既可以译成肯定形式，也可以译成双重否定的形式。

> We will **never forget** the moment.
> 我们会永远记得这一刻。

> This activity is **not meaningless**.
> 这项活动不是没有意义的。

> We see him **not infrequently**.
> 我们时常见到他。

实战演练

1. Because of the financial crisis, days are gone _____ local 5-star hotels charged 6,000 yuan for one night.
   A. if   B. when   C. which   D. since
2. The girl arranged to have piano lessons at the training center with her sister _____ she would stay for an hour.
   A. where   B. who   C. which   D. what
3. News came from the school office _____ Wang Lin had been admitted to Beijing University.
   A. which   B. what   C. that   D. where
4. The traffic rule says young children under the age of four and _____ less than 40 pounds must be in a child safety seat.
   A. being weighed   B. to weigh   C. weighed   D. weighing
5. The fact has worried many scientists _____ the earth is becoming warmer and warmer these years.
   A. what   B. which   C. that   D. though
6. _____, the more expensive the camera, the better its quality.
   A. General speaking   B. Speaking general
   C. Generally speaking   D. Speaking generally
7. Your performance in the driving test didn't reach the required standard, _____, you failed.
   A. in the end   B. after all
   C. in other words   D. at the same time
8. It is so nice to hear from her. _____, the last time we met is more than thirty years ago.
   A. What's more   B. That is to say   C. In other words   D. Believe it or not
9. Never waste anything, and _____, never waste time.
   A. after all   B. at all   C. in all   D. above all
10. His father came home at midnight, and _____, he was drunk.
    A. as a result   B. that is to say   C. what's more   D. sooner or later
11. I've become good friends with several of the students in my school _____ I met in the English speech contest last year.
    A. who   B. where   C. when   D. which
12. Two middle-aged passengers fell into the sea. _____, neither of them could swim.
    A. In fact   B. Luckily   C. Unfortunately   D. Naturally
13. _____ his clothes, he may be an artist.
    A. Judging by   B. Judged by   C. To judge by   D. Judge by
14. It's no trouble at all. _____, it will be a great pleasure to help you.
    A. On the contrary   B. In general   C. For example   D. In brief
15. _____, the task was finished in only one week.
    A. To my surprise
    C. To my sorrow
    B. To my sadness
    D. To my disappointment

实战演练参考答案

第一部分　基础语法

第一章　名词、代词

CADCA　　CBDCA　　ADCDB

第二章　冠词、数词

BCBAD　　ABBDB　　AABDA

第三章　动词

CACDC　　BDCBA　　DDBBB

第四章　形容词、副词

BDDBC　　ACCBA　　ACCBC

第五章　连词、介词

ADABC　　BCDBD　　AABBA

第二部分　核心语法

第一章　简单句

一、判断下列句子属于哪种基本句型

1. He sent me a letter yesterday.　　主语+谓语+间接宾语+直接宾语

2. We named our baby John.　　主语+谓语+宾语+宾语补足语

3. She looks so beautiful today.　　主语+系动词+表语

4. He looks at the beautiful girl under the tree.　　主语+谓语+宾语

5. They often play chess in the park.　　主语+谓语+宾语

二、将下列句子转换为否定句和一般疑问句

1. She is a teacher.

   否定句：She is not a teacher.

   一般疑问句：Is she a teacher?

2. She has finished her work.

   否定句：She hasn't finished her work.

   一般疑问句：Has she finished her work?

3. I forgot my homework.

   否定句：I didn't forget my homework.

   一般疑问句：Did you forget your homework?

4. She will finish her work soon.

   否定句：She won't finish her work soon.

   一般疑问句：Will she finish her work soon?

5. My friends can play basketball.

   否定句：My friends can't play basketball.

   一般疑问句：Can your friends play basketball?

三、单项选择

DDAAB　　CACAB

第二章　时态

CABAB　　CCBAB　　BACDD

第三章　语态

BAABD　　ACBDC　　BBAAC

第四章　主谓一致

ABABA　　DAACB　　BBBCB

第五章　从句

DBBDA　　ABDBB　　AAADC

第六章　非谓语动词

DBACB　　CDBAA　　ACBDA

第七章　特殊句型

CBCDB　　ACBCC　　DACBA

第八章　其他结构

BACDC　　CCDDC　　ACAAA

附录 不规则动词变化表

1. AAA 形式

动词原形	过去式	过去分词
cost	cost	cost
cut	cut	cut
hurt	hurt	hurt
hit	hit	hit
let	let	let
put	put	put
read	read	read
set	set	set
spread	spread	spread
spit	spit/spat	spit/spat
shut	shut	shut

2. AAB 形式

动词原形	过去式	过去分词
beat	beat	beaten

3. ABA 形式

动词原形	过去式	过去分词
become	became	become
come	came	come
run	ran	run

4. ABB 形式

(1) 在动词原形后加一个辅音字母 d、t 或 ed 构成过去式或过去分词。

动词原形	过去式	过去分词
burn	burnt	burnt
deal	dealt	dealt
dream	dreamed/dreamt	dreamed/dreamt
hear	heard	heard
hang	hanged/hung	hanged/hung
learn	learned/learnt	learned/learnt
light	lit/lighted	lit/lighted
mean	meant	meant
prove	proved	proved/proven
shine	shone/shined	shone/shined
show	showed	showed/shown
smell	smelled/smelt	smelled/smelt
speed	sped/speeded	sped/speeded
spell	spelled/spelt	spelled/spelt
wake	waked/woke	waked/woken

（2）把动词原形的最后一个辅音字母"d"改为"t"构成过去式或过去分词。

动词原形	过去式	过去分词
build	built	built
lend	lent	lent
rebuild	rebuilt	rebuilt
send	sent	sent
spend	spent	spent

（3）原形→ought→ought。

动词原形	过去式	过去分词
bring	brought	brought
buy	bought	bought
fight	fought	fought
think	thought	thought

(4) 原形→aught→aught。

动词原形	过去式	过去分词
catch	caught	caught
teach	taught	taught

(5) 变其中一个元音字母。

动词原形	过去式	过去分词
dig	dug	dug
feed	fed	fed
find	found	found
get	got	got/gotten
hold	held	held
lead	led	led
meet	met	met
sit	sat	sat
shoot	shot	shot
spit	spit/spat	spit/spat
stick	stuck	stuck
win	won	won

(6) 原形→lt/pt/ft→lt/pt/ft。

动词原形	过去式	过去分词
feel	felt	felt
keep	kept	kept
leave	left	left
sleep	slept	slept
sweep	swept	swept

(7) 其他。

动词原形	过去式	过去分词
lay	laid	laid
pay	paid	paid
say	said	said
stand	stood	stood
understand	understood	understood
lose	lost	lost
have	had	had
make	made	made
sell	sold	sold
tell	told	told
retell	retold	retold

5. ABC 形式

(1) 原形→过去式→原形+(e)n。

动词原形	过去式	过去分词
blow	blew	blown
drive	drove	driven
draw	drew	drawn
eat	ate	eaten
fall	fell	fallen
give	gave	given
grow	grew	grown
forgive	forgave	forgiven
know	knew	known
mistake	mistook	mistaken
overeat	overate	overeaten

续表

动词原形	过去式	过去分词
prove	proved	proven/proved
take	took	taken
throw	threw	thrown
ride	rode	ridden
see	saw	seen
show	showed	shown/showed
write	wrote	written

(2) 原形→过去式→过去式+(e)n。

动词原形	过去式	过去分词
break	broke	broken
choose	chose	chosen
get	got	got/gotten
hide	hid	hidden
forget	forgot	forgotten
freeze	froze	frozen
speak	spoke	spoken
steal	stole	stolen

(3) 变单词在重读音节中的元音字母"i"分别为"a"(过去式)和"u"(过去分词)。[i→a→u]。

动词原形	过去式	过去分词
begin	began	begun
drink	drank	drunk
sing	sang	sung
sink	sank	sunk
swim	swam	swum
ring	rang	rung

(4) 其他。

动词原形	过去式	过去分词
be(am, is, are)	was/were	been
bear	bore	born/borne
do	did	done
fly	flew	flown
go	went	gone
lie	lay/lied	lain/lied
wear	wore	worn